Shabbat as Revolution

SHABBAT AS REVOLUTION

39 Ways to Renew Creation and Change the World

RABBI DR. SHMULY YANKLOWITZ

KTAV Publishing House
New York

URIM PUBLICATIONS
Jerusalem • New York

Shabbat as Revolution:
39 Ways to Renew Creation and Change the World
by Rabbi Shmuly Yanklowitz

Typeset by Ariel Walden

Printed in Israel

First Edition

ISBN 978-1-60280-475-3

KTAV Publishing House
527 Empire Boulevard
Brooklyn, NY 11225
www.ktav.com

Urim Publications
P.O. Box 52287
Jerusalem 9152102
Israel
www.UrimPublications.com

Library of Congress Cataloging-in-Publication Data in progress.

This book is dedicated to Shoshana, the love of my life,
who makes Shabbos so special every week
of our precious lives together.

Contents

Introduction

And the Children of Yisrael shall observe Shabbat ... between Me and the Children of Yisrael, it is a sign forever.

(Exodus 31:16)

God's creation is called *melacha*.[1] We learn from the Mishnah[2] that there are thirty-nine categories of prohibition on Shabbat, also referred to as *melacha*[3] (forty minus one in the Mishnah's parlance), equal to the thirty-nine tasks that were needed to build the *Mishkan* (Tabernacle).[4] It is suggested that just as there were thirty-nine dimensions to building the *Mishkan* and thus thirty-nine prohibitions on Shabbat, there were also thirty-nine dimensions to the creation of the world. It has also been suggested that the *melachot* were used by the Divine in the creation of the world.[5]

Furthermore, the Talmudic sage Rabbi Chanina bar Chama teaches that the thirty-nine *melachot* (the plural form of the term)

---

1. Genesis 2:2, 2:3.

2. Mishnah Shabbat 7:2. It is instructive to note that the Torah itself does not mention the number of *melachot*, nor does it specify any of them besides *mav'ir* (kindling a fire).

3. Exodus 35:2.

4. BT Mishna Shabbat Ch. 7, Mechilta de-Rabbi Yishmael, "Ki Tissa" and "Vayakhel," BT *Shabbat* 73–75, Jerusalem Talmud Shabbat 7:2.

5. Tanhuma, Pekudei 82.

are direct corollaries of the thirty-nine activities related to the service in the *Mishkan*.[6] The Jerusalem Talmud derives the specific number thirty-nine from *gematria* (numerology).[7] In addition, the Talmudic rabbis also propose that there are thirty-nine *toladot* (sub-categories) of each of the *melachot*.

The late biblical scholar Nechama Leibowitz offered seven language parallels between Genesis chapters 1–2, which describe the creation story, and Exodus chapters 28 and 39, which describe Shabbat, to demonstrate clearly how connected the *melachot* of creation are with the *melachot* of the *Mishkan*. In this conception of the expansive nature of the *melachot*, God engages in *tzimtzum* (Divine retraction) on Shabbat, to create space for rest one day of the week; both creation and rest are tasks for us to emulate and are two sides of the same coin. Without rest, we will eventually burn out and cease to create; without further creation, rest serves no function.

Thus, we might ask: Is Shabbat about becoming our ideal self on that particular day, or about restoring ourselves to be our best during the other six days of the week?

In the mystical Zohar, it is asked: "What is Shabbat?"[8] The answer: "It is the name of God!" Indeed, to learn about observing Shabbat is not merely about a positive, balanced, healing lifestyle. It is also a journey toward discovering the deepest mystical secrets of existence. If Shabbat is the name of God, then going deeper into Shabbat is a revelation into the mind of God. As the mystics relate to us mortals: "Shabbat is one-sixtieth of the world to come."[9]

---

6. BT Shabbat 49b.

7. JT Shabbat 7:2. Regarding the forbidden *melachot* of Shabbat, Exodus 35:1 states: "*Eileh hadevarim*," "These are the words" which God commanded to Moshe. In *gematria*, the word "*eileh*" is equal to 36; the word "*hadevarim*" is written in the plural form, which connotes (at least) 2; finally, the word "*hadevarim*" is also written with a definite article, equaling 1. The total then is 36+2+1=39.

8. Zohar II 88b.

9. BT Brachot 57b.

"Shabbat is the day of the Torah"[10] because before the first sin (in the Garden of Eden), there was light everywhere. On Shabbat, through Torah, we restore that light in the world. Even the skin of the first humans was light. But then, darkness emerged, and the skin of light turned into garments.[11] We are therefore commanded to light the Shabbat candles, which emerges as the mitzvah to bring back the light of creation, as the "original light" (referred to in the Zohar as *ohr haganuz,* literally "stored light") is now hidden. In our own ways, we light up the world. We bring redemption. We light up our souls, the channel for Divine presence and vision in the world. As the verse states: "The candle of God is the soul of the human."[12]

Shabbat practice was never intended to be only about behavior or limiting it. Built into the halachot (Jewish laws) are deep psychological concepts. One of the most fascinating dimensions of the *melachot* is the need for acts to be intentional *and* constructive. This concept is referred to as *melechet machshevet.* If someone does an act unintentionally, it is not fully considered a biblical *melacha*. The same is true with one doing an act that would normally be a *melacha,* but doing it with destructive, rather than constructive, intentions. Such actions avoid biblical categorization although they may still be rabbinic prohibitions. Here are several of those categories, in brief:

- *Melacha she'eina tzericha l'gufa* – Doing an action that is not needed for its own sake. The classic example mentioned in the Talmud is digging a pit for the sole purpose of the dirt, with no need for the pit itself.
- *Davar she'eino mitkaven* – Doing an action where one doesn't

---

10. Zohar III 95a.

11. This description in the Zohar is clearly meant to be understood on a mystical, and not physical, level.

12. Proverbs 20:7.

intend for a *melacha* to occur. An example is dragging a table across a lawn, thereby creating a ditch.

- *Pesik reisha* – Doing a *davar she'eino mitkaven* (unintended *melacha*) and yet the *melacha* is inevitable and foreseeable.[1] A distinction is made between *pesik reisha d'nicha leih* (when the one engaging in *pesik reisha* will benefit from the action) and *pesik reisha d'lo nicha leih* (when the one engaging in *pesik reisha* will not benefit from the action).
- *Mitasek* – Doing an action while thinking it is permissible, but it turns out not to be. An example is picking up a vegetable off the ground thinking it was not connected to the earth only to find that it was in fact attached.
- *Shinui* – Doing a *melacha* in an abnormal fashion. An example is tearing open a package with one's teeth.
- *Mekalkeil* – Doing a *melacha* not in a constructive manner but rather in a destructive fashion. An example is opening a box from both ends, rendering it no longer usable.
- *Shnayim she'asa'uha* – Two people doing a *melacha* together that could have been done alone by one person. An example is two parents carrying a child home together, outside of an *eiruv*, when one could have done it alone.
- *Grama* – Doing a *melacha* indirectly. An example is pushing an object that in turn pushes an electric switch.[2]

In this book, we will explore the *melachot* through a philosophical lens. Philosophy, of course, is a broad field and an unwieldy

---

1. *Pesik reisha* literally means "cutting off the head." The Talmud presents a case of a child coming to his father, asking him to cut off the head of the chicken for him to play with (apparently this was an acceptable "toy" in talmudic times). The father responds: "If I cut off its head, won't it surely die?" That is to say, *shechita* (killing the animal), a *melacha*, is unavoidable in this case.

2. As always, there is great debate among the Talmudic rabbis about what these categories entail. In each case, here we just chose one explanation rather than all of the various approaches in the Talmud (such as between Rabbi Shimon and Rabbi Yehudah) and among the *rishonim* (medieval commentators, such as Rashi and Rambam).

term. We will not primarily look at logic (the study of the validity of arguments), metaphysics (the study of abstract concepts of reality), or epistemology (the study of truth), although those three branches of philosophy remain fascinating and of great importance. Rather, we will explore the thirty-nine dimensions of Shabbat through the four philosophical branches of aesthetics (the study of beauty and art), politics (government, citizens, and rights), ethics (the study of how to morally live), and existentialism (the study of individual freedom and personal choice). We are also less interested in the Greek philosophy embraced by medieval Jewish philosophers. Instead, we will utilize modern and postmodern philosophical techniques that are more closely connected to the problems and questions that people need to be answered today.

At this juncture, we will draw upon the famous case of Plato's Cave. Here, Plato describes the foolishness of prisoners in a cave who mistake shadows on a wall for reality since they do not know anything about the reality outside the cave; the *Matrix* film series is also premised on a similar theme. Indeed, one can live a full existence focused on the shadows rather than upon the reality outside the cave. Even if set free, in Plato's Cave, it would be far too frightening, for most, to actually step out of the cave, out of reality as it has been known. Or, in the case of the *Matrix* films, to choose the pill that liberates one to see true reality.

One lives in a false reality if they only exist in the sphere of seeking constant pleasure. In philosophy, hedonism is a theory of value. For a hedonist, the only thing intrinsically positive to all people at all times is pleasure, and the only thing that is intrinsically negative and of no value is pain. For the hedonist, to be sure, this notion applies both to mental and physical phenomena. So, this is not just about the drunken glutton.

Others, rather than seeking pleasure, seek power. But mastering the world creates new challenges we may not be able to master. We must be called toward humility in our relationship to the planet and humankind at large. Pirkei Avot (Ethics of the

Fathers) teaches: "Love work, hate power."[3] Here, we are taught
not only to be uncomfortable with those in power – and those
who seek to be in power – but also that we are to love *melacha*.
The *melachot*, on Shabbat, are not negative. They are positive.
But they can only be fully positive if we reserve them for six
days of the week and reflect on them on the seventh. In loving
this "work," we also come to "hate power" because stepping
back from the work itself is a humble act of disempowerment.
We remind ourselves humbly of our limitations and that our
desire is not to conquer but to repair. And yet we also learn in
Pirkei Avot: "*Lo alecha hamlacha ligmor*" ("It is not on you to
complete the work"), but at the same time, "*v'lo atah ben chorin
l'hibateil mimenah*" ("and you are not free to refrain from it").[4]

We must engage in the work to repair the world even though
we will not complete the work. We are in this world together and
each of us must do what we can.

In his commentary on Pirkei Avot 1:10, Rabbi Yitzchak Eisik
Safrin, (known as the Kormorna Rebbe, 1806–1874) teaches that
we need to perform all of the thirty-nine *melachot* to uplift the
souls and lifeforce in them. He also teaches that eighteen times
thirty-nine equals *tal tehiya* (the dew of resurrection) in *gematria*,
which also equals Shabbat.[5] A *talmid chacham* (Torah scholar),
however, can accomplish all of this through learning Torah in
place of physically performing the *melachot*, he suggests. Furthermore, Avot d'Rabbi Natan (an aggadic work, circa 700–900)
teaches that just as the Torah was given to *Am Yisrael* with a *brit*
(covenant), so too the skilled labor (*melachot*) was given with
a special *brit*. This is demonstrated by the fact that God didn't
allow the *Shechinah* (the Divine presence) to dwell among them
until they did the *melachot* in building the *Mishkan*: "Make me a

---

3. Pirkei Avot 1:10.
4. Ibid. 2:16.
5. 18 × 39 = 702, and Shabbat = 702. Further, 18 × 39 is *Tal Tehiya*, the 18
being the *tehiya* (*hai*) and the 39 being *tal*.

Temple, and I will dwell within you."[6] And so, when we perform the *melachot*, our souls will cleave to us in our labor, and our mind expands, drawing new light (*mochin*).

We normally think of the *mitzvot* as a way to elevate sparks but, in fact, the *melachot* have that exact same potential. When we live with the *melachot* that are connected to one's soul root, we elevate.[7] And so, the thesis of this book is that the *melachot* offer *tikkunim* (ways to repair the world). In performing the *melachot* and taking the necessary space to step back and reflect on them as both a unit and each of them individually, we bring repairs to the world. Each *melacha* offers a different potential for repair.

Join me on this journey as we take the steps to repair the world through the ethical realities of the mystical dimensions of Shabbat.

Appreciation

I want to express my sincere appreciation to Rabbi Avram Herzog, Judry Subar, and AJ Frost for their feedback and edits. I also am grateful to the KTAV team and all of the editors involved. Further, I want to express gratitude to the dozens of Jewish learners who joined my classes where I originally shared these ideas.

---

6. Exodus 25:8.

7. Consider here Karl Marx and how he taught about the connection between the dignity of labor and the birth of consciousness.

1.

Zorei'a (Seeding)

IN THE POPULAR imagination (at least, in the ideas instilled within us during Hebrew School) Shabbat is the day of rest. It's a day when we shun driving, electricity, handling money, and exercising any of the conveniences that we utilize during the week. For many Jews, let alone the vast majority of the world population that doesn't celebrate Shabbat, the prohibitions inherent in the holiday seem to be of a more archaic time. Doesn't rest mean having the ability to turn on the TV, veg out, and retreat from the world?

In the view of the Rabbis of the Talmud, the Shabbat prohibitions of certain activities went beyond the mundane. The ability to not light a fire, for example, is a powerful tool. An intellectual tool. It might not seem apparent at first glance, but as we will see in these succeeding 39 weeks – one dedicated to each prohibitive dimension of work (_melacha_) – there is much wisdom to be gained from exploring these activities that are forbidden on Shabbat.

The first set of _melachot_ – categories of _melechet machshevet_, or thought through activities – that are prohibited on Shabbat, are those that relate to agricultural activity. The first of those that we will address here, as per the order of the _melachot_ in the Talmud, is the prohibition of _zorei'a_, understood as sowing or seeding or planting (i.e., anything that enables vegetative growth). Given that the entire experience of Shabbat can be seen as _zeicher_ *l'ma'aseh bereishit* (a commemoration of the Divine act of creation) as well *zecher l'yetzi'at Mitzrayim* (a commemoration of the exodus from Egypt), this *melacha*, just as all 39 categories of activity prohibited on Shabbat,[1] can be seen as having two spiritual origins. Firstly, the prohibition of *zorei'a* from day three of the Creation story, the day on which God enables the growth of vegetation.[2] This category of *melacha* (*av melacha*), one of the 11 *melachot* concerning what goes into making the bread and dyes,[3] further emerges from the construction of the *Mishkan*, the Tabernacle, that the Israelites built just after they emerged from slavery in Egypt; the designers of the *Mishkan* planted herbs to create dyes used for many of the *Mishkan*'s components, and in keeping the Tabernacle as a going concern, wheat was grown to produce the *lechem hapanim* (showbread) which was used in the *Mishkan* every week. We have the opportunity to reconnect with the agricultural experience. We are all too often too disconnected from our food systems today.

The prohibition of planting is understood in both negative and positive terms. Just as on Shabbat we should refrain from planting or doing anything that would further the growth of vegetation, so too, on the other six days of the week, we should foster creation and build a *mishkan* in our time. What does that look like?

Most obviously, it means planting new crops and protecting existing ones. Particularly in an age when we recognize (or should recognize) the importance of plants to the ecological health of the world, this sort of activity is key.

In addition to seeding, it applies to all that goes into improving the ability for a plant to grow (watering, pruning, weeding, etc.), not only outdoor plants but indoor plants too, not only to

---

1. The 39 are listed in the Mishnah, BT Shabbat 73a.

2. Genesis 1:11–12.

3. (1) sowing, (2) plowing, (3) harvesting, (4) binding sheaves, (5) threshing, (6) winnowing, (7) selecting, (8) grinding, (9) sifting, (10) kneading, (11) baking.

living plants but even dead ones, not only if the planting activity produces results. On a deeper halakhic level:

- If one were eating watermelon, one would want to avoid dropping seeds over the grass or dirt (but it would not be a problem over concrete)
- One would want to avoid rinsing one's hands over the grass
- One would want to avoid opening the window shade if it was only being done in order to get sunlight
- If gifted fresh cut flowers, one would want to avoid putting them into a vase with water
- It would not be a problem to provide seeds to chickens in a coop where the intention and likelihood is that, before the seeds can germinate, the chickens will eat all of the seeds, assuming that the seeds will be eaten on that day; it would be problematic, however, to fill a bird feeder in one's yard, as the birds are free to find food elsewhere and do not rely only upon the birdfeeder for sustenance

What a relief it can be to be free of yard responsibilities for one day of the week (for those fortunate to have a yard and the physical capability of tending to it)!

But more deeply, the prohibition – against the physical insertion of seeds into the ground for them to sprout – is so that, instead, we meditate about the spiritual seeds of Torah, of timeless wisdom, and tending to seeds of potentiality within ourselves and within others.

Let's examine the process of creating spiritual vegetation through the lens of the Neo-Aristotelean Capability Approach.[4] Don't worry, it's not as esoteric as it might sound. Essentially, through this framework, we learn about the idea that everyone with a capability should have the freedom to thrive in order to actualize that capability. This is a philosophy of ethics focused

---

4. See the works of Amartya Sen and Martha Nussbaum.

on individual well-being, education, and thriving in all of one's ways. Because this approach focuses on the full-self (and even the fully-formed realized self), it goes beyond utilitarian metrics which views thriving purely through the lens of happiness. It also goes beyond the materialist approach to well-being (i.e., wealth). This follows a Kantian approach, that each person is an end in and of themselves yet strays from the Kantian approach by embracing a deeper plurality of values in assessing the good life for each unique person. It is not Kant's categorical imperative (universal mandate that all act the same). We are concerned with equity (what individuals need) in addition to equality (ensuring everyone has their basic human needs met). Each of us has seeds of potentiality within us yearning to grow. Each of us has the opportunity to advocate for a society that enables each person to grow.

Indeed, there is a Jewish concept that every object of creation has deep potential and enormous capability. Consider this midrashic passage: "There is no blade of grass below that does not have a star and angel which strikes it and tells it to grow."[1] This image might be viewed as proto-Chasidic, as it evokes a sense of such closeness between the celestial and the terrestrial spheres.

Thought leaders of the Chasidic movement itself have suggested still more vividly how deep a connection exists between nature and God. The Degel Machaneh Ephraim, for example, points out that *Elokim* (God), has the same *gematria*, or numerical value, as *hateva* (nature), (86), suggesting that the Divine and nature are interfused with one another (panentheism). He uses this idea as part of a distinctive immanentist theology (that is, one that promotes the idea that the spiritual world permeates the mundane) but it is not a secularized mysticism, which is more in the realm of Spinoza.

Our spiritual life is also interconnected with the plant kingdom. Rebbe Nachman writes about *sichah* (meditation, prayer)

---

1. Bereshit Rabbah 10:7, Zohar I, 61a.

and how it has the same root as *siach* (bush). He argues that every bush yearns to live and grow, and depicts vegetation as adding strength to our prayers.[2] From Rebbe Nachman's theological vantage point, this mystical understanding of the natural world is yet another proof for why the open field – where things grow – is the best place to pray.[3] Perhaps this is related also to the power of the moment that Moshe (Moses) experienced at the burning bush.

The Slonimer Rebbe explains that the term *ein od mil'vado* ("there is no other besides God") doesn't mean that there is no other God but that there is nothing but God. In all of nature, there is only God. Each seed can remind us of this if we consider that by sowing a seed, we are attempting to actualize a representation of the Divine.

Further, each seed within a fruit reminds us of the soul within each person. We are challenged to see beyond the surface into the hidden mystical dimension where there is wisdom buried within the universe.

When we refrain from *zorei'a* on Shabbat, we are not just avoiding the idea of seeding. Rather, we are interested in the notion of how souls grow through the nourishing liquids of Torah, wisdom, and reflection. In this way, we shift our consciousness from an external physical planting process to a deeper spiritual and intellectual consciousness around human potentiality and dignity. We can't create growth in the material world on Shabbat, but we can nurture growth in the spiritual world. God is infused with everything, and the seed – which itself is infused with an inner light that allows it to germinate – is the proof of that presence. We must "water" our inner "seed" and nourish the gift of being created in the image of God. "Planting" a seed within another may be considered an act of violence since that person

2. Rebbe Nachman's Wisdom #98 and Likutei Moharan II, 1.
3. Rebbe Nachman's Wisdom #163 and #227.

has their own seed. Rather, our job is to help them water and nourish their seeds.

Thich Nhat Hanh writes[4] about how we can nourish our seeds of love and compassion and avoid nourishing the seeds of anger and resentment. The seeds we water will flourish. He explains that this is true not only for ourselves but for our loved ones as well as we choose which of their seeds to water each day. We must lovingly engage in this "selective watering" for our life partners.

The metaphor of plant seeds as a methodology to think about the human soul offers a transcendent dimension to the relationship between *zera*, or "seed," in its genealogical sense and the experience of seeding a field to make vegetation flourish. In the Creation story, humans are instructed to be fruitful – that is, in a sense, to experience the growth of humanity as the planting of fruit trees – and to multiply.[5] And, in the course of the Exodus narrative, we're told that the Israelites did indeed follow that directive and were fruitful.[6] We're reminded, then, of a connection between the significance of planting in the ground and the concomitant prohibition of this on Shabbat, on the one hand, and the process of growing humanity in general, and of growing the Jewish people – *Zera Avraham, Zera Yisrael* – on the other.

In addition, our seed is about looking back (our seed as our ancestry) and about looking forward (our seed as our perpetuation of life). The first mitzvah of the Torah is *peru urvu* (the mitzvah to procreate) and it lines up with the first *av melacha* (seeding). Having children (spreading our seed) is a great act of hope in the future, choosing to invest new humans into the future faithfully. Indeed, seeding (sexual relations within a loving committed relationship) is itself a mitzvah on Shabbat. This is

---

4. Thich Nhat Hanh is a Vietnamese Buddhist monk who lives in France and has written many books. This is from his book *Anger: Wisdom for Cooling the Flames* (New York: Riverhead Books, 2001).
5. Genesis 1:28.
6. Exodus 1:12.

because, at its best, this is not merely a physical act but a deeply spiritual one.

This is the story of Choni HaMe'agel[7] and the tree planted for future generations.

> One day [Choni] was journeying on the road and he saw a man planting a carob tree; he asked him: How long does it take [for this tree] to bear fruit? The man replied: Seventy years. He then further asked him: Are you certain that you will live another seventy years? The man replied: I found [ready grown] carob trees in the world; as my forefathers planted these for me, so I too plant these for my children.

Here we might ask: What are the consequences of our moral actions for the future? What are the seeds we are planting for the future (for future generations, for the future of earth, for the future of society)?

Now, we know there is a soul (*neshama*) within every person and a Jewish spiritual dimension (*pintele Yid*) within every Jewish person. This respectively makes us human and Jewish. Nonetheless, as we identify the seed (the inner spiritual depths), we want to avoid philosophical essentialism. This is to say, we want to avoid the idea that humans are fundamentally monolithic and predictable and also the idea that Jews are in some way instinctively or biologically distinct. Rather, humans have a spiritual essence, but that essence is not predictive of one's identity or choices because of human freedom.

Within the word *zorei'a* is *zar* (foreign) and *ra* (evil). Here we might suggest that when we make our seed (our inner light and essence) foreign, we become capable of evil. We must see our own shadows, own them, and refine them.

Perhaps what makes us human more than anything else is our capacity for kindness, and thus to be partners with the Divine in

---

7. BT, Taanit 23a.

creating a world built on compassion. Rabbi Shlomo Wolbe,[8] a
20th-century teacher of *mussar* (the Jewish spiritual and ethical
development field) in Jerusalem, wrote:

> I declare, "The world is built of your love." (Psalms 89:2) ...
> Every act of *hesed*, even a small one, is an actual act of building
> and creation, enlivening the spirit of the downtrodden and the
> broken-hearted.

Indeed, we continue to build the world each day, planting seeds
of kindness, partnering with the Divine as we lift up the hidden
and revealed sparks within us and beyond us. In refraining from
zorei'a on Shabbat, we can be renewed to return to the physical
work of tending to the earth and planting seeds. We can also
realign ourselves to our mission within our inner seeds recon-
necting to our deeper essence, actualizing our unique potential,
and flourishing in our holy capabilities.

---

8. Rabbi Shlomo Wolbe, *Alei Shur*, Vol. 2. (Jerusalem, Israel: Bais Hamussar,
1967), p. 198.

2.
Choreish (Plowing)

THE SECOND CATEGORY of work that we are going to explore is the *melacha* of *choreish*, plowing. When one digs into the earth, one loosens the soil and makes the land more fertile for planting crops, flowers or trees. So, we learn that we should avoid scraping the ground on Shabbat. This action is one of the first eleven *melachot* associated with growing the herbs and vegetation needed for dyes and the wheat needed for the breads of the *Mishkan* (the Tabernacle). So, as with the first *melacha* of *zorei'a*, planting, we, traditionally, on Shabbat, avoid directly interacting with the earth: digging, fertilizing, weeding, mowing, raking, scraping one's plow along the fertile ground, or even dragging chairs along the earth (if making an impression on the earth is inevitable).

The main purpose of plowing in farming is to turn over the top layer of soil in order to bring up the fresher nutrients to the surface. On a deeper level, what are we looking at with *charisha*, the process of plowing? We perform an act that is about going below the surface of the physical world as we know it. By plowing deeper, we can discover nutrients that can nourish our physical and spiritual planting. If we remain merely on the surface level, we can experience decay and lose access to a deeper life source.

First, we don't know what we'll find when we dig below the surface. Consider political philosopher John Rawls' "veil of ignorance" exercise. He suggests that we should imagine our moral decisions such that we do not know where our decisions will lead us, such as which chair in "musical chairs" we will end up in. Will it be the chair where we'll make $2,000 a year or the one where we'll make $2 million a year? Will it be the chair where we'll be perceived to have white skin or the chair that says we have black skin? In exploring our moral imaginations, we start to wonder what it might be like to be reborn into a different group. Indeed, below the surface of how society operates, there are unjust systems, human biases, and a lottery (of randomness? of Divine plan?) as to how we end up where we end up. *Charisha*: we dig deeper to see what's really going on in our society.

What else happens when we dig deeper into the human mind and human experience? We will discover something that cannot be expressed or measured. Galileo saw the world around him and wanted to know more. Thus, he began to develop a quantitative vocabulary for existence.[1] But he also acknowledged that consciousness is something that cannot be measured in physical terms. Consciousness poses challenges to our study of the brain. Neuroscience is crucial, but it has its limits, as does every hard science. Some believe that physical science will eventually have a breakthrough and be able to "see" or "measure" consciousness. But Galileo specifically approached physical science as excluding consciousness for a reason. Scientific understanding of the brain

---

1. In Jewish law, we can find at times that Ashkenazi legal authorities (those of Jews originating from Europe) might take a more quantitative approach in reaching halachic conclusions, while Sefardi authorities (those of Jews originating from the North African and Mediterranean region) take a more qualitative approach. Consider, for example, the idea of how we assess *bateil b'shishim* (a prohibited food item being voided if mixed with at least sixty times that amount. For example: If a drop of milk falls into a pot of chicken soup, the milk is voided as long as it comprises no more than 1/60 of the total). Ashkenazim turn purely toward mathematical measurement to assess if there is more than 1 piece of non-kosher food to 60 parts of kosher food. Sefardim turn toward taste and having a gentile taste the food to see if the non-kosher part is noticeable at all. This second approach is known as *notein ta'am* (literally meaning that it gives off a taste).

can show correlation but not causation. This is to say, if part of the brain becomes activated by a stimulus, we see that there is a correlation involved but the cause still cannot be explained.

Here we need consciousness. Consciousness is at the core of human identity. We live not just in an objective realm of tangible objects but rather the intangible subjects that occupy our minds (emotions, values, perceptions, perceptions of our perceptions, etc.).[2] Today, there are prominent voices that (perhaps nonsensically) suggest that we need to only talk about "facts, not feelings," as if the former is objective and real and the latter is flimsy and fabricated. The reality is not so simple. Whether what happens in our minds consists of a cartesian self-definition or a postmodern articulation of mindfulness, we can understand it as an aspect of what it means to be human. We can undertake the digging represented by *charisha* in an effort to excavate the limits of our humanity. We need *charisha*; we need to dig deep into the human consciousness to explore the depths of our reality. This digging will help us navigate the furrows that seem to separate the physical world that we believe we perceive and the spirituality that we might experience.

Three components are needed for a rainbow to exist: sunlight, rain, and a conscious eye at the correct geometric location. It is the human being that is necessary for a rainbow's existence. So, in a sense, there is no rainbow if we are not there. But it's also true that there are countless rainbows around us if we just reposition ourselves. Similarly, does a tree falling in the forest make a noise if no one is there to hear it? The easy answer is no. Noise needs a subject to be a noise. Human subjectivity is required for objectivity to exist at all. Dr. Robert Lanza, a professor at Wake Forest University, writes:

> When studying subatomic particles, the observer appears to alter and determine what is perceived. The presence and methodology

---

2. See Immanuel Kant on primary vs. secondary qualities.

of the experimenter are hopelessly entangled with whatever he
is attempting to observe and what results he gets. An electron
turns out to be both a particle and a wave, but how and, more
importantly, where such a particle will be located remains dependent upon the very act of observation.[3]

In an old Chassidic parable, a person seeks to journey toward
the inner palace of the king, requiring him to travel far, get over
walls, and past gatekeepers. But in the end, the traveler realizes
that wherever he's standing he's already within the inner chamber
of the King. One merely needs to break down the illusion of there
being walls at all. The journey to the King is entirely internal,
subjective, and accessible.

The philosophical basis of Shabbat is freedom, breaking down
the illusion of walls. Not only is Shabbat connected to the Exodus
from Egypt – objective freedom – but also to the creation of the
world – subjective freedom). Regarding the latter, we deal with
free will, a foundational element in Jewish thought. Shabbat is
about reclaiming our freedom. We can start and we can stop, and
our stopping on Shabbat is not controlled by government, profit
motive, our cultural zeitgeist (albeit time or location), or our
mood. We choose to stop regardless of any extraneous factors.
It is a volitional and intentional reclaiming of our freedom. We
have moral agency when we embrace Shabbat amidst no shortage
of other opportunities to choose from. Determinism, on the rise
today, argues that all of human psychology can be contained
within the hard sciences. Shabbat argues that we have a soul
(indeed, a *neshama yeteira*, an "extra" soul on Shabbat) that
transcends the physical boundaries of the self.

The ability to embrace Shabbat – however that might look – is
morally important because we suffer when our inner lives are out

---

3. Robert Lanza, *Biocentrism: How Life and Consciousness are the Keys to
Understanding the true Nature of the Universe* (Dallas, TX: Benbella Books,
Inc, 2009), p. 49.

of touch with our outer lives. This misalignment leads to alien-
ation. As an alternative, through spiritual attunement, we work
to line up reality as we know it with reality as we experience it.
Before we can plant seeds of potentiality, before we can receive
insight, we need to dig down, go inwards, and create inner space
to see anew.

Charisha also gives a nod to a peaceful utopia to come. As the
prophets explain:

> They shall beat their swords into plowshares, and their spears
> into pruning hooks; nation shall not lift up sword against na-
> tion, neither shall they learn war anymore.[4]

Darwin's notion of progress does violence to the past; the past
dies off. In Jewish thought, we might suggest that a dialectical
spirit be conserved, where creation and progress are neither violent nor separate from the past. This is why the broken tablets are
kept in the Ark of the Covenant with the new tablets, and why
minority opinions are preserved in the Talmud. Rather, the old
must live alongside the new. In this spirit too, the sword is never
fully eradicated in that messianic vision, but rather is turned into
a plowshare.

Rabbeinu Bachya, a 13th-century Spanish rabbi, wrote that
a crucial part of human success is to set the stage economically,
through toil, to enable spiritual life. Here, he specifically relates
this process to plowing the earth.

> People are involved with *Takkanat HaOlam*, repairing the
> world, in plowing and harvesting, in buying and selling, and in
> other activities people do for *Yishuv HaOlam*, i.e., maintaining
> human habitation of the natural world.[5]

---

4. Micah 4:3, Isaiah 2:4.
5. Noam Zion: *Gates of Heshbon HaNefesh* (Jerusalem, Israel: Shalom
Hartman Institute, 2015), Chapter 22.

Plowing, on one hand, may be viewed as an act of violence, putting swords into the earth, forcing the earth into new patterns of being. After all, the sword was developed, historically, at the same time as the plowshare, in order to foster human power and dominance (over other humans, beasts, and earth). Or the plowshare may be viewed as a vehicle of fertility, enabling a nurturing experience. This will depend on whether one takes a more anthropocentric approach (a teleological approach that the earth's purpose is serving humans) or an approach validating the earth as an end in itself that deserves rest and preservation.

But some shun this kind of work and prefer strict spiritual asceticism. Most famously, we think of the Rashbi (an acronym for Rabbi Shimon bar Yochai) and his exit from the cave, only to detest the sight of farmers plowing their fields.

Ultimately, *Charisha* is about work, both physical and spiritual, work that allows us to get beneath the surface. We each must go deeper, on a personal level, into our consciousnesses. We must act as individuals but also as a collective as we go deeper into societal problems that confront us on a collective level. Only by going deeper, can we reach a truer experience of reality. By embracing the Divine limits in creation (a day to stop physical creation), we can learn about our own human limits in creation. This humility can in turn inspire growth and new creativity.

3.

Kotzeir (Reaping)

THE *MELACHA* IS about removing vegetation from the earth. In the *Mishkan* (Tabernacle), this type of cutting was done to gather herbs for the dyes used in construction and to harvest the wheat to produce the flour needed for showbread. The Hebrew word *kotzeir* translates most literally as "harvesting." But because *kotzeir*, as one of the thirty-nine *melachot*, has to do more generally with taking plant life from wherever it's growing, it entails avoiding engaging with trees, bushes, and flowers at all during Shabbat (with or without a tool), to avoid any possible removal of vegetation from its source. Shaking a tree, for example, in order for fruit to fall to the ground, is encompassed in *kotzeir*.

We celebrate the holiday of Shavuot, which is referred to as *Hag Ha'Katzir* (the Feast of the Harvest); so, in addition to Shabbat, we have that special opportunity to reflect on *kotzeir*. What is it that we're trying to focus on during Shabbat regarding our relationship to cutting plants? Every aspect of life has roots that provide living things with nourishment. As humans, we have our own physical life sources (from which we meet basic human needs such as water and food), and we have our own spiritual life sources as well. On the latter point, we might investigate what it is exactly that each of us needs in order to be nourished spiritually and connected to our respective souls and to the Divine.

Rabbi Dr. Arthur Green, a professor and widely-respected

authority on Kabbalah, writes that the first sin in the Garden of Eden (and thus, the first sin perpetrated by emerging humanity) involved picking fruit – a quintessential act of *kotzeir* – and what was really at stake there.

> The early kabbalists offer another profound teaching about the tale of Eden. Reading the text closely, they say, shows us that there were two trees at the center of the garden: The Tree of Knowledge and the Tree of Life. These two trees were joined to one another, knowledge and life (or Creation and Revelation, World and Torah), being, in their essence, one. Adam and Eve's sin was plucking the fruit. In doing so, they separated the two trees, tasting only of knowledge, but in such a way that it was cut off from its root in the Tree of Life. Their sin was separation, breaking apart the unity of being. The kabbalists understood the break between the two trees as dividing the sefirot (spiritual emanations), seeking to worship *Shekinah* (God's presence) alone, cut off from her deeper roots within the Godhead.[1]

Why is it such a problem for the tree of knowledge of good and evil to be separated from the tree of life? One possible answer might lie in the atrocious genocide of the Holocaust. This was an enlightened society that embraced philosophy and knowledge. And yet, it destroyed life wantonly. Almost inevitably, when knowledge is detached from life and the absolute infinite value of human life, mass atrocities can occur. The French philosopher Emannuel Levinas urges us to keep the two intact, moving ethics from metaphysics back to the face of the other, reuniting the tree of life with the tree of knowledge. Rabbi Adin Steinsaltz taught that even though the Garden of Eden decree of expulsion occurred before Shabbat, Adam and Eve were given Shabbat in the Garden first and weren't actually expelled until after Shabbat.

---

1. Rabbi Dr. Art Green, *Ehyeh: A Kabbalah for Tomorrow* (Woodstock, Vermont: Jewish Lights Publishing, 2004), p. 144–145.

So, he asks, why didn't they then eat from the tree of eternal life to overturn the decree of mortality? He explains that sometimes when we're too immersed in complex truth, we forget simple truth. We must ensure that our critical thinking enables us both to hold on to complex truths while also living by simple truths.

Against this kabbalistic backdrop which imagines trees as evoking separation rather than cosmic unity, we gain insight into why the rabbis caution the engagement with plants during Shabbat. Consider this Talmudic passage.

> Rabbi Yaakov said: One who walks on the road while reviewing (a Torah lesson) but interrupts his review and exclaims "How beautiful is this tree! How beautiful is this plowed field!" – Scripture considers it as if he bears guilt for his soul.[2]

Can we miss the forest for the trees? Indeed, an overemphasized singularity distracts us from bigger truths that we must hold in our consciousness.

Trees have a central role in kabbalah.[3] Avoiding cutting vegetation helps us to focus on the interconnectivity of all life and the oneness of all beings. Professor Daniel C. Matt writes:

> Maybe I should just stick with "tree?" But is there really a separate, self-contained thing I can call by that name? Down below, the roots absorb water and minerals from the soil. Up above, the chlorophyll in the leaves traps and stores the energy of sunlight. The leaf is not separate from the tree; the tree is not

---

2. Pirkei Avot 3:9.

3. "When Israel engages in the mystical unification of the Shema with a perfect will, a light emerges from the secret supernal world, and the light strikes the sparks of blackness from within and splits up into seventy lights, and these seventy shine on the seventy branches of the Tree of Life (Tiferet). This tree then exhales perfumes and spices, and all the trees in the Garden of Eden exhale perfumes, and praise their Master, for then the consort is adorned for entry into the chamber with her husband." Zohar 2:133b–134b, in Tishby, *Wisdom of the Zohar* (London: Littman Library of Jewish Civilization, 1989), p. 1023.

separate from the earth and atmosphere. If I pause and reflect, I realize that nothing is entirely separate from anything else. A faint memory of the cosmic seed lingers.[4]

The notion of separation is an illusion, a face that hides a deeper reality and truth. We often talk about the elevated status of the human being, uniquely created in the image of God. But, in *Hasidut* (mysticism), it is also true that Divinity is infused into all of creation. The Baal Shem Tov, the founder of *Hasidut*, taught:

> This is an important principle: everything in this world contains the Divine sparks. There is nothing in this world that is devoid of these sparks – not even trees and rocks. There are even the sparks from the breaking of vessels in everything we do, even in the sins we commit.[5]

The Maharal of Prague (Rabbi Judah Loew) writes about how interconnectivity offers a new perspective on epistemology and mores specifically of hermeneutics. He describes the multiple ways of understanding biblical texts by drawing on images from the plant kingdom. "*Pardes,*" according to the Talmud, not only means an orchard but also connotes four levels of interpretation. Once again, we see the interconnection between vegetation and reality-interpretation.

> We must never uproot [i.e., lose sight of] the *peshat* (literal meaning). It remains intact, while the midrash or *derash*, the allegorical interpretation, probes the depth of the text. Let me cite a parable to explain this point. The roots of a tree are deeply embedded in the ground, while the tree produces branches, fruit,

---

4. Daniel C. Matt, *God & The Big Bang* (Vermont: Jewish Lights Publishing, 2015), p. 22.

5. I. Baal Shem Tov and Jacob Immanuel Schochet, *Tzavaat HaRivash: The Testament of Rabbi Israel Baal Shem Tov* (New York: Kehot Publication Society, 1975), pg. 54.

and leaves. Everything emanates from these roots. The *peshat* constitutes the root of the text, which expands and expands, sprouting branches in every direction.[1]

Israeli Professor Mordechai Rotenberg builds off this idea:

The Maharal's metaphor is similar to the one by Hegel cited in the introduction to this book. Hegel conceives of a conflict: the flower negates the bud and the fruit negates the flower. In contrast, the Maharal brilliantly interprets the word *peshat*, the literal meaning of the biblical text, in association with the *Hitpashut*, "expansion" (both words share a common verbal root, P-SH-T, which connotes simplicity). According to the Maharal's metaphor, the tree expands into branches and fruit, all of which stem from the same root. Hence the apparent contradiction between the literal and non-literal interpretations does not generate a tension between them in representing the truth; they coexist peacefully and enrich our lives.[2]

A fascinating midrash explores how the trees feared the creation of the ax precisely because, for trees, the act of *kotzeir* creates an existential challenge.

When the world was created God first made the trees.... afterward, God made iron. The trees shook with terror as they foresaw now the making of axes and their eventual demise. Said God: "Don't be afraid. If you give none of your wood, there can be no handles with which to make axes."[3]

Beautiful things can be exploited toward violent and oppressive

1. A. Kariv, *Kitvei Maharal MiPrag* (Jerusalem, 5720 [1959–60]), vol. 2, pg. 283.
2. Mordechai Rotenberg, *The Psychology of Tzimtzum: Self, Other and God* (Jerusalem: Koren Publishers, 2015).
3. Genesis Rabba, 5:9.

ends. We are learning, through *kotzeir*, to see the fullness of the tree, the fullness of being. Buber taught that we cannot see only a part of another person but rather we should see their wholeness, their fullness.

> As long as love is "blind" – that is, as long as it does not see a whole being – it does not yet truly stand under the basic word of relation.[4]
>
> The basic word I-You [I-Thou] can only be spoken with one's whole being.[5]

This is not only the work toward the other but also the relationship toward the self. Dr. Mona Fishbane writes:

> Buber's insight here is profound. I can only see you in your wholeness when I embrace my own wholeness, when I reintegrate my split-off parts. Then I do not need you to carry my parts, and I do not need to do the dance of projective identification.[6]

Dr. Max Klau writes about the work of Dr. Yaneer Bar Yam on complex systems theory.

> Bar Yam's overview of interdependence invites us to consider three different types of systems and imagine what happens when a piece of the system is removed:
> The first example is a material like a piece of metal or a glass of water. In these instances, it is possible to remove a component of the system (by cutting off a corner of the metal sheet or removing a spoonful of water from the glass) without profoundly changing the system. . . .

---

4. Martin Buber, *I and Thou*, translated by Walter Kaufmann, 1970 (NY: Charles Scribner's sons – German, 1921), p. 67–68.

5. Ibid, p. 54.

6. Dr. Mona Fishbane, "I, Thou, and We: A Dialogical Approach to Couples Therapy," in *Journal of Marital and Family Therapy*, 1998, Vol. 24, No. 1, p. 46.

A second example of a more interdependent system is a plant or tree. Imagine what happens [if] you cut some roots or branches from a tree: While the tree as a whole may continue to grow, it will surely be impacted by the loss of the part. And the part itself will be profoundly affected (it will die) because of the removal.

We see an even higher level of interdependence [that] appears when we look at a more complex system like an animal. Remove a leg or a lung, and both the animal and the part are – to put it mildly – profoundly affected. Unlike a tree, the attempt to separate almost any component part from the whole in a living animal is sure to have a major impact on both the whole animal and the part that was removed.

Dr. Bar Yam states:

> These three examples show very different kinds of interdependence. Recognizing that these different behaviors exist is an important part of characterizing all of the systems we are interested in. Consider the family or organization you are a part of. How strong are the dependencies between the parts? ... These are key questions for understanding the system and how we might affect it by our actions. Just asking these questions when we think about our world is an important part of understanding relationships.[7]

So, in this approach of complex systems theory, when the less complex controls the more complex, a system cannot develop. If a dictator controls the masses, the country cannot develop and evolve. When the power is given to the people (through democracy rather than tyranny) the complexity of the system is given the freedom to evolve and adapt.

---

7. Bar-Yam, "General Features of Complex Systems," in Knowledge Management, Organizational Intelligence and Learning, and Complexity, Vol. I, 2001, p. 8.

In the broadest sense, we are assumed to work the land and take advantage of the availability of vegetation to provide food for our families and our communities. In a fascinating midrash,[8] the rabbis specifically reflect on how, if the Messiah is arriving, he will actually disappear if we stop our planting. Indeed, the redemption of the world cannot emerge without us engaging with the world, and in particular the vegetative aspect of the world.

We also reflect on our unfortunate destruction of the environment. Jewish law, originating in the Torah itself, specifically states that we may not destroy fruit trees in a time of war. This is the basis for *bal tashchit* (literally "do not destroy," the environmental mitzvah to preserve and conserve):

> When you shall besiege a city a long time, in making war against it to take it, you shall not destroy its trees by forcing an ax against them; for you may eat of them, and you shall not cut them down. For is the tree of the field a man that it should be besieged by you? Only the trees which you know are not trees for food, you shall destroy and cut them down; and you shall build siege works against the city that makes war with you until it is subdued.[9]

Maimonides builds off this:

> It is forbidden to chop down fruit trees and to deny them water so they will dry, as it says in the Torah "do not destroy its trees." And anyone who does so will be given lashes. This applies not only during a siege, but in all instances that one chops down a fruit tree in a destructive manner; but one may destroy a fruit tree if it is harming other trees, or it is harming the field of others, or if its maintenance is expensive. The Torah only prohibits destroying trees for the sake of destruction. Any

8. Avot D'Rebbe Natan.
9. Deuteronomy 20:19–20.

non-fruit-bearing trees one is allowed to destroy, even for no purpose. One can do the same for a fruit tree that has aged and bears little fruit and is not worth maintaining; it is permissible to cut it down.

This is true not only of trees, but whoever breaks vessels or rips clothing or destroys a building, or blocks up a water source, or destroys foodstuffs in a destructive manner, has violated the prohibition of *bal tashchit* – do not be wasteful....[10]

The Midrash reminds us of our moral responsibility:

When the Holy One be Blessed created the first man, God took him and led him around all the trees of the Garden of Eden, and said to him, "Behold My works, how beautiful and commendable they are! All that I have created, for your sake I created it. Pay heed that you do not corrupt and destroy My universe; for if you corrupt it there is no one to repair it after you."[11]

This offers an anthropocentric worldview; albeit one in which we are charged with deep responsibility and cannot pray our way out of our crisis. To be involved in the act of *kotzeir* means to be caught up with some of the challenging actions and thoughts that plants allow us to engage in. And so, pausing from *kotzeir* on Shabbat enables us to recommit to physical conservation and spiritual interconnectivity.

As we recite in Psalms, "Those who tearfully sow will reap in glad song" (*Hazorim b'dimah, b'rina yiktzoru*). Indeed, may your *kotzeir* be joyful, and may our glories transform our traumas.

---

10. Maimonides, *Mishneh Torah*, "The Laws of Kings and their Wars," 6:8–10.
11. Ecclesiastes Rabba, 7.19.

4.

Me'ameir (Bundling sheaves)

THE MELACHA OF *me'ameir* is concerned with the act of gathering (and particularly, the gathering of produce or bundling of sheaves), once again connected to the totality of the agricultural experience. What's interesting about this stage in the agricultural process is that produce is moved from the ground towards its ultimate use. And by this time in the agricultural cycle, the farmer is engaged in gathering what has been harvested. The farmer is – or hopes to be – close to seeing a profit since the crop is now being prepared for the marketplace. The Midrash warns us of the moral dimensions of this final stage.

> It is like the case of a man who had bought a sheaf of corn which he placed upon his shoulder and then walked in front of the donkey who was longing to eat it. But what did the owner do? When he reached home, he tied the sheaf high above the donkey so that the animal could not reach it. People said to him, "You cruel man; the animal has been running the whole day for the sake of the sheaf, and now you refuse to give it to him." So, it is with the hired worker; the whole day he has been toiling and sweating, hoping for his wages, and you send him away empty-handed.[1]

---

1. Tanchuma, Mishpatim 10, commentary on Exodus 22: 25–26.

40

Professor Amartya Sen invites us to consider a flute found in a village. Who should get to keep the flute? The child who made the flute? The child who can play the flute the best? Or the child who will never be able to afford a flute? Here, crucial issues of political theory and economics are raised. So too, in our gathering of the profits, how should profits be divided?

When we gather our figurative (or literal) crops with our own hands, we risk thinking that we deserve to take for ourselves whatever the marketplace offers us and might find ourselves forgetting that we must share credit for what we reap with those who helped us grow it.

On a philosophical level, we reflect on what it means to gather ideas. In reflecting on real-world ethics, we might consider all the dimensions we need to gather together to get a full picture of the world around us, including the principles, context, data, history, perspectives, experiences, dialogue, situation, and consequences that define the universe around us. We don't just smack down the abstract principle or law on the table and expect it to give us all the answers. Rather, we need to go through the process of gathering. And what we gather will allow us to recognize the multi-dimensionality of the decisions that face us daily. Can we gather together, and hold together, all the complexity in our moral deliberations? Just as we string together chords to make music, we can string together various ideas to get a more clear and profound perspective. This is about moral pragmatism, a holding of resistance to hard absolute theories. In doing so, we embrace a plurality of values. Rabbi Walter Wurzburger, the late student of Rabbi Joseph Soloveitchik, writes:

> The pluralism of Jewish ethics manifests itself in the readiness to operate with several independent ethical norms and principles such as concern for love, justice, truth, and peace. Since they frequently give rise to conflicting obligations, it becomes necessary to rely upon intuitive judgments to resolve the conflict. There is, however, another dimension to the pluralism of Jewish

ethics: it is multi-tiered and comprises many strands. It contains
not only objective components such as duties and obligations
but also numerous values and ideals possessing only subjective
validity. Moreover, the pluralistic thrust of Jewish ethics makes
it possible to recognize the legitimacy of many alternate ethical
values and ideals.[1]

In the process of committing to moral pluralism, however, we
run the risk of social chaos; when we try to operationalize the
moral compasses that set the paths that we perceive to be purely
on a theoretical plane. For example, we know, on various levels,
that we need herd immunity in order to deal with communicable
diseases. The population has to agree to immunization for the
necessary herd immunity to develop optimally. People need to
live by a social contract to ensure there is some degree of societal
trust and cooperation. So, here we engage in organizing. Each
of us must gather together all the unique factors to resolve our
personal moral dilemmas, but then collectively we need discourse
and organizing – that is, community gathering – to become
aligned on collective issues. We embrace a pluralism of "live and
let live" at times, and at other times of moral concessions, we
must make sacrifices in our commitments for collective consensus
and cooperation. We take a majoritarian approach but also need
to hold on to minority views. We hold on to the individual's
liberty along with the collective's well-being. So too, we offer the
democratization of knowledge and observe the cyclical nature
of how different values are emphasized. At times, we may select
to prioritize the collective well-being (like in a pandemic and the
need for immunization). At other times, we prioritize the freedom
of minorities from over-reaching religious approaches.

When we think about the need to gather together the different perspectives that allow for this pluralism, we recognize that each of us only has access to partial truth. God is the infinite kaleidoscope holding all the partial truths. Our job is to gather the sparks from all the partial truths to participate in a fuller Godly existence. Rav Avraham Isaac Kook, the first Ashkenazi chief rabbi of pre-state Israel, taught that remaining only in one's own partial truth is to remain in the dark.

We can consider the gathered pieces of the Divine, kaleidoscopic truth through the prism of the Jewish holidays. For one, the holiday of Sukkot is referred to as *Chag Ha'Asif* (the Feast of Ingathering, the Festival of Gathering).[2] This refers to the gathering of the harvest but also recognizes the importance of having our families and communities gather together in celebration.

Related to the word *me'ameir* is the counting of the *Omer* (these words share the same root – *ayin, mem, reish*). We count the days between Passover, when barley was gathered together for the *omer* sacrifice brought in the Temple,[3] and Shavuot, another agriculturally significant holiday which we mark today, in part, by reading of how Ruth met Boaz when she was gathering food for herself and her mother-in-law. When we count the *Omer* today, we gather together the weeks that transition our psyche from freedom, represented by Passover and the Exodus, to responsibility, which is reflected in the Torah, given to Moses on Shavuot. Just as during the period of the *Omer* when we look to ascend in our spiritual consciousness, so too, in our refraining from physical *me'ameir* on Shabbat, we refocus ourselves on gathering together more perspectives to deepen and expand our consciousness.

---

2. Exodus 23:16.

3. The term *omer* is technically a measurement, equivalent to roughly 1.5 pounds, and refers to the amount (of barley) gathered for this sacrifice. The specific measurement of *omer* is first found in the Torah in relation to the daily amount of *manna* to be collected by each and every individual in the desert. We can perhaps suggest that *omer* represents the reciprocal relationship between us and God. God gives an *omer* to us, and we in turn offer an *omer* to God.

Maimonides writes that the goal of this counting (or gathering of the weeks) is about a love relationship with God.[4]

> Shavuot is the time of the Giving of the Torah. In order to honor and elevate this day, we count the days from the previous festival until it [arrives], like someone who is waiting for a loved one to arrive, who counts the days by the hours. This is the reason for counting the *Omer* from the day that we left Egypt until the day of the Giving of the Torah, as this was the ultimate purpose of leaving Egypt: "And I will bring them to Me."[5]

Rabbi Aryeh Carmell teaches that the goal in counting is to transition from being a non-human animal to becoming human.

> The *omer* on Pesach was from the barley harvest. The offering on Shavuot was of wheat. Barley is mainly food for animals. Wheat is food for human beings. The Torah hints to us that physical independence by itself still leaves man – from the Torah perspective – on the animal level. The counting of the forty-nine days signifies a sevenfold refining process and marks our progress to full human status with our acceptance of the Torah at Sinai, seven weeks after the Exodus.[6]

The Zohar reminds us that part of the *Omer* counting experience is also the day of Lag Ba'Omer,[7] where we gather together to create light and reflect on the revelation of the Zohar.

---

4. Maimonides, *Guide for the Perplexed* 3:43.
5. Exodus 19:4.
6. Rabbi Aryeh Carmell, *Masterplan, Judaism: Its Program, meanings, Goals* (NY, Jerusalem: Feldheim, 1991), p. 205.
7. *Lag* is comprised of the Hebrew letters *lamed* and *gimel*, and is the numerical equivalent of 33; Lag Ba'Omer, then, is the 33rd day of the *Omer* period.

On the day that Rabbi Shimon bar Yochai was to leave this world, he organized his teachings. His friends came to his room and he said to them, "Now is a time of favor. I can now reveal to you holy things that have not been revealed until now." ... All that day the fire never left his room, and ... no one who was able to approach as the light and the fire were surrounding him ... [After he passed away, and they came to bury him] the fire flew into the air and danced before him. A voice was heard [from Heaven] saying, "Come and gather [every year] for the *hilulah* (anniversary) of Rabbi Shimon bar Yochai."[8]

Indeed, central to kabbalah is the idea of *tikkun olam* (repairing the world) through the gathering and elevating of the sparks.

On the level of global justice, we can also pull out and see the fuller human experience shared by the individuals who, gathered together, make up humanity which collectively faces bundles of challenges. The Midrash says:

If all the suffering and pain in the world were gathered [on one side of a scale], and poverty was on the other side, poverty would outweigh them all.[9]

Indeed, when we gather the evidence at large, we can refocus ourselves on the largest moral problems. This is also true on an existential level when we reflect on life and death. Consider how the Book of Genesis refers to the death of the three patriarchs as a gathering to one's people (*va'yai'asef*, literally meaning "he was gathered").

And Abraham breathed his last, dying at a good, ripe age, old and contented; and he was gathered to his ancestors.[10]

---

8. Zohar, Idra Zuta, Devarim, Parshat Ha'azinu, p. 296.
9. Exodus Rabbah 31:14.
10. Genesis 25:8.

He (Isaac) was gathered to his kin in ripe old age.[11]

When Jacob finished his instructions to his sons, he drew his feet into the bed, and breathing his last, he was gathered to his people.[12]

We can refer to gathering as *oseif* (as just seen above), as *mekabeitz* (hence the name kibbutz, a gathering of a collective), and here as *me'ameir*. In this world, we gather together as families and as communities. We gather together ideas and information. In death, we return to our ancestors and are gathered together by them and with them, and as those still on earth and in mourning, we gather together to remember.

---

11. Genesis 35:29.
12. Genesis 49:33.

5.

Dash (Threshing)

As part of the agricultural experience, the act of *dash* (threshing) involves loosening grain kernels from their stalks; the process of removing the edible grain from the chaff is the next step in the process after reaping and gathering. Threshing is labor-intensive when it's done by hand, so some ancient farmers – and even some contemporary ones – would beat the grain using a flail on a threshing floor. Some would have their donkeys or oxen walk in circles on the grain on a hard surface. In modern times, some farmers would put grain on the road so vehicles could drive over them.

This *melacha* is, ultimately, concerned with extracting edible food from inedible objects. Traditionally, this *melacha* is treated hand-in-hand with *boreir* (selecting) and is extended to milking cows[1] and even to a nursing mother expressing milk to be saved for later use. The halacha (Jewish law) distinguishes between removing a banana or an orange from a peel that is snug and removing peas from an inedible pod that are not snug and which

---

1. Milking cows, while technically problematic, is permissible on the grounds that not milking would place the cows in severe pain and perhaps even danger. Similarly, a woman may express milk even if it were not to be used on Shabbat, providing that she feels pain and reckons that she cannot wait until after Shabbat. Putting it another way, *tza'ar ba'alei chayim* (pain experienced by all living creatures) is a prime factor in determining the permissibility of an otherwise problematic act on Shabbat.

are normally removed well before eating. The former, peeling bananas and oranges, is not problematic from the outset, as removing the peel earlier could ruin the food, whereas the latter is also considered permissible even though care could have been taken to remove the pod beforehand.[1] A derivative of *dash* is *sechita* (squeezing), such as wringing out a wet towel or squeezing a lemon into a cup of tea.

The act of threshing is important in halachic contexts beyond the laws of Shabbat. For example, a quandary emerged that pitted a halachic imperative relating to the need to support community leaders against another having to do with animal welfare. The laws of *terumah*, which require that portions of the harvest of Israelites and Levites be given to the *kohanim* (priests), forbid an animal working on the threshing floor from eating the grain at its feet. Yet, at the same time, muzzling an animal engaged in threshing is biblically prohibited, presumably in recognition of the discomfort that an animal, engaged in hard work, would feel if it is muzzled with food just below its mouth.[2] The sages developed a creative solution, suggesting that the owners muzzle their animals with a feedbag containing grain similar to that being threshed, so the animals would not feel frustrated while at their labors.[3]

So, too, when slaves were freed, the Torah instructs that they be supplied from the threshing floor:

> If a fellow Hebrew, man or woman, is sold to you, s/he shall serve you six years, and in the seventh year, you shall set him/her free. When you set him/her free, do not let him/her go empty-handed: Furnish him/her out of the flock, threshing floor, and vat, with which God has blessed you. Bear in mind that you

---

1. Here we see the Sages' sensitivity even to an individual's desire to fulfill *oneg Shabbat* (physical enjoyment of Shabbat).
2. Deuteronomy 25:4.
3. Terumot 9:3; also cf. Bava Metzia 90a. Another solution would be to employ the animal of a kohein, which may be fed *terumah*.

were slaves in the land of Egypt and your God redeemed you; therefore, I enjoin this commandment upon you today.

But should he say to you, "I do not want to leave you" – for he loves your household and is happy with you –you shall take an awl and put it through his ear into the door, and he shall become your slave in perpetuity. Do the same with your female slave. When you do set him free, do not feel aggrieved; for in the six years, he has given you double the service of a hired slave. Moreover, your God will bless you in all you do.[4]

Here, we're dealing with slave reparations paid directly from the threshing floor. This is also an important point concerning prisoner re-entry. One of the reasons why the recidivism rate is so high is due to improper re-entry into society. We must ask and address the issue of what freed prisoners need to re-enter society in order to succeed.

The Sages further required that there be some distance created from the threshing floor:

A fixed threshing floor must be kept fifty cubits from a town. A man should not fix a threshing floor on his own estate unless there is a clear space all around of fifty cubits. He must keep it away from the plantation of his neighbor and his plowed fallow a sufficient distance to prevent damage being caused.[5]

Rashi explains that the primary reason for the distance is to protect those passing by as well as people in the fields. Indeed, this is another lesson about how we think about food sources. We must do the necessary work to feed ourselves and our families, but we can't hurt others in the process. In fact, we need to put special precautions in place to protect workers, animals, the land, and society at large. We must consider the "essential workers"

---

4. Deuteronomy 15:12–18.
5. Mishna, Tractate Bava Batra 2:8.

and the precarious positions they are put in each day in fields and factories, for such low wages, to ensure that we have the fruits, vegetables, and other essentials we need on our plates and in our homes.

The threshing floor also plays a role in other areas of the Torah. God instructs David to build an altar on top of a threshing floor and he does.[6] From this passage, we see that the threshing floor is a space that can be made sacred. A Middle Eastern outdoor threshing floor was typically on a hill with decent but not overly strong breezes (for winnowing after threshing) and that space was paved flat. Thus, David building an altar on a threshing floor meant that rather than take over an existing hilltop altar to a pagan god, David found an appropriate spot in a grain-fertile area in which to build an altar to engage in Divine worship, thanking God for providing the harvest bounty. Further, the fact that this was the threshing floor of a Jebusite – even as Araunah (the owner of this threshing floor) was reimbursed – means that no Israelite's land was confiscated, expropriated, or taken possession of by the right of eminent domain.

Similarly, Ruth orchestrated her key encounter with Boaz to take place at the threshing floor.[7] That story reminds us that choosing the right time, place, and manner to interact with another person helps us relate to others with the dignity that their humanity requires. Historically, threshing floors were out of town and the family normally slept on those floors during the season of threshing and winnowing. Boaz, being alone on the threshing floor, shows that he had wealth, that he was single, and that he might be secluded enough to consider marital relations and start a family.

On a mystical Jewish level, the connection to threshing is most obvious. As the kabbalah teaches, the hidden sparks of goodness are trapped within *kelipot* (shells) and our *mitzvot* can shatter

---

6. Samuel II, chapter 24: 18–25.
7. Ruth 3: 6–8.

the outer shells – threshing the shells, so to speak – and liberate and elevate the sparks.

On a moral level too, we want to free the good and noble from the sort of entrapment that a kernel of grain experiences within the imprisonment of chaff. But how can we do that when entrapment is all around us? In Michel Foucault's book "Madness and Civilization," he explores the history of how reason and madness have normally been contrasted; madness is seen as the dark side of reason. But he challenges this binary notion, suggesting that madness, such as that seemingly exhibited by a prophet or seer, offers a new form of insight and truth. But such people are (perhaps incorrectly) marginalized along with others who are criminalized. He shows a historical progression in the societal shared understanding of madness, demonstrating that madness is still not validated but at least is seen as something to cure rather than to criminalize. Later, Foucault goes deeper into the history of torture and punishment at large. Most famously, he explores Jeremy Bentham's panopticon. Bentham, a late 18th-century/early 19th-century British philosopher, considered the first proponent of utilitarianism, imagined a world where the greatest pleasure led to the greatest good for society. His imagined prison model – the panopticon – is a massive institution where everything is hyper-structured and everyone is observed. He extends this idea of "discipline" to various other institutions beyond just the prison where we turn subjects into objects.

Foucault suggests that power is spread throughout all practices and that there is a race to accumulate power in order to modify others' behaviors in all areas of society. Yet, one might suggest that he is not cynical since he does also argue that power can be productive, such as in education. Power is an inevitable dynamic of our lives. He wants to see us engage in the just distribution of power rather than falling into systems of dominance. There will, for example, inevitably be a power dynamic between lovers, yet we can think carefully about how to balance that out.

What we cannot do is be blind or naive to the power dynamics around us. After all, such illusions lead to greater suffering for all. We have to engage in processes of distinguishing the true from the untrue, the good from the evil. We have to differentiate food from the inedible, that which can nourish us from that which cannot. This is where our pluralism or relativism has its limits. There still need to be some binaries within our more complex epistemological structures; there need to be limits and definitions and separations. We need to be able to separate the chaff from the wheat.

Now, there are cases where we don't just want to discard the negative. Consider our emotional life, for example. We are invited to serve God *bechol levavcha*[8] ("with all our heart"), and not just with our positive emotions. So, our negative emotions can be our teachers. Rather than feel bad about bad feelings, we can work to integrate all of our emotions into a fuller self and fuller service.

Stepping back on Shabbat from the process of threshing (and thus removing food from non-food) helps us to focus on the gray areas in our lives, but also helps us maintain focus on the black and white areas of our lives.

---

8. The Torah could have used the word *libcha* rather than *levavcha* (the non-possessive forms of these words are *lev* and *levav*, the former containing one Hebrew letter *bet*, the latter containing two. It is this choice of *levavcha* that lead our Sages to state that we are to worship God with both our positive and negative emotions, with both our wheat and our chaff.

6.

Zoreh (Winnowing)

THE NEXT MELACHA is *zoreh* (winnowing), another step in the agricultural process of removing the chaff from the grain. Winnowing involves using a tool to throw threshed produce into the air so that the wind blows the lighter chaff from the heavier kernels. Similar to the previous *melacha* of *dash* (threshing), this process is about removing food from non-food.[1] Some think it's specifically about using wind for such a process, and others suggest that wind is not necessary for an action to come within the scope of *zoreh*. And so, one traditional extension of this *melacha* would perhaps prohibit shaking a tablecloth outside to remove crumbs from the tablecloth.[2] Wind can be very dangerous (tornados) or quite delightful (summer breeze). Here, we see wind as something helpful and useful.

In thinking about how the weekday activity of winnowing is dependent upon the airspace and the air that fills it, we can reflect on the idea that we are all interconnected through our breath. Today, we are quite aware of the phrase "I can't breathe" that accompanied the tragic murder of George Floyd (and Eric Garner

---

1. It is interesting and instructive to consider the act of removing excessive amounts of cellophane from an airline kosher meal (removing the destructive inedible portion from the edible portion). Similarly, perhaps we should ponder the excessive amount of plastic used in the wrapping of toys.

2. Common practice is to permit shaking out a tablecloth, as is wiping crumbs off of a tablecloth while still on the table.

in 2014), a phrase that now represents the work that so many are doing to make up in some way for that tragedy and others like it. And as we confront the COVID-19 pandemic, we're aware that we wear masks because we share the air. Also, with a rising climate change crisis, we see how interconnected our actions are in surviving together in this ecology that's made up, in large part, of the air that we all hope remains clean.

Rabbi Moshe Feinstein, considered one of the greatest halachic decisors of the 20th century, taught how second-hand smoke was real damage. To demonstrate this point, he quoted a Talmudic case where a bird took a berry from one yard and dropped it on the roof of another yard (leaving a stain). Indeed, the first owner has responsibility even though they didn't actively cause harm, and the berry traveled through the air, not at the control of the owner. So too, with secondhand smoke, one doesn't intend to harm others, nonetheless, the unintended consequences create harm to others. In our pandemic times, we understand more than ever the power of saving lives through taking responsibility for our own space, our own breath, and the airspace around us.

Here we can reflect on the Tragedy of the Commons, a theory which originated in an essay in 1833 by British economist William Forster Lloyd. This is a term often used in environmental contexts with regard to sustainable development, representing a system in which individuals who all need a shared resource behave independently according to their own respective self-interests, contrary to the common good of the collective, in a way that depletes or ruins the shared resource. What do we do about the problem of those pushing fiercely for economic growth without environmental regulation? What will happen to our shared spaces and resources, our oceans, rivers, and clean air, if everyone does their own separate *zoreh*, throwing whatever pollution they want into our collective airspace?

Professor Daniel Matt, a noted scholar of Jewish mysticism, asks:

Why is the sky blue? Among the wavelengths of light in the sun's spectrum, blue oscillates at the highest frequency and is, therefore, scattered effectively by molecules of air in our atmosphere. Because the blue light is bouncing off air in all directions, the sky turns blue. To me, this is more amazing than ancient Mesopotamian and biblical beliefs that the sky is blue because of all the water up there.[1]

We can experience the Divine gift of breathing space, of experiencing the visible and invisible at once.

Likewise, Rabbi Dr. Arthur Green writes:

We are urgently in need of ways to renew our sense of human responsibility for preserving the natural world around us. As we call for less abusive treatment of earth's resources; for a more reverent protection of air, soil, and water; and for the preservation of species in both plant and animal realm, we need a theological language that will serve as the basis for such a change in human attitude. The age in which we live cries out for a religious language that speaks of the underlying *unity* of all existence, a unity that is manifest within life's diversity, rather than of the struggles of species against species. This unity is that of Creation, of the sense that all beings emerge from a single source.[2]

Consider this idea from the new Koren Rav Kook prayer book which addresses how to stand during prayer:[3]

This is not merely a matter of which direction one must face during the Amidah prayer. Rather, a visualization is called for.

---

1. Daniel Matt, *God and The Big Bang* (Woodstock, Vermont: Jewish Lights Publishing, 1996), page xiii.

2. Arthur Green, *Seek My Face, A Jewish Mystical Theology* (Vermont: Jewish Lights Publishing, 2012), Page 51.

3. *Koren Rav Kook Siddur* (Toby Press LLC, 2017), p. 95.

In one's mind's eye, one must imagine that one is actually facing
the Temple. Rav Kook's eminent disciple, Rabbi Ya'akov Moshe
Harlap wrote[4] to his son in America that through meditative
prayer one actually extends the "airspace of the Land of Israel"
(*avira de'Eretz Yisrael*)! Earlier, Rabbi Nahman of Breslov taught
that by clapping one's hands during prayer, one is able to purify
the contaminated air outside of the Land of Israel. "And then
the air of the place where the Israelite prays is purified, and he
draws the holy air as in the Land of Israel."[5]

Through this radical theology which one might even anachronis-
tically term a Hasidic framework for post-Zionism, we change
the air around us. Our minds determine where we are. As the Baal
Shem Tov, the founder of Hasidism, taught, each of us is where
our respective minds are. The mental and spiritual realm, for
these thinkers, matters more than the physical, objective reality
around us. The self follows the mind; the truest reality is found
in the soul.

The philosopher Philo, writing in the first century (one of the
most fascinating periods in human history), wrote about how
reflecting on the air, among many other magnificent wonders,
can bring us closer to our Creator:

> Who can look upon statues or paintings without thinking at
> once of a sculptor or painter? Who can see clothes or ships or
> houses without getting the idea of a weaver and a shipwright
> or a house builder? And when one enters a well-ordered city in
> which the arrangements for civil life are very admirably man-
> aged, what else will you suppose but that this city is directed
> by good rulers? So then, one who comes to the truly great city,
> and beholds hills and plains with animals and plants, the rivers,

4. Rabbi Ya'akov Moshe Harlap, *Mikhtevei Maron*, ed. Ze'ev Wolf Charlop
(Jerusalem, 1988), Letter 1 (p. 9).
5. Rabbi Nahman of Breslov, *Likkutei Moharan* I, 44.

spring-fed or winter torrents, streaming along, the seas with
their expanses, the air with its happily tempered phases, the
yearly seasons passing into each other, and then the sun and
moon ruling the day and night, and the other heavenly bodies
fixed or planetary and the whole firmament revolving in rhyth-
mic order, must one not naturally or rather necessarily gain the
conceptions of the Maker and Father and Ruler also?[6]

Meditating on our breath, we might wonder: Why does God
require humans to breathe in order to live? Certainly, a Divine
plan could have fashioned human beings in another way. Is it to
remind us, with each breath, of the relationship between our inner
world and our outer world? Is it to give us the gift of meditation
and spiritual attunement with the miraculous experience of life?
Perhaps the answer is clearer in our peculiar time than it was in
the past. Perhaps we were fashioned in a way that requires us to
breathe so that, existentially, we never forget the interconnectivity of all life. We are one fabric, intricately interwoven: Humans
with other humans, with non-human animals, with trees, with air
and water. With each breath in, we inhale all the life force around
us, and all the interconnected life force everywhere, from all time.
With each exhale, we return the conscious gift of compassionate
interconnectivity. Today, many of us wear masks. (Hopefully,
every one of us who is privileged to be able to spend some time
in public wears a mask, in the interest of keeping us all safe.)
These masks can remind us of the gift of life, the gift of breath,
the gift of the interconnectivity of all life. We are one. There is
only the One.
   Before we encountered the hyper-challenged world of 2020,
some were thinking that we had mastered the ideal form of government with hyper-unregulated capitalism. Some were investing

---

6. "De Specialibus Legibus" I:6 (Loeb Classical Library; London and Cambridge, MA: William Heinemann Ltd. and Harvard University Press, 1950),
vol. 7, p. 119.

millions in immortality as if we'd wiped out disease and were ready to conquer death. Some, growing ever richer, claimed they were invincible and unstoppable and fully in control of their fate. Some laughed that God was dead and the individual was now all-powerful. Some thought that, as Americans, we could have literally everything we wanted. To destroy the planet but to be okay. To exploit the poor but to be okay. To block out asylum seekers but still breathe the same air as everyone else on the same planet. To live selfishly and privately but to be safe from the chaos of the world. To exploit, but to be safe in mansions. And, we've once again been reminded that we must wake up from such delusions. It is hard to know what to reach for in order to feel a sense of security today. But if we reach for anything, it should start with humility.

We don't have all the answers. None of us is in control.

We don't know where we're headed. But humility can lead to solidarity. Humility can lead to love. And that can help us work together towards the answers we all need.

This gem on healing penned by Rumi, a 13th-century poet and Sufi mystic, touches on our experience of the air.

> Lord, the air smells good today,
> straight from the mysteries
> within the inner courts of God.
> A grace like new clothes thrown
> across the garden, free medicine for everybody.
> The trees in their prayer, the birds in praise
> the first blue violets kneeling.
> Whatever came from Being is caught up in being, drunkenly
> forgetting the way back.

In thinking of the airwaves, we can also reflect on the power of speech and the importance of putting healthy, positive, truthful speech into the air. Indeed, we can never take back what we have put out there. There is the power of an apology but it can only repair and never completely remove harm. Just as God created the first human beings through breath (*nefesh Elokim*), so too each of us is recreated with each breath, and we can create worlds or destroy worlds through our breath turned into speech.

In working for a healthy emotional life, we can think about processes of separation as well. In evolutionary psychology, there is value to guilt, as it can lead to necessary repairs to rejoin a group. On the other hand, we know there can be destructive rather than reparative guilt. So too with shame; there can be both healthy and toxic forms of shame. In exploring our emotional lives, we can separate out the parts in our airspace. For Rebbe Nachman, this was literally done through speaking, even yelling.

Zoreh reminds us that we each individually need air in order to breathe and live. *Zoreh* equally reminds us that the air we breathe impacts others as well. Through our breathing, our constant act of *zoreh*, we have the power to impact all humanity and all living beings. We can choose to leave an imprint of harm or of benefit to the world. Let us choose breathing "life" into the world, impacting the planet for the good and doing our part to ensure its survival.

7.
Boreir (Sorting)

WE CONTINUE OUR discussion about separation. *Boreir* is the *melacha* of separating what we want from what we don't want. In the *Mishkan*, after the winnowing process (*zoreh*) separated kernels from their chaff, a pile of kernels would be left mixed with the debris. *Boreir* was the process that selected the kernels from the rest of the debris.

Traditionally, the rules surrounding this *melacha* require that we avoid sorting that which is mixed together. The practical applications are complex and multifaceted. One may move food that is already on a plate while eating, separating the different items and organizing them, since that's the process of eating normally; it's done for the purpose of eating food immediately. It seems that, even subconsciously, our minds are programmed to separate the good from the bad or the desirable from the undesirable and not vice versa. If one is to remove the undesirable, it should be removed along with some of the desirable. For example, when someone removes an undesirable bone from a bowl of soup, it should be taken out with a spoonful of the desirable broth. Similarly, watermelon seeds should be removed with a bit of watermelon.

Professor Robert Kegan, a professor at the Harvard Graduate School of Education and a developmental psychologist, has elucidated an important model of separation that manifests itself psychologically, particularly in adult development. Kegan shows how one develops by moving the structure of one's knowing (what can be seen as a subject) to the content of one's knowing (what can be seen as an object). It is through this separation process that one becomes able to hold what one feels and knows, rather than be held by it.

This is also true with regard to our emotions as they relate to injustice. In his new book, *Love and Rage: The Path of Liberation Through Anger*, which delves into the subject of systemic injustice, Lama Rod Owens teaches about an approach that validates our anger but also transcends it, another process of psychic separation that helps us grow. Consider these words from James Baldwin:

> I can only tell you about myself as much as I can face about myself. And this has happened to everybody who's tried to live. You go through life for a long time thinking, No one has ever suffered the way I've suffered, my God, my God. And then you realize – You read something or hear something, and you realize that your suffering does not isolate you; your suffering is your bridge. Many people have suffered before you, many people are suffering around you and always will, and all you can do is bring, hopefully, a little light into that suffering. Enough light so that the person who is suffering can begin to comprehend his suffering and start to live with it and change it, change the situation. We don't change anything; all we can do is invest people with the morale to change it for themselves.

Most studies of emotions are concerned with negative emotions: sadness, anger, and anxiety for example. I would argue instead that we should explore the experience of laughter, a universal experience found in all cultures. In an authentic experience of laughter, one steps away from an experience in order to play with it, to observe it, and to see it differently. Such is the experience of laughter that it has the power to reduce our adrenaline and decrease our stress; in other words, laughing is healthy for us.

Non-human animals laugh too. Studies show that rats that are tickled to laughter during their juvenile stage are more likely to laugh in later stages of life. And chimpanzees, humanity's closest related cousins, laugh through inhaling and exhaling while humans laugh only through exhaling.

Cognitive neuroscientist Sophie Scott, a fellow at University College London, has commented about how laughter connects, creates bonds, and unites all of humanity. The contagion of laughter is more powerful with the familiarity of a person. But, ultimately, laughing with someone else or not doing so is about separation, about who is in and who is out. It's related to feelings of exclusivity and is about affiliation. The ability to laugh with others depends on who or what is being laughed at. We laugh, most frequently, because we like being on the inside. Scott shows how we rarely laugh at a joke itself but rather in order to connect with the other, sharing the laughter experience together. It's intentionally communicative and connective. It's often highly nuanced and indicates who is in the group and who is not; it's about power. Who laughs at you? Who laughs with you and who does not? Most of one's childhood can be consumed with these dynamics and how we navigate our relationship to laughter.

Still, we know that cultures differ. In America, it has been shown that, in the workplace, we don't tolerate laughter in different frequencies other than the norm. In Japan, any laughter is considered inappropriate at work. Some cultures laugh at bad news. In traditional Christianity, great pains are taken to show that Jesus never laughed. He must be serious; it wouldn't be appropriate for such a figure to laugh. For some, laughter is a sign of weakness, reducing one's power and strength.

So, how does Jewish thought understand laughter?

The most obvious case of biblical laughter is the teaching that our great patriarch Yitzchak – Isaac – is named for his mother's laughter.[1] Interestingly enough, we can also learn from his

---

1. Genesis 21.

half-brother Yishmael's laughter and the different reaction that laughter evokes.

The rabbis of the Talmud considered laughter to be of considerable importance, in both a positive and a negative sense. Thus, Rabbah teaches that one should open up learning experiences with a joke because "Laughter opens the soul to moral and spiritual imagination."[2] And the Gemara tells us that the Prophet Elijah told Rabbi Berokah Hoza'a that two people who made a living by making people laugh merited to be included in the World to Come.[3] At the same time, the Talmud also warns of excessive merriment.[4]

The Talmud tells of a rabbinic discussion about God's predilection to laugh and to play, with some rabbis describing how God sets aside a portion of each day for such activity.[5] Consider this famous story of how the rabbis imagine God laughing:

> Said Rabbi Jeremiah: "The Torah had already been given at Mount Sinai; we pay no attention to a Heavenly Voice, because Thou hast long since written in the Torah at Mount Sinai, 'After the majority must one incline.'"
>
> Rabbi Nathan met Elijah and asked him: "What did the Holy One be Blessed do in that hour [when Rabbi Jeremiah uttered this truth according to which a majority view on a legal question can outweigh the pronouncement of a Heavenly Voice]? – God laughed [with joy], and replied, saying, 'My children have defeated Me. My children have defeated Me.'"[6]

God releases control over humans as humans mature. There is joy (even delight or humor), like the joy of a parent, in seeing one's child progress.

---

2. Pesachim 117a, Shabbat 30b.
3. Taanit 22a.
4. Berachot 30b–31a.
5. Avodah Zara 3b.
6. Bava Metzia 59a.

In other cases, laughter can be shown to demonstrate one's foolish certainty:

> If someone removes stones from his field and puts them into the public road, and someone else came along and was injured by them – he is liable, even though they [the Talmudic rabbis] have said that he is tantamount to one who removes stones from what does not belong to him and puts them into an area that does belong to him. A man once removed stones from his own field and put them into the public road. A pious man there argued with him and said, "Why are you taking stones from what is not yours and putting them into what belongs to you?" The man laughed at him. After a while, the same man fell into poverty and sold his field, and was walking along in that very place until he stumbled [on the rocks he had earlier tossed out]. He said, "It was not for nothing that that good man said to me, 'You are removing stones from what does not belong to you and putting them into what belongs to you.'"[7]

It's a tragic story. The role of laughter exposes deep theological dynamics.

Elsewhere, laughter – and reaction to laughter – is characterized as powerful, even violent. After the people laugh at the Talmudic sage Reish Lakish, he kills them all.[8]

In some cases, laughter is a true outlier. Most famously, consider Rabbi Akiva:

> When they reached Mount Scopus, they tore their clothes. When they reached the Temple Mount, they saw a jackal come out of the Holy of Holies. They began to cry, and Rabbi Akiva began to laugh. They said to him: "Why do you laugh?" He said to them:

---

7. Tosefta, Bava Kamma 2:12–13.

8. Gittin 47. This statement regarding Reish Lakish may be regarded metaphorically and not literally.

"Why do you cry?" They said to him: "Jackals now walk upon
the place of which it is written 'And the stranger that comes near
shall be put to death' (Numbers 1:51). Shall we not cry?" He
said to them: "That is why I laugh. For it is written 'And I took
unto me faithful witnesses to record, Uriah the priest, and Zach-
ariah the son of Jeberechiah' (Isaiah 8:2). What has Uriah to do
with Zechariah? Uriah [lived at the time] of the First Temple,
and Zechariah [at the time] of the second Temple? Rather, the
verse linked the prophecy of Zechariah to the prophecy of Uriah.
Regarding Uriah it is written 'Therefore shall Zion, because of
you, be plowed as a field' (Micah 3:12). Regarding Zechariah,
it is written 'There shall yet old men and old women dwell in
the streets of Jerusalem' (Zechariah 8:4). Until the prophecy
of Uriah was fulfilled, I feared that the prophecy of Zechariah
would not come to be. Now that the prophecy of Uriah has come
to be, it is known that the prophecy of Zechariah will come to
be." They said to him in these words: "Akiva you have comforted
us. Akiva you have comforted us."[1]

We learn from medieval Jewish scholars some of the challenges
presented by laughter. Maimonides considered laughter to be
potentially problematic. He articulated his understanding that
it is forbidden for judges to laugh when engaged in their serious
work:

> Every Jewish court which is appropriate has the Divine Presence
> with it. Therefore, the judges need to sit in awe and dread,
> enwrapped, and with gravitas, and are forbidden from levity,
> laughter, or idle speech in the court. Rather, they should engage
> in Torah and wisdom.[2]

Ibn Ezra taught that the word for cruelty (*achzar*) comes from

---

1. Makkot 24b.
2. Mishneh Torah, Hilchot Sanhedrin 3:7.

ach-zar (treating someone like a foreigner). Indeed, excluding and putting others on the outside through jokes can enable acts of dehumanization and cruelty.

Many centuries later, the Hasidic Masters had much to say about laughter. The first of them, the Baal Shem Tov, emphasized that by laughing we grow emotionally and come to a greater state of *dveikut* (clinging to the Divine).[3]

Rebbe Nachman built on the Baal Shem Tov's idea by telling of someone of diminished social stature who laughed at the world and considered it a place of play, and thereby lived a true life filled with truth and brought great merit to the world.[4]

The Kotzker Rebbe also responded to the laughter:

> "Where is the dwelling of God?"
> This was the question with which the rabbi of Kotzk surprised a number of learned men who happened to be visiting him.
> They laughed at him: "What a thing to ask! Is not the whole world full of God's glory?"
> Then he answered his own question:
> "God dwells wherever people let God in."[5]

Secular thinkers across the ages have also demonstrated some difficulty in finding positive aspects to laughter. In his *Republic*, Plato famously sought to abolish laughter from his ideal state, claiming that laughter was an irrational and unstable human behavior that negated self-control. Laughter, Plato thought, had no place in a rational society. Plato was either playing a rather elaborate philosophical prank or he would simply faint at the decorum (or more accurately, lack thereof) in parliaments today. Thomas Hobbes (1588–1679), the great English political philosopher, was also dismissive of laughter. Hobbes felt that laughter

---

3. Keter Shem Tov 27.
4. Chayei Moharan 400.
5. Martin Buber, *Tales of the Hasidim* (NY: Schocken Books, 1975), p. 277.

was a product of man's selfishness and reflected a cowardly desire to ridicule others.

Other writers, Jewish and otherwise, have found great importance in laughter. In 1900, the French philosopher Henri Bergson wrote his *Laughter: An Essay on the Meaning of the Comic*. Bergson felt that we laugh at society's inconsistencies and paradoxically strange habits. Such laughter allows us to live with, and perhaps even correct, our quirks. In 1905, Sigmund Freud published a book dedicated to analyzing jokes and their relationship to our consciousness. Freud argued that history's most successful leaders, Moses in particular, had a sense of humor.

This trend affected more specifically Jewish thought as well. In 1905, Rabbi Pinchas Kohn of the Hildesheimer seminary published a book entitled *Rabbinic Humour: From Ancient to Modern Times*. Kohn argued that a good sense of humor and the ability to laugh can be traced to the very first moments of the Jewish tradition. Of course, when it comes to self-deprecating humor, it may be appropriate for oneself to say but not for others. Jews can make Jewish jokes that playfully critique Jewish culture, but if gentiles were to do so it would perhaps be considered anti-Semitic. This is true, of course, for other cultural groups as well.

Khalil Gibran, an early 20th-century Lebanese American poet, suggests laughter is necessary for wisdom:

> Wisdom ceases to be wisdom when it becomes too proud to weep, too grave to laugh, and too selfish to seek other than itself.

We see, through all of this, that when we laugh, we might be emulating Divine activity, or we might be demonstrating an all-too-common human tendency to separate acquaintances into two groups: those with whom we feel comfortable to have fun and those whom we would just as soon exclude from our frivolity. Indeed, when we return to the beginning of this discussion and contemplate Sarah's laughter upon being told that she, a woman of advanced age, would have a child, in fact, her husband Abraham also laughed, and we can wonder whether either or both of them did so in a joyful manner or in a fashion that simply mocked the unbelievable.

As we contemplate this question, we would do well to associate laughter with the totality of wisdom.

For Rebbe Nachman, *bereirah* (clarifying or choosing) is a spiritual activity where we learn to clarify the *tov* (the good) and the *ra* (the evil) in everything. It is a psychic-spiritual introspective process of intellectual deliberations. This is similar to *boreir*,[6] separating out the *ochel* (food) from the *pesolet* (undesirable or inedible portion). This is a purely binary approach. There is good and evil; there is edible and inedible.[7]

Boreir and *bereirah*, however, are not just about the binaries of virtue and vice. We can differentiate without creating hierarchies. Consider, for example, the ritual of *havdalah*, where we celebrate distinctions. We appreciate both Shabbat and the weekdays, Jews and gentiles, the holy and the mundane; but we acknowledge the different kinds of relationships we have to each. We live with division and unity, with duality and with paradox, particularism, and universalism, with difference and similarity. It is all good, but we must differentiate to maximize the potential for good.

The famous work of *mussar* (moral and ethical behavior) "Orchot Tzaddikim,"[8] teaches that there is no such thing as a purely negative emotion or trait (except for a display of anger). Rather, every emotion can be good or bad, depending on the circumstances. As put succinctly by Shlomo HaMelech (King Solomon), *lakol zeman, v'eit l'chol cheifetz tachat hashamayim*

---

6. The words *boreir* and *bereirah* share the same Hebrew root.

7. This division of edible and non-edible finds its way into halacha as well. If one is going to eat a food in a non-normative state, one does not recite a *berachah*. For example: Today it is common to eat raw carrots. In the time of the Talmud, however, carrots were not eaten raw. Therefore, the Talmud teaches, that if one were to eat a raw carrot, they would not recite a *berachah*.

8. Author unknown.

("There is a season for everything and a time for all desired emotions under the sky").[9]

Boreir is about sensitizing ourselves to the power of separation, to the politics of exclusion. Perhaps when we avoid *boreir* on Shabbat, we remind ourselves of the dangers presented by separating humanity into in-groups and out-groups. At a minimum, it allows us to contemplate several important questions. Who is in and who is out? How do we engage humor to draw the lines? How should we and how should we not – when should we and when should we not – draw such lines?

Through refraining from the act of *boreir* on Shabbat, we are reminded that while selecting and separating out has its place, not doing so – not excluding others, either outright or indirectly through our behavior – has its equal place.

9. Ecclesiastes 3.

8.
Tochein (Grinding)

THE MELACHA OF *tochein* concerns the process of grinding, used in the *Mishkan* to grind the previously separated wheat into flour to make the *lechem hapanim* (showbread) and also to offer on the *mizbei'ach* (altar) as a *korban* (sacrifice). In addition, *tochein* is the mechanism by which large objects are deconstructed into pieces that are small enough to be fit for a use different from their original purpose. For example, the workers in the *Mishkan* would grind herbs into a powder before mixing it with water. There are exceptions to the prohibition of *tochein* on Shabbat, as there are to all the *melachot*. One rule is *ein tochein achar tochein*, the idea that grinding after grinding is not a problem; If something was ground already, we don't worry about grinding it again. In addition to this permission, similar to *boreir* (selecting), we have the permission to grind something *samuch lise'udah* (if it's being done right before a meal), if it's *miyad* (for immediate use) and with a *shinui* (in an abnormal manner). So, traditionally, one would avoid dicing vegetables finely. As another practical example, the Sages prohibited even the act of taking most medicines, as in talmudic times preparation of medicine involved grinding. Today, medicines that are made earlier, such as pills and liquids, are not deemed to be as problematic, as there is no concern that one may come to grind them.

The process of grinding is one of the most powerful human acts because it transforms the ground substance so radically;

material changes from being a solid to being a powder and can never be reconstructed to its original form. Perhaps this is why the rabbis suggest that this act will have its limits in the messianic era. Especially, the midrash says that grinding won't work on what the rabbis knew as the *luz* bone,[1] the bone, only the size of a kernel of barley, that is at the top of the spine right below the brain. The *midrash* engages a dialogue (likely a product of rabbinic moral imagination) between a rabbi and Hadrian, the 2nd-century Roman emperor who was a cruel imperialist:

> Hadrian – may his bones rot – once asked Rabbi Yehoshua ben Chanania, "From what part of the body will the Holy One be Blessed, cause humanity to blossom forth in the future?" "From the *luz*, the 'nut' of the spinal column [the prominent bone just below the back of the neck]," he replied. "How do you know that?" he asked. "Bring me one and I will prove it to you," he replied. He ground it in a grinder but it did not get ground; he threw it into the fire, yet it was not burnt; he put it in water, but it did not dissolve; he placed it on an anvil and hit it with a hammer, but the anvil split and the hammer broke, yet the "nut" was not damaged at all.[2]

This story suggests that elements of human physicality share an element of eternality with the Divine; it also underscores the reality that that's not entirely correct. This is one reason why crematoria, and why modern cremation, are so troubling in Jewish tradition; this *midrash* indicates the precise problem – the capacity of the act of pulverization to transform the human body into powder.

Rebbe Nachman taught that no matter how low we fall, there

---

1. There is a Jewish custom (recorded in Sefer Ta'amei Haminhagim 425) to eat a meal on Saturday night (known as the *melava malka*, literally "accompanying the Sabbath Queen" as it departs) to feed that bone, the bone with which the resurrection of the dead will begin.
2. Bereishit Rabbah 28:3.

is an indestructible part of each person from which one can rebuild oneself. We must ask ourselves, in regards to resilience: what is the indestructible part of myself that cannot be ground up beyond recognition?

And from little things, little moments, little ideas, we can zoom out to the grandiose. A little snowflake can fill us with wonder for the cosmos. A little musical note can be strung with others to create a symphony. The large dimensions of life, ground up into little bits, can be combined into something new and marvelous.

Thus, *tochein*, concerning food, is the physical act that is done as a food preparation stage. But is it ever part of the consumption stage? One Talmudic commentary implies that *tochein* within one's mouth is actually something of a positive experience:

> Avimi, the son of Rabbi Avahu, taught: It is possible to serve one's father the finest delicacies and in doing so, forfeit his right to existence.[3]
>
> The Tosafot (Tosafists)[4] explain: The Jerusalem Talmud illustrates this with an example. It once happened [regarding] someone who regularly served his father a fine type of fowl: One time his father inquired, "How are you able to obtain this delicacy on a regular basis?" The son responded, "What do you care, old man? Just keep grinding and eat," as if to say, "just keep chewing and keep quiet."[5]

Then again, consider how the manna – the substance that kept the Israelites alive during their wanderings in the desert, is kabbalistically understood to have been ground in the heavens for the righteous to consume on Earth (thereby not requiring further grinding):

---

3. Kiddushin 31a.

4. The Tosafot (literally meaning "additions") were comprised primarily of Rashi's grandchildren, who wrote a detailed explanation of the Talmud.

5. Tosafot commentary on Kiddushin 31a.

"Let the skies rain down righteousness" – when the "heavens" receive from above, from the supernal site that abides above them, then "the skies rain down righteousness." What are "the skies"? The site where they grind the manna for the righteous ... For whom? For the site called "righteous one," for they grind the manna that comes from "above," and all the goodness is gathered in them to bestow it on the rung of the "righteous one," so that "righteousness" will be blessed from their flow....[6]

What about *tochein* as an intellectual process? We see how *tochein* is used to understand Talmudic debate:

Ulla said: One who saw Resh Lakish in the *beit midrash* (study hall) [engaged in debate] would think that he was uprooting mountains and grinding them against each other![7]

Today, we refer to "grinding teeth" to mean intellectual grappling.

Consider, however, that the prophet Isaiah uses *tochein* regarding abuse of the poor:

The Lord stands up to plead a cause, God rises to champion peoples. God will bring this charge against the elders and princes of God's people: "It is you who have devoured the vineyard, the spoil of the poor is in your houses. What do you mean by crushing My people, by grinding the face of the poor?" says God of hosts.[8]

But what does it mean to grind the face of the poor? Today, we still speak of "grinding poverty" to mean overwhelming, overbearing oppression. One is reduced from a whole self into a partial self by being crushed in exploitation. Similarly, we refer

6. Zohar, Vayikra 25b–26a.
7. Sanhedrin 24a.
8. Isaiah 3:13–15.

to "the daily grind" as a response to our workday lives, as if our souls are crushed by the weight of our responsibilities, whether it's school, work, or family.

Further, grinding in the agricultural process is used by the rabbis to remind us of our own character development:

> A philosopher asked R. Hoshaya: "If circumcision is so precious, why was it not given to Adam?" … "I cannot send you away empty-handed," said he; [the real reason is this:] "whatever was created in the first six days requires further preparation, e.g., mustard needs sweetening, vetches need sweetening, wheat needs grinding, and human beings (Adam) also need tikkun [fixing]."[9]

The *mitzvot* are here to refine our character. That's how we know we have done them right. So, too, stepping back from *tochein* to reflect on our relationship to grinding, in various ways, is about our growth.

We see from all of the above that *tochein* has the power to be both constructive and destructive. It is thus instructive to remind ourselves that just as we must take God's creation and work it to make it into food, so too we must take our created selves and work ourselves to become our best selves. This is *tochein*: grinding humanity's raw nature into a new substance that resembles the old but at the same time is something quite new. This process is natural but also supra-natural in that our finely ground selves are our true selves, but our true selves transformed into service. Given that Shabbat is *me'ein Olam Haba*, a taste of the World to Come, it makes sense that we experience ourselves on Shabbat as not requiring a typical measure of self-transformation in order to serve the Divine element of the world in which we live.

---

9. Bereishit Rabba 11:6.

9.

Merakeid (Sifting)

I N THE NINTH *melacha,* we look at the process of *merakeid* (sifting), which mirrors the sifting that was done in the *Mishkan* when flour was readied to make bread, or when a sifting-like action was done in the herb-preparation process. The *melacha* encompasses sifting or straining using a sieve or a filter. In modern Shabbat observance, one might avoid making coffee with a pour-over filter or straining excess salad dressing from a salad. This prohibition, like the other *melachot* concerning separation, is about removing the undesirable from the desirable. In the case of this particular *melacha,* the separation is put into effect specifically by the use of a utensil.

Stepping back to observe the fact that sifting is just one among many other agricultural processes reminds us to be grateful for how labor-intensive food production truly is. As is recorded in the Talmud:

> Ben Zoma saw a multitude (of Jews) while he was standing on a step of the Temple Mount. He said (the blessing) "Blessed.... the Sage of the Secrets." And (he also recited) "Blessed.... Who created all these to serve me."
>
> He used to say: "How many exertions did Adam, the first man, make until he found bread to eat: He plowed, he sowed, he reaped, he gathered (stalks) together, he threshed, he winnowed, he selected, he ground (grain into flour), he sifted, he kneaded,

he baked, and afterward he ate the bread. But I (Ben Zoma) rise early in the morning and find all these (labors) prepared before me."[1]

Sifting is helpful not only in an agricultural process but also in helping us determine the status of a lost object:

> When a person sees a colleague's dinar (a coin of that era) fall into sand or dust and escape the colleague's vision, it is as if it fell into the sea or a river, and it belongs to the finder. For the owner despairs of its recovery, since it does not have a mark by which it can be identified. Even if he saw the original owner bring a sifter to search for the lost dinar, the owner is considered to have given up hope. He is searching out of wishful thinking, as would other seekers who search in the dust, although they have not lost anything, in the hope that they will find what someone else has lost. The owner is searching in such a manner; it is not that he has not despaired of the recovery of his money.[2]

We can wonder, though, whether we should act *lifnim mishurat hadin* (beyond the letter of the law), by returning an article that has been so thoroughly lost by its owner that the owner cannot sift through a world of objects to locate it. The way we search for lost objects helps us think about how we view the world. We hold within ourselves notions of subjectivity to avoid viewing the world outside ourselves as a conglomeration of objects upon which we can act with attention only to our own interests.

At the same time, we can also ask how people might themselves undergo a kind of sifting process in relation to others. In particular, we can consider how we distinguish, or sift, those people with whom we have an affinity from "the other." How often do we judge others? Do we engage in racial profiling to let most

---

1. BT Brachot 58a.
2. Rambam, Mishneh Torah. *Hilchot Gezeilah V'aveida,* chapter 14.

pass but filter out those who "look" more suspicious? Indeed, do we go so far as to sift with a utensil, as the *halachot* of *merakeid* tell us not to do on Shabbat, when we help perpetuate systems to differentiate among people, leading to systemic racism? Are we similarly at fault when we succumb to the inherent racism that we all must recognize in ourselves? In the Book of Amos, it says:

> For I will give the order, and shake the house of Israel, through all the nations, as one shakes (sand) in a sieve, and not a pebble falls to the ground.[1]

Here, in a problematic fashion, we similarly see the idea of sifting as a form of punishment or filtering out the sinful from the pure.

Then again, we also see some positivity in the act of using a sieve. Thus, in the writings of the kabbalist Rabbi Yehuda Ashlag, we find the idea of the Creator positively sifting through humans:

> And this is the key to an understanding of the incapacity of [so-called] world-reformers (*metaknei olam*) that arose through the generations. For they saw a human being in the image of a machine that is not working properly and needs repair (*tikkun*). This means, to remove the corrupted parts and replace them with others that are fixed (*metukanim*). And that is the whole tendency of these world-reformers – to eradicate anything bad and harmful in the human species – and the truth is, were it not that the Creator was standing against them, they would certainly have already had enough time to sift humanity like a sieve, and to leave only [what is] good and useful. But because the Creator watches over all the elements in [the Divine] Creation with such great care ... no allowance is made for anyone to destroy a single thing in [God's] domain – but only to turn it and transform it to be good ...[2]

---

1. Amos 9:9.
2. Michael Berg, Ed. *On World Peace: Two Essays by the Holy Kabbalist*

Indeed, it is not only Shabbat that reminds us of the work of sifting; looking up at the moon does as well. This Talmudic passage talks about *kiddush levanah* (the prayer of sanctifying the new moon):

> R. Aha b. Hanina also said in the name of R. Assi in R. Yohanan's name: "Until what day of the month may the benediction over the new moon be recited? – Until its concavity is filled up. And how long is that?" – R. Jacob b. Idi said In Rav Yehuda's name: "Seven days." The Nehardeans said: "Sixteen [days]." Now, both agree with R. Yohanan, but the one [explains it as meaning]: "Until it is like a strung bow; the other: Until it is like a sieve."[3]

Also, the *shemitah* (sabbatical) year, and the justice-focused messages in the *halachot* of that year, are quite relevant to how we think about lending a sieve:

> A woman may lend to her neighbor suspected of transgressing the Sabbatical Year law a fine sieve, or a coarse sieve, or a handmill, or an oven, but she must not sift nor grind with her. The wife of a fellow may loan to the wife of an illiterate man a fine sieve or a coarse sieve, and she may winnow, or grind, or sift with her; but when she pours out the water, she must not touch it with her, because they must not assist and thus, themselves, commit a transgression. And all these have they [the Sages] enjoined for the sake of peace. And they may encourage non-Jews in the Sabbatical Year but not Jews, and they may offer them greetings for the sake of peace.[4]

Consider how Rebbe Nachman thinks about sifting in our internal obligations to work on the spiritual side of our psyche:

Rav Yehuda Ashlag, by Yehuda Ashlag. Kabbalah Publishing, 2013.

3. BT, Sanhedrin 41b.
4. Mishna, Gitten 5:9.

9. *Merakeid* (Sifting)

In just the same way you must carry on searching until you find another good point. Even if you feel that this good point is also full of flaws, you must still search for some good in it. And so, you must continue finding more and more good points. This is how songs are made.

In essence, music is made by sifting the good from the bad. The musician has to find the "good spirit" and reject the bad. A musical instrument is basically a vessel containing air. The musician produces the sounds by causing the air to vibrate. One's task is to move one's hands on the instrument in such a way as to produce good spirit, "good vibrations," while avoiding the "bad vibrations" – the dissonant winds of gloom and depression.

When a person refuses to allow himself to fall into despair but instead gives himself new life by finding and gathering their positive points, this makes melodies. They can then pray, sing, and give thanks to God.[5]

Rav Abraham Isaac Kook deals with sifting concerning how we think about our ideas, our beliefs in particular:

Knesset Yisrael is the distilled essence of all existence, and in this world, this distillation is devolved onto the Israelite nation, truly, in its materiality and spirituality, its generations and faith. And the Israelite history is the idealized distillation of general history, and there is no movement in the world, in all the peoples, whose like is not to be found in Israel. And its faith is the sifted essence of all beliefs, and the source from which idealism and the good flow to all the beliefs, and thus necessarily the force which distinguishes among belief concepts until it brings them to the level of *clear speech "so that they all may call out in the Name of God"* (Zephaniah 3:9) *"and your redeemer, the Holy One of Israel, will be called Lord of all the Earth"* (Isaiah 54:5).[6]

---

5. Likkutei Moharan I, 282.
6. Source Number 6, Rav Kook, Qovetz 2:157 (Arpilei Tohar) [circa 1913],

Indeed, sifting is something we do in learning to find intellectual clarification. We learn in Pirkei Avot (Ethics of Our Fathers):

> There are four types of students that sit before the sages: A sponge, a funnel, a strainer, and a sieve: a sponge, which absorbs everything; a funnel, which lets in from one end and lets out from the other; a strainer, which lets the wine flow through and retains the sediment; and a sieve, which allows the flour dust to pass through and retains the fine flour.[7]

We are to be like a sieve. In sifting, we can gain clarity. Who is in and who is out? What is in and what is out? We can see differences more clearly when we separate one concept, or one object, from another, but in seeing those differences, how will we judge them? And how will we decide? It is not only cognitive and intellectual discernment we're exploring, but the realm of empathy. How can we learn to listen compassionately to others and hold their pain with them, but also not allow the toxicity of pain to penetrate us?

Also, consider Piaget's developmental stages. We may, at times, want our children to be like sponges (in the right environments) but then as adults, or young adults, to be like sieves that are more discerning within the ambiguities of complex public life. Also, there are times, in spiritual experiences, that we want to immerse uncritically and absorb like sponges. And, yet, other times, intellectually, when we want to embrace skepticism and filter out the unneeded or harmful.

Merakeid, then, reminds us that the process of learning how to sift is indeed the work of a lifetime. After all, what could be more precious to guard than our minds and souls?

---

p. 292–293, Orot, p. 138.
  7. Pirkei Avot 5:18.

10.
Lash (Kneading)

T HE TENTH MELACHA is *lash* (kneading), which is the first prohibition that is distinct from the first nine *melachot* we've already looked at. The first five, *zorei'a* (planting) through *dash* (threshing) dealt with planting and reaping, and beginning with *zoreh* (winnowing), we explored *melachot* that share the characteristic of differentiation: separating objects to make them smaller. *Lash*, however, changes the paradigm. Now, the prohibition is about joining together smaller items into one larger mass. *Lash* was done in the *Mishkan* to produce the *lechem hapanim* (showbread) and to produce the dyes by mixing ground herbs and water into a paste. When we talk about *lash*, typically the discussion is in regard to the process of mixing flour and water to make dough or making a thick salad dressing. (Making a salad dressing by combining an already viscous substance, such as mayonnaise, with other ingredients, would be permitted). But *lash* goes beyond food as well, extending to other realms such as mixing sand or dirt with liquid, and perhaps even hair braiding (as one is taking strands of hair and turning them into one larger mass).

There is power to the hands. Through our hands, we have the power to transform. This is referred to in halachic sources as *koach gavra* (the power of man). Using one's hands to knead can be cathartic, it can be healing, it can transmit energy. Kneading is laborious but connecting. In reflecting on the spiritual nature of kneading, one might think about the process as joining together the physical and the spiritual. Flour is clearly a physical, material object. Water, in Jewish thought, is Torah: the spiritual dimension. The Talmud articulates the metaphor beautifully, as it says: "there is no water other than Torah."[1] When kneading (or even when eating bread that has been kneaded), one might reflect on our power to elevate the physical toward spiritual ends.

To think about *lash* invites us to focus not only on the process but also on the people who effectuate the process. Due to the laborious nature of kneading, we can turn our consciousness toward the workers. We can remind ourselves of the story of Rabbi Yisrael Salanter and how he taught his students that the most important thing to check for in the matzah factory was not ritual *kashrut* but how the women kneading the dough were being treated.[2]

We see the idea that kneading deserves some emphasis quite early in the Torah:

> God appeared to him [Avraham] in the plains of Mamre while he was sitting at the entrance to the tent in the heat of the day. He lifted his eyes and there were three men standing before him. He saw them, and ran to greet them from the entrance to the tent, and bowed toward the ground. He said: "My Lord, if I have found favor in Your eyes, please do not leave your servant. Let water be drawn, and wash your feet, and rest under the tree. I will fetch some bread and you will satiate yourselves, then go on – in as much as you have passed your servant's way." They said, "Do so, just as you have said."
>
> So, Avraham hurried to the tent, to his wife Sarah, and said, "Hurry! [Take] three measures of fine flour – knead them and make cakes!" Then Avraham ran to the cattle, took a good,

---

1. Baba Kamma 82a.
2. Martin Buber, in *Tales of the Hasidim*, says there is a similar story about Rabbi Levi Yitzchak of Berditchev.

tender calf and gave it to the youth who hurried to prepare it. He took cream and milk, as well as the calf which he had prepared, and he placed these before them. He stood before them, under the tree, and they ate.[1]

Why does Avraham instruct Sarah to knead? Why not just say "make cakes?" Why does Avraham want to demonstrate his awareness of the extra steps involved in the process? Was it a sensitivity toward how laborious it would be for Sarah? Perhaps. Or maybe Avraham acknowledged that Sarah would be kneading the dough from which she would make cakes to make clear to her that he recognized that he was asking a lot of her: he requested that she hurry to undertake a difficult, multi-step task because of her love for him and her respect for the strangers. In this way, we might actually imagine Avraham talking in this manner because he wanted to honor both the quality and quantity of her work.

By mentioning the necessity of kneading the dough, Avraham also commented on the status of the strangers for whom he and Sarah were preparing a meal. He wanted to ensure that the strangers would be honored with fresh bread of a high quality, even though he didn't know them or their mission. He wanted to give them the best, simply because they were hungry and in need.

Furthermore, the process of kneading has to do, in part, with making dough even and uniform. Avraham was, therefore, perhaps making a statement about how people whom we see as strangers are entitled to be treated – and to be seen – as elements of a uniform whole that make up humanity. At the same time, when we're instructed not to knead on Shabbat, we're reminded that the other side of the humanity-is-uniform coin is that our respective ethnic, religious, racial, and other identities are to be celebrated. That is, even though one theme of Shabbat is *zeicher l'ma'aseh bereishit* (a remembrance of the six days of Creation), another Shabbat theme is *zeicher l'yetziat Mitzrayim* (a reminder

---

1. Genesis 18:1–8.

of the Exodus from Egypt), when we were taken *goy mikerev goy*,[2] one nation, with its own history, culture, and relationship with the Divine, from the midst of another nation. We celebrate the universalistic theme of creation and the particularistic theme of freedom from slavery.

The Torah also ties *lash* to serving others in another respect. The act of kneading is connected to *tzedakah* through the mitzvah to be *mafrish challah* (separate challah).[3] We read in the Torah:

> God spoke to Moshe, telling him to speak to the Jewish people and say to them, "When you come to the land to which I am bringing you and you eat the land's produce, you must separate a portion for God. You must separate the first portion of your kneading as a dough offering. It must be separated just like the elevated gift that is taken from the threshing floor. You must give the first of your kneading as a portion to God for all generations."[4]

Consider how the Zohar understands the problem of being unaware of how something was kneaded:

> There was a man who lived in the mountains. He knew nothing about those living in the city. He sowed wheat and ate the kernels raw. One day he entered the city. They offered him good bread. The man asked, "What's this for?"
>
> They replied, "It's bread, to eat!"
>
> He ate, and it tasted very good. He asked, "What's it made of?"

---

2. Deuteronomy 4:34.

3. Although we typically refer to challah as the loaf of bread itself, the origin of the term derives from the piece of dough which was separated from the larger batch and given to the kohein (priest). Hence the *berachah* recited upon setting aside that piece: *l'hafrish challah min ha'isah* ("to separate the challah from the dough"). Today, in the absence of the Beit Hamikdash (Temple), when the priestly rituals are not in place, we typically burn that piece of dough, as no one, other than the kohein, is entitled to it.

4. Numbers 15:17–21.

They answered, "Wheat."

Later they offered him thick loaves kneaded with oil. He tasted them and asked, "And what are these made of?"

They answered, "Wheat."

Later they offered him royal pastry kneaded with honey and oil. He asked, "And what are these made of?"

They answered, "Wheat."

He said, "Surely, I am the master of all of these since I eat the essence of all of these: wheat!"

Because of that view, he knew nothing of the delights of the world, which were lost to him. So, it is with one who grasps the principle but is unaware of all those delectable delights deriving, diverging from that principle.[5]

Further, the midrash teaches that kneading (and producing bread in general) is connected to our process of hermeneutics and interpretation:

To what can it be compared? To a king of flesh and blood who had two servants and loved them both with a perfect love. He gave each of them a measure of wheat and each a bundle of flax. What did the wise servant do? He took the flax and spun a cloth. He took the wheat and made flour. He cleaned the flour and ground, kneaded and baked it, and set it on top of the table. Then he spread the cloth over it and left it until the king would come. The foolish servant, however, did nothing at all. After some time, the king returned from a journey and came into his house. He said to his servants: "My sons, bring me what I gave you." One servant showed the wheat still in the box with the bundle of flax upon it. Alas for his shame, alas for his disgrace. When the Holy One gave the Torah to Israel, God gave it only

---

5. Zohar 2:176a–b. See Daniel Matt, *The Essential Kabbalah*: The Heart of Jewish Mysticism (HarperCollins, 1983), p. 207; and *The Zohar*: Pritzker Edition, Vol. 5, (California: Stanford University Press, 2009), pp. 531–34.

in the form of wheat, for us to make flour from it, and flax, for us to make a garment from it.[6]

Indeed, our job is to work with what we've received in this world in order to refine and develop it further. We need to take the disparate ingredients of life – love, death, justice, peace – and form them, knead them, into one structure: ourselves. This is true not only with the physical object that we have but also, as we see, how we interpret our texts. As we interpret our texts, we realize that this is true not only regarding our physical selves, but with our spiritual selves as well. Just as *lash* represents the power of our hands, so too we must harness that power to transform our physical and spiritual selves, and in turn, the entire world.

---

6. Seder Eliyahu Zuta 2.

11.
Ofeh (Baking)

THE ELEVENTH *MELACHA* is *ofeh* (baking), and by extension includes *bishul* (cooking). This prohibition is concerned with enhancing and preparing food, or even non-food items, through heat. This *melacha* is based, like *lash* (kneading), upon the work in the *Mishkan* of baking the showbread and producing dyes from the necessary herbs. To determine whether a solid food is altered enough to reach the level of *bishul* is measured by considering whether it has become a *ma'achal ben Drusai*[1] (about two-thirds cooked); the measure for cooking a liquid is based on whether it has reached *yad soledet bo* (the point when one's hand would singe in it), determined by if one would pull his hand back from the heat (understood to be approximately 110 degrees Fahrenheit).

There are a lot of rich stories in the Torah about cooking and the family dynamics and politics involved. Some examples: Consider the story of Cain and Abel offering their gifts to God;[2] of Jacob cooking lentil stew and selling it to his brother in exchange for the birthright;[3] of Jacob and Esau each cooking for

---

1. Ma'achal ben Drusai refers to a food item cooked just enough for a ben Drusai, a member of a family (or perhaps clan) of robbers, to eat it. As they were forever on the run, they often resorted to eating foods not cooked all the way through.
2. Genesis 4.
3. Ibid 25.

their father to win his heart.[4] Or consider the idea of cooking and offering *korbanot* (sacrifices) for God in the Mishkan (Tabernacle) and Beit Hamikdash (Temple).

Fire, the force that effectuates *bishul*, is a crucial ingredient not only of the physical world but also of our spiritual lives. Fire can be the "yin and yang," representing both a constructive or a destructive element. Just as emotions can be channeled in either direction (consider "fire" as enthusiasm vs. "fire" as zealotry and acting impulsively), fire can be channeled to consume or to illuminate, to bring destructive heat, or healing light.

Concerning fire as a spiritual energy, Rabbi Yehudah Aryeh Leib Alter, known as the Sfat Emet, writes:

> ...The Baal Shem Tov taught that there must always be a point of [fiery] enthusiasm in our hearts. This is the meaning of the phrase "A perpetual fire shall be kept burning and shall not be extinguished" (Leviticus 6:6). The altar symbolizes the heart [and the fire is our enthusiasm].
>
> When Scripture here says "perpetual," it does not mean only in terms of time [i.e., that our enthusiasm must always exist], but suggests that the enthusiasm must be because of the promise of perpetuity [in other words, we are enthusiastic because of the promise that our inner fires will never go out]. When we commit to sustaining our engagement with all our heart and soul, then that inner fire will "not go out."
>
> When our enthusiasm [toward our service] is correct, then any "distracting thought" [of fatigue or disinterest] that arises in our hearts will automatically be consumed in the heat of the heart, like wax before a flame. When this distracting thought is burned in the heart, a new light will arise there. This is why "upon the altar all night" (ibid 6:2) is followed by "in the morning the priest shall feed wood to it" (ibid 6:5) [new energy follows the darkness of doubt].... And through the burning of distracting

---

4. Ibid 27.

thoughts there is renewal of energy in the morning.... Nevertheless, it is still up to us to apply effort to bring this about.[5]

Indeed, God speaks to Moses from the fire both at the Burning Bush and in the fiery lightning witnessed at Sinai.[6] Fire creates both a locus and an experience within which to encounter the Divine. On the other hand, fire also defines a spiritual place as dangerous. As it says: "For the Lord your God is a consuming fire."[7] Or consider the idea that fire represents hell and forms of damnation for those who dishonor the Torah. The Talmud indicates that fire is one-sixtieth part of *Gehinnom* (hell).[8] Or the idea of fire as punishment: "They issued a proclamation in Sodom saying, 'Everyone who strengthens the hand of the poor and the needy and the stranger with a loaf of bread shall be burnt by fire.'"[9]

Similarly, we are told about the dangers of fire in the following story: "Rabbi Akiva taught: 'If a husband and wife are worthy, the Divine Presence dwells in their midst. If they are not worthy, a fire consumes them.'"[10]

So, too, in the *Unetaneh Tokef* prayer recited on Yom Kippur, we see the tension between the themes of fire as a Divine invitation and of flames as a reminder of Divine dominion. The strength of the prayer lies in its juxtaposition of powerful imagery regarding Divine might, on the one hand, and with the idea that Divine closeness and mercy are accessible on the other. These two elements of the human relationship with the Divine are played against each other throughout until, towards the end of the prayer, we read of Divine decrees issued on Rosh Hashana as to who will be saved and who will not, and who among those

---

5. Sefat Emet, Parshat Tzav 5640 (1880).
6. Exodus 3:2.
7. Deuteronomy 4:24.
8. BT Brachot 57b.
9. Pirkei D'Rebbe Eliezer 25.
10. BT Sotah 17a.

destined to perish will face a fiery end while others will be challenged by water.

This poetry is ambiguous as to whether fire, in this context, bears more of a positive or a negative connotation. On the one hand, there is Divine mercy and the potential for prayer and repentance. On the other hand, we feel the terrifying consequences of our mortality and our moral failings. Perhaps that ambiguity is a necessary outgrowth of an image that appears earlier in this prayer. Early in *Unetaneh Tokef* we're told that a great shofar will be sounded but that the sound that will be heard will be a still, small voice. This line reminds us of the considerable drama that follows the faceoff between Eliyahu Hanavi (the prophet Elijah) and the prophets of Ba'al (a form of idolatry) when Elijah has an encounter with the Divine.[1] Elijah witnessed a great wind, followed by an earthquake, and ultimately a blazing fire. But the divinity that Elijah seemed to assume he would find in those powerful forces was not there; even a raging conflagration did not contain the Divine reality. That force actually appeared in a "*kol demama dakka*," a still, small voice, described in precisely the words borrowed to invoke the immanent, merciful God in *Unetaneh Tokef.*

The rabbis of the Talmud use an image of fire to answer a question that they raise when they wonder how, on a practical level, the Torah could be written in heaven:

> On what was the primordial Torah written? On parchment? But the animals had not been created yet, so how could one use their skins for parchment? Maybe on gold or silver? But the metals had not been created, refined, or unearthed! Maybe on wooden tablets? But the trees had not yet been created! So, what was it written on? It was written with black fire on white fire and wrapped around the right arm of the Holy One, as it is written [Deuteronomy 33:2]: 'On God's right arm, the fiery law.'[2]

---

1. 1 Kings 19:11–12.
2. Midrash Konen, Beit Hamidrash II p. 23. Also see the Jerusalem Talmud

In our previous *melacha* of *lash* (kneading), we explored how the Torah is called water. But, also, at times, Torah is called fire. Consider this midrash:

> Why was the Torah not given in the land of Israel? ... To avoid causing dissension among the tribes. Else one might have said: "In my territory the Torah was given." And the other might have said: "In my territory the Torah was given." Therefore, the Torah was given in the desert, publicly and openly, in a place belonging to no one. To three things the Torah is likened: to the desert, to fire, and to water. This is to tell you that just as these three things are free to all who come into the world, so also are the words of the Torah free to all who come into the world."[3]

Torah is also likened to fire because it brings light and warmth. Consider the Zohar:

> On the day that Rabbi Shimon bar Yochai was to leave this world, he organized his teachings. His friends came to his room and he said to them, "Now is a time of favor. I can now reveal to you holy things that have not been revealed until now." ... All that day the fire never left his room, and there was no one who was able to approach as the light and the fire were surrounding him ... [After he passed away, and they came to bury him] the fire flew into the air and danced before him. A voice was heard [from Heaven] saying, "Come and gather [every year] for the *hilulah* (anniversary) of Rabbi Shimon bar Yochai."[4]

Shekalim 6:1: "The Torah that the Holy One of Blessing gave to Moses (at Mt. Sinai) was white fire inscribed by black fire." On this Rabbi Levi Yitzhak of Berditchev teaches: "In this world we read the letters; in the future we will know how to read the spaces."

3. *Mekhilta B'Chodesh* 5.

4. Zohar, Idra Zuta, Devarim, Parshat Ha'azinu, p. 296 – Revelation of the Zohar. This story is the source of the custom to light bonfires on Lag Ba'Omer, as the tradition has it that Rabbi Shimon bar Yochai passed away on Lag Ba'Omer.

Now, when it comes to mixing the physical and spiritual – food and fire, which are mixed when we perform *bishul* – it sounds mystical and exciting. But our tradition also teaches that cooking can be cruel. Nahmanides writes:

> The understanding of "You shall be a holy nation to Hashem your God" has to do with "You shall not cook a kid in its mother's milk." Because it [milk mixed with meat] is not a disgusting food, but rather is prohibited because we must be deal with our food in a holy way, or that we must be holy and not be cruel by milking a mother and taking that milk to cook in it her offspring. And even though this prohibition will get extended to include all milk, because all nursing mothers are called "eim" (mother), and all offspring who nurse are called "gedi" (a kid), any cooking of this type is cruel.[5]

Maimonides explains how cooking is only one of the three prohibitions that emerges from this animal welfare principle:

> ... And at this point, it is proper that I should draw attention to an important principle, which I have not yet mentioned. The words 'You shall not cook a kid in its mother's milk' occur three times in the Torah, and according to those who hand down the tradition, each of these prohibitions has a different purpose. One, they say, forbids eating it, one forbids deriving any benefit from it, and one forbids cooking it.[6]

But, cooking, of course, can also be compassionate. We cook for those we love.[7] We cook for guests. We cook for the hungry. Further, the ability to cook is not only about ethics towards

---

5. Ramban's commentary on Deuteronomy 14:21.
6. Rambam, Book of Commandments, Negative Commandment 187.
7. In fact, the midrash informs us that the lentil stew that Yaakov (Jacob) was cooking was indeed for his father, who was mourning the passing of his father Avraham. Round foods represent the cycle of life, which would explain

animals and generosity to other humans, but also about our own health. Cooking is a spiritual practice of *yeish miyeish*, creating something new from something older. Through unique combinations, we transform existing objects into something palatable, nourishing, and enjoyable. This is how all of life should be: We take the raw and transform it into something wholesome.

Every Shabbat, when we pause from our normal cooking and reflect upon that which has already been cooked, we have the opportunity to realize this gift that we have been given; indeed, it is a gift that can be passed forward for all to cherish.

---

why Yaakov was cooking lentils, which are round, and is the reason why one of the foods customarily eaten after burying one's beloved is an egg.

12.

Gozeiz (Shearing)

WHILE THE FIRST eleven *melachot* we discussed were related to agrarian activities based around the production of the dyes and the *lechem hapanim* (showbread), our next thirteen *melachot* are concerned with producing coverings and curtains for the *Mishkan*. The first of these is *gozeiz*, which is shearing sheep or cutting hair. While this *melacha* has been extended to pulling out human hair, getting a haircut, shaving, etc., it originally concerned the specifics of shearing sheep.

Unfortunately, there are many cruelties shown toward sheep in the shearing process. Some suggest that shearing, if done humanely (which is rarely the case), is good for sheep. For example, one commentator suggests:

> When domesticated sheep cannot shed their fleece themselves, their wool will grow longer and longer while flies lay eggs in the moist folds of their skin. The hatched maggots can eat the sheep alive.

But, is it really true that sheep need human's help to survive naturally? Before domestication, sheep didn't need to be sheared by humans and survived fine without us. Throughout the centuries, however, human beings have specifically bred sheep to grow thick wool that won't shed so we can use more of it (similar to how we've bred chickens to have more meat and to lay the most eggs, even if it means the chickens could collapse from their own weight), making human shearing necessary. Domesticated sheep have been bred to grow a tremendous amount of wool, which, if not sheared, will cause them harm, although older sheep will produce less and will not need to be sheared as often.

Many animal rights advocates would ideally want to end the wool industry entirely, even if it means fewer sheep existing since that industry takes something from an animal. An animal welfarist, on the other hand, would be more open to the idea of humane shearing for the sheep which already exists or to shearing sheep who live on a local, humane, sustainable farm, and are treated like pets and not raised for wool or meat.[1]

Here is a response from a farmer who discusses the question of what would happen to domesticated animals if humans were suddenly gone and unable to care for them:

> Most of the domesticated breeds of livestock will NOT survive. They all depend on human care, and would quickly decline.
> … Sheep would die quick[ly], especially wool sheep. There are breeds of sheep that do not grow a wool coat that would last longer, but they would die off soon too. Wool sheep cannot suddenly just stop growing wool. It cannot be bred out in a generation or two, it would take hundreds of years to breed wool growth completely out of sheep. Wool sheep need to be shorn once a year at least. If not, the wool keeps growing and will inhibit movement. The animal will go "wool blind" and not be able to see, they would not be able to eat, and the wool around their butt would get covered in feces. They would get an infection or flystrike. They could not get bred or give birth.

For wild sheep – which now sadly comprise only a small percentage of sheep – sheep-shearing is entirely unnecessary

---

1. Read about a sanctuary that discusses what they do and why: https://far msanctuary.typepad.com/sanctuary_tails/2009/04/shearing-rescued-sheep.html

because sheep shed naturally as warranted by their bodies and the conditions in which they live. As such, sheep-shearing is a practice designed by humans to commoditize sheep that, in the process, causes them pain and distress and leaves them subject to slaughter when the wool extracted from them is no longer marketable.

I suppose it is true that once individual sheep are sheared, it is necessary to continue shearing those sheep because their wool grows back longer than is healthy for them in that the initial shearing disrupts their natural bodily rhythms. At industrialized sheep farms, this continuous cycle of shearing typically occurs in a harmful fashion. At smaller, family-run sheep farms, I think it is likely that sheep are treated more sensitively.

The Torah takes the need to be discriminate in deciding when to shear seriously. There is a Torah prohibition against shearing the wool of one's *bechor* (firstborn male):

> Every firstling that shall be born among your cattle and flock – the males – you shall sanctify to the Lord your God. Do not work with the firstling of your cattle and do not shear the firstling of your flock.[2]

At the same time, shearing is also presented in a positive light. For example, the firstborn has the status of a sanctified animal that was redeemed. Indeed, one midrash compares the Jewish people's commitment to *tzedakah* (charity) to sheep shearing.

> No one should say that I will have depleted my property if I give to the poor. Rather one should look and see that all who do not deplete, do not replenish. Thus, the hair of one's head and one's beard which is trimmed – always grows back, while the hair of one's eyebrows which are never trimmed do not grow. Israel is

---

2. Deuteronomy 15:19.

analogous to a lamb that is sheared and yet every year it grows new wool, while the pig is never sheared and never replenished.[1]

Rabbi Yishmael extends this idea beyond the nature of the Jewish people toward the issue of Divine reward and punishment:

> Whoever shears off part of their possessions and dispenses them in *tzedakah* will be rescued from the punishment of Hell. Imagine two sheep crossing a river, one shorn and the other not shorn. The shorn one gets across, the unshorn one does not.[2],[3]

The *melacha Gozeiz* raises interesting questions around property ownership as well. The Talmud records of one who sells an animal yet retains for themselves its shearings and offspring.[4] The purchaser is entitled to do with the animal whatever they wish. Nevertheless, the purchaser's ownership is limited. Regarding shearings and offspring, the animal is considered as if it still belongs to the seller. This opens up some questions about how we might think about worker rights and property rights in our own messy systems of commerce today.

On a deeper level, the capacity to shed hair and grow anew represents our capacity to renew ourselves, which is a true spiritual gift. Rabbi Menachem Froman, the late Hasidic peace activist, wrote about the religious capacity for renewal:

> The event of the new moon (*hiddush*)[5] was, for the Sages, the most intense instance where we encounter the Creator and

---

1. Midrash Song of Songs Zuta 1:15.
2. Indeed, sheep can swim. And indeed, sheep with too much hair can be weighed down and drown.
3. Gittin 7a.
4. BT Bava Metziah 34a.
5. The term *kiddush hachodesh* refers to both the beit din's (Jewish court's) declaration of the new moon in Talmudic times, and to the monthly prayer in which we sanctify the moon to this day. The word *kiddush* (sanctification) is closely related to *chiddush* (renewal), and it is therefore suggested that the

Renewer of the world. Revolutionary Marxism went to war against religion, primarily because it saw it as an anti-revolutionary force. Religious faith can lead us to conservative conclusions. Religion can sanctify the status quo as the handiwork of the Creator. However, we might also come to the exact opposite conclusion. If a person believes that the world is created (*mehudash*, "made anew," in medieval terminology), then he believes that the world could be radically remade anew.[6]

On this topic, Rav Kook wrote:

The world is renewed through novel interpretations of Torah. This is simply because the innovation revealed to us in limited form comes to us as an infinitely diminished essence after the tremendous spiritual waves have flooded and flowed away, rolled from one world to another, becoming ever more constricted and diminished, until they, at last, appear before us in the form of some innovation.

At its source, this innovation is not a private lightning flash of intellect but rather the renewal of a new land, all according to the nature of what is renewed.[7]

Perhaps you've heard this simple story before.

A man found a cocoon of an emperor moth. He took it home so that he could watch the moth come out of the cocoon. On the day a small opening appeared, he sat and watched the moth for

---

original term for *kiddush hachodesh* was *chiddush hachodesh*. Furthermore, the Mishnah records that the new month was decreed in Talmudic times by the pronouncement *mekudash hachodesh, mekudash* ("the new month is sanctified, it is indeed sanctified"). There is a theory that this is recorded in error, and that the pronouncement was actually *mechudash* ("renewed") and not *mekudash*.

6. Menachem Froman, *Give Me Time: Ideas on the Time of the Year and the Space of the Land (Ten Li Zeman: Ra'ayanot al Tzir Hashana Umerchav Haaretz)* (Jerusalem: Maggid Books, 2017), p. 119.

7. *Orot Hakodesh*, vol. 1, p. 179.

several hours as the moth struggled to force the body through that little hole.

The moth seemed to be stuck and appeared to have stopped making progress. It seemed as if it had gotten as far as it could and it could go no farther. The man, in his kindness, decided to help the moth; so, he took a pair of scissors and snipped off the remaining bit of the cocoon. The moth then emerged easily. But its body was swollen and small, its wings, wrinkled and shriveled. The man continued to watch the moth because he expected that, at any moment, the wings would enlarge and expand to be able to support the body, which would contract in time. Neither happened! In fact, the little moth spent the rest of its life crawling around with a small, swollen body and shriveled wings. It never was able to fly. The man in his kindness and haste did not understand that the struggle required for the moth to get through the tiny opening was necessary to force fluid from the body of the moth into its wings so that it would be ready for flight upon achieving its freedom from the cocoon. Freedom and flight would only come after the struggle. By depriving the moth of a struggle, he deprived the moth of health.

Sometimes struggles are exactly what we need in our life. If we were to go through our life without any obstacles, we would be crippled. We would not be as strong as we could have been. We can give every opportunity a chance, leaving no room for regrets, and not forgetting the power of the struggle. To be sure, we don't want to romanticize struggle or make meaning of others' pain or struggle. We can, however, make meaning of our own struggle while we work to remove the pain and suffering involved in another's struggle.

Our lives are like sheep that can be sheared. We constantly drop an old coat – whether that be our hopes or our desires – and grow a new one. On Shabbat, and in general, many of us are removed from animal care. But this *melacha* reminds us that human interference can have the ability to disrupt the natural order.

One look at the world today shows how destructive humans can be when living with great hubris. Yet, when we really take the time to dig deeper and consider how our personal choices and actions can have an effect on the world around us, we then have that sacred opening to reflect on our capacity for renewal.

13.
Melabain (Whitening)

THE THIRTEENTH MELACHA is *melabain,* from the root word *lavan* (white), and means whitening (bleaching or laundering). In this *melacha,* we are concerned mostly with removing stains from garments. The idea of this action as a melacha emerged from the *Mishkan* with regard to bleaching wool as part of the process of producing the tapestries.

What is the moral cost to us doing our laundry? Consider this tosefta:

> A cistern provides water for a town [in a time of drought]: concerning the townspeople and others, the townspeople have precedence to the water.
>
> The towns animals and the lives of others: the lives of others have precedence over animals. Rabbi Yose says that the animals have precedence over the townspeople.
>
> The animals of the town and the animals of others? The animals of the townspeople have precedence.
>
> The lives of others and the laundry of the town? The lives of others have precedence over the water. Rabbi Yose says that laundry of the townspeople comes before the lives of others.[1]

It may seem disgusting that the people choose laundry over human lives, right? But don't we all do that? Don't we all allocate

---

1. Tosefta, Bava Metzia, chapter 11.

funds to machines, detergents, and water that clean our clothes?
Funds that could have been donated to save lives? We wish for
our clothes to look good and smell good. How much is that
worth to us?

What does white symbolize in Jewish thought? Let's start with
the idea of aging and wisdom.

> "And Abraham became old (Genesis 24:1)." Until Abraham,
> there was no old age, so that one who wished to speak with
> Abraham might mistakenly find himself speaking to Isaac, or
> one who wished to speak with Isaac might mistakenly find him-
> self speaking to Abraham. But when Abraham came, he pleaded
> for old age, saying, "Master of the universe, You must make a
> visible distinction between father and son, between a youth and
> an old man, so that the old man may be honored by the youth."
> God replied, "As you live, I shall begin with you." So, Abraham
> went off, passed the night, and arose in the morning. When he
> arose, he saw that the hair of his head and of his beard had
> turned white. He said, "Master of the universe, if You have given
> me white hair as a mark of old age, [I do not find it attractive]."
> "On the contrary," God replied, "the hoary head is a crown of
> glory."[2]

God loves the maturity and the wisdom that comes along with
age and the color white represents this process. But thinking
about the whitening of hair over time allows us to focus not so
much on age but rather on the wisdom for which the whiteness
serves as a metaphor, as the sages emphasize in another story:

> [Rabbi Eleazar's wife] said to him: You have no white hair. He
> was eighteen years old that day, and a miracle was wrought for
> him and eighteen rows of hair [on his beard] turned white. That

---

2. Bava Metzia 87a (quoting from Proverbs 6:31), Bereshit Rabbah 65:9.

is why R. Eleazar b. Azariah said: Behold it is as if I am seventy years old, and he did not say [simply] seventy years old.[3]

We might also consider the idea of *lavan* as light, represented by the moon which is called *levanah*. We look up into the starry night and witness marvelous revelation and the blessing of light within the dark. We gain hope from the whitening or lightening of the sky. And we understand that wisdom and hope come not only from inherent light, such as that in the sun, but also reflected light – shared and dispersed light, wisdom, and insight of a quality worthy of being shared and dispersed – that the moon symbolizes.

On the other hand, there is also the idea of white as representing a plague. As it says:

> Miriam and Aaron spoke against Moses, concerning the Cushite wife he had married ... They said, "Has God only spoken through Moshe [in prophecy]? He has spoken through us, as well!"
>
> And God heard. ... God said, "Now hear my words. If there shall be prophets among you, I appear to them in visions, I speak to them through dreams. Not so my servant, Moses. He is trustworthy in My entire house. I speak to him mouth to mouth, with clear vision and not in riddles. Why did you not fear speaking about my servant, about Moshe?"
>
> And God became angry with them and God left. And the cloud left the tent and Miriam was white as snow with *tzara'at*. Aaron turned to Miriam and she had *tzara'at*. ... Miriam was quarantined outside the camp for seven days, and the people did not journey until Miriam was brought in.[4]

Here white is a sign of plague, of punishment, of *lashon hara*. We are reminded by this story that if we speak about someone inap-

---

3. Berachot 27b–28a.
4. Numbers 12:1–15.

propriately, if we improperly suggest that that person's totality is defined by one feature, one relationship, one action – that is, that the individual's personality is monochromatic, or even without any color but simply white – we can find ourselves responsible for the plague of communal stasis, the inability of a community to accomplish the growth that accompanies recognition that every person has so many colorful facets.

White also can represent friendliness. Rabbi Yohanan said: "Better to whiten one's teeth with a smile to one's friend than to feed them milk.[5],[6] On the other hand, whitening another's face can mean shaming them. As the Sefer Hachinuch writes, the Rabbis referred to the sin of publicly shaming another person as *malbin pnei chaveiro barabim*, causing another's face to become pale.[7] *Halbanat panim* (whitening of the face) refers to embarrassing another, symbolized by the face turning pale with shame. Rabbi Moshe Alshikh wrote:

> Do not be surprised that one can deserve capital punishment even though one has not actually ended a life, for has not a person's face been created in the image of God, and without which one would be comparable to an animal? Therefore, one who whitens the face (humiliates a person), where the image of God resides, is deserving of death for one has blemished the site of the image of God."[8]

On a similar note:
One who whitens [shames] a fellow's face in public has no

---

5. BT Ketubot 111b.
6. Related to teeth being white for all humans, we also share white fingernails. We wash our hands after a haircut or after cutting our fingernails to represent the separation of death from life (i.e., a part of our body is being removed, a dead part from the rest of our life).
7. Sefer Hachinuch, mitzvah 240.
8. Rabbi Moshe Alshech's commentary on the verse "one who spills the blood of a person, in a person, his blood shall be spilled" (Gen. 9:5) (Torat Moshe).

place in the world to come even if they have accrued Torah and good acts, for the human being is created in God's image.[1]

On the opposite end, white represents purity, particularly as contrasted with red which represents sin:

How do we know that they tie a crimson thread on the head of the scapegoat [which is sent forth on Yom Kippur]? Since it says, "Though your sins be as scarlet, they shall be white as snow."[2]

Related to Yom Kippur, we, traditionally, wear a white *kittel* (a white linen or cotton robe worn by some Jews on some holidays). Many also wear the *kittle* under the chuppah (at marriage), for burial shrouds, or as the leader of the Passover seder. In each case, we are reflecting on rebirth and the humility of our mortality.

While white can positively portray purity, we should also be careful not to think of red as impure. Consider for example the blood of the heifer to purify. Consider the idea a menstruating woman, who should not be deemed impure or unclean during menstruation and pure or clean at other times. The blood can be viewed positively in regards to the covenantal blessing of procreation and fertility.

Nevertheless, the idea that white and red stand in stark contrast is hardly clear. Jacob had negative experiences with our matriarch Rebecca's brother, Lavan – Jacob's father-in-law whose name literally means "white" – and Esau, who was sold his red soup to Jacob and who went on to be embodied in the nation of Edom whose name means "red." Jacob knew, at least, where he stood with his brother. His father-in-law tried to appear white as the driven snow even as he dealt underhandedly with Jacob, maneuvering Jacob into a marriage with one sister although Jacob expected to marry the other. The problematic nature of Lavan's nature is related, in the English language, to "whitewashing," which is used to signify a lack of transparency and honesty.

---

1. Cited in Daniel Sperber, *Darka shel Halakha, Keri'at Nashim baTorah: Perakim biMediniyyut Pesikah.* (Jerusalem: Reuven Mass., 2007), p. 85 fn. 117.
2. Mishnah, Yoma 6:8 (quoting Isaiah 1:18).

Lavan doesn't see the dignity of Jacob, as a family member, as a worker, or as a person. Rather, one might suggest that he is a founder of white supremacy, where value is only given to others for what they are able to produce. Other people are disposable and abusable if they are different from the norm. All that matters is what they can produce for you. In the Passover seder each year, we read about how Lavan is the paradigmatic antisemite, "Go and learn what Lavan, the Aramean, sought to do to our father Yaakov. A Pharaoh made his decree only about the males, whereas Lavan sought to destroy everything." We can learn from Lavan about the history of the Jewish people and the threat that still remains today.

In "Skin in the Game: How Antisemitism Animates White Nationalism," Eric K. Ward writes:

> American White nationalism, which emerged in the wake of the 1960s civil rights struggle and descends from White suprema-cism, is a revolutionary social movement committed to building a Whites-only nation, and antisemitism forms its theoretical core. That last part – antisemitism forms the theoretical core of White nationalism – bears repeating.

Ward argues here that white nationalism is a genocidal movement fueled by antisemitism.

We must remember that equating whiteness with purity is socially problematic, just as the idea of light and dark can be concerning. We can't explore the process of whitening without looking at the reality of whiteness in people. White people often talk about people of color and discuss blackness. But have white people grappled with their own – our own? – whiteness? What does it mean to carry the privilege of whiteness? Does complicity come along with this privilege? How might one leverage their own power to amplify access and deepen potential for those without that privilege?

Sometimes, those who seek to shame others have their own

internal work to do. Sometimes they might consider refraining from externalizing their pain and rather holding their pain. Consider this short teaching from a Chassidic teacher, Rabbi Usher Freund:

> A tale of one who had a stone within their heart.
> And it hurt them.
> And they grew bitter.
> And they sought all sorts of ways to throw away the stone.
> And nothing worked.
> Until they came to a wise man, who told them:
> Stop trying to throw it away, carry it.[3]

We need to carry our pain rather than throw it away, even as we have to be careful to avoid hiding it – making it invisible in the sense of being without color, or only white – when we have to let it out. Each of us has different traumas and different glories to carry along with us in our journeys. We protect each other by doing our own inner healing work, by carrying and tending to our burdens and wounds rather than ignoring them or attempting, fruitlessly, to merely toss them aside. Each of us is given different challenges, different opportunities to serve, and different spiritual paths. Consider the pluralism taught here by Rabbi Akiva Eiger based on a passage at the end of the Talmudic tractate of Ta'anit suggesting that in the future the righteous ones ("the tzaddikim") will dance together in a circle in the Garden of Eden. Each righteous person, dancing around the Creator, will point to God and say: "This is our God; this is Hashem, Whom we have so longed to behold!" Rabbi Akiva Eiger explains here the symbolism behind the idea of why the dance around the Divine is in a circle and the broader lessons behind the dance of the righteous:

---

3. https://twitter.com/jorosenfeld/status/1496497575314313218?s=20&t =j9buRCXROppEq-EIrOJVtg.

In this world, every Tzaddik has a unique, individual approach to serving Hashem. On the surface, every one of them appears to be heading in a completely different direction. The truth is, however, that this is not the case. All of the different Tzaddikim are united by a common goal – to draw closer to Hashem and fulfill His will in the best possible manner. In the World to Come this will become apparent to all. The Tzaddikim will dance around Hashem "arranged in a circle." In a circle, every individual is facing a different direction – yet they all revolve around the same central point. The Tzaddikim, although each has a unique approach, are all trying to accomplish the same goal. Their lives revolve around the same central point, the point where "Hashem is sitting." In the World to Come, each of them will point to Him and announce to all that this is their G-d, to Whom they had strived to come close and serve throughout their lives!

Indeed, the Baal Shem Tov taught[4] that each of us must listen to their own soul (neshama) to discover our unique *avodah* (service in the world).

We need not shame others who are on a different spiritual path from us. We also don't have to be embarrassed by our unique calling within our spiritual path. The *melacha* of *melabain* reminds us of the warmth exuded by the white of our smiles but also the pain that can be caused by the whitening of another's face. Each day, we can reflect on our relationship to the color white, both in actuality and symbolically, and what it means for human dignity, in human history, and in our own quest for spiritual purification and ethical growth.

---

4. J. Immanuel Schochet, *Tzavat Harivash, the Testament of Rabbi Israel Baal Shem Tov* (New York: Kehot Publication Society, 1998), p. 41.

14.

Menapeitz (Combing)

As we continue on the theme from the last two *melachot*, the fourteenth *melacha*, *menapeitz*, involves disentangling, brushing, or combing clumps of tangled material (typically hair). This prohibition, as we have seen in previous weeks, goes back to the practices surrounding the *Mishkan*. In this case, the custom would be to cut the hair of a sheep, after which the hair would still be tangled and would need to be sorted out in order to process it into fabric. In some cases, the hair would be brushed or combed before shearing to facilitate the cutting itself. As in the *melacha* of *gozeiz* (shearing), it extends to human beings as well; combing or brushing one's hair on Shabbat is indeed problematic and can only be done under certain conditions.

How does the act of brushing correspond to the higher echelons of Jewish wisdom? Among practitioners of mindfulness, the act of brushing – one's teeth, one's hair – is often treated as a good example of something common and mundane that can be elevated by being mindful of the activity. There are often quieter moments to step away from the hustle and bustle of the world to focus exclusively on the self. It's not vanity to take care of one's physical appearance if it provides moments of reflection. It's worth considering this notion.

On the topic of hair, the Talmud teaches that God pays attention to each individual hair – of which there are hundreds of thousands on every person's body – to teach a lesson about the depth of Divine concern:

> Job complained about his suffering to God: Perhaps a storm passed before You causing You to confuse me with Your enemy? God replied: I have created many hairs in people, and for every hair I have created a separate pit so that two hairs should not take nourishment from the same source. For if they were to take nourishment from the same place it would cause blindness. If I don't confuse one hair pit with another, why should I confuse Job with another man?[1]

This is, of course, an intense issue of theology (theodicy) concerning how God cares for and looks after people. But here, of interest, is the idea that God cares for each and every hair. The hair symbolizes the multiplicity of the human being, the various dimensions and aspects of our lives.

On a similar note, let's think of the Jewish custom not to cut a baby boy's hair until his third birthday. Influenced by kabbalah, this custom rests on the idea that a young boy might be protected from harm if his appearance is not made distinctive by cutting his hair in some individualizing way. Lilith, the seducer, might not be able to tempt the little boy since he appears to be a little girl to her. Yet, perhaps a better understanding of this practice takes an opposite approach. Parents who allow their child's hair to grow wild are parents who recognize the importance of a child being allowed to find his or her own way to become a tame, responsible, helpful member of society. We wait to cut our child's hair until necessary, then, to remind ourselves that as they get older and reach adolescence, they should be given time to express their authentic selves without us making undue educational interventions in their natural development. We want

---

1. BT Bava Batra 16a–b.

them to discover their own nature before we try to intervene in cultivating it.

Jean-Jacques Rousseau argued, in his work *Emile*, that children should be removed from school, which pushes conformity. Rather, students should be educated in isolation where their unique natures could develop.[2] Philosophically, if not in practice, he believed in breaking from indoctrination and institutionalized educational systems.

Unfortunately, there is not a parallel tradition of waiting to cut hair for girls. This is particularly unfortunate because for many, not cutting a little girl's hair would be even more desirable to the family than not cutting the little boy's hair, due to societal norms. Interestingly enough, the rabbis suggested that God braided Eve's hair.[3] It's also worth noting that, in anthropomorphic kabbalistic texts, God himself is depicted as having ringlets.[4]

A comb doesn't always carry with it a warm feeling in Jewish lore. Consider this famous Talmudic story:

> At the hour when Rabbi Akiva was taken out for execution, it was the time for the recital of the Shema. Thus, while they were combing his flesh with iron combs, he was accepting upon himself the yoke of the kingdom of heaven.
>
> His students said to him: "Our master, even at this point?"
>
> He said to them: "All my days I have been troubled by this verse [and its proper interpretation], *b'chol nafshecha* ('with all your soul') – even if God takes away your soul. I said: When will I have the opportunity of fulfilling this? Now that I have the opportunity shall I not fulfill it?"
>
> [In reciting the Shema] he prolonged saying the final word *Echad* ('One') of "Hear O Israel, the Lord is our God, the Lord is One" until his soul departed.

---

2. It appears that Rousseau unfortunately abandoned his own children.
3. Brachot 61a, Shabbat 95a.
4. See Sefer Yetzirah. See Shiur Hakavod.

A heavenly voice went forth and proclaimed: "Happy are
you, Rabbi Akiva, that your soul has departed with the word
'One!'"[5]

There is another story involving Rabbi Akiva and hair, a story
that can be read in a positive vein. Rabbi Akiva's wife sold the
braids of her hair and used the proceeds so that he could go
study Torah.[6] Although this might be seen as a touching story of
humble self-sacrifice, Rabbi Dr. Rachel Adler offers a feminist
critique of this story that focuses on how Rabbi Akiva's wife
negates who she is:

> How is it that the *tzaddikim* [righteous men] seem so individ-
> ualized and the *tzidkaniot* [righteous women] so generalized?
> I would advance two reasons. First of all, the mitzvot of the
> *tzadeket* are mainly directed toward serving others. She is a
> *tzadeket* to the extent that she sacrifices herself in order that
> others may actualize themselves spiritually. One has no sense
> of an attempt to cultivate a religious self, built out of the raw
> materials of a unique personality. The model for the *tzadeket*
> is Rachel, the wife of Rabbi Akiva, who sold her hair and sent
> her husband away to study for twenty-four years, leaving herself
> beggared and without means of support;[7] or the wife of Rabbi
> Menachem Mendel of Rymanov who sold her share in the next
> world to buy her husband bread.[8]

Rabbi Harold S. Kushner pointed out the significance of the fact
that hair is dead and unfeeling:

---

5. BT, Brachot 61b.

6. JT, Sotah 9:15.

7. This case reminds me of Fantine, in Les Misérables, selling her hair to
take care of her daughter Cosette.

8. Rachel Adler, "The Jew Who Wasn't There: Halacha and the Jewish
Woman." Response: A Contemporary Jewish Review, Summer 1973, p.79b.

Pain is the price we pay for being alive. Dead cells – our hair, our fingernails – can't feel pain; they cannot feel anything. When we understand that, our question will change from, "Why do we have to feel pain?" to "What do we do with our pain so that it becomes meaningful and not just pointless empty suffering?[1]

This is why traditionally, I might suggest, we wash our hands after a haircut or after cutting our nails. This is to deepen our relationship to death, and to the affirmation of life.[2]

In the Torah, one of the rules for the *nazir* (Nazarite) is that he not cut his hair.[3] Perhaps, in this line of traditional thinking, haircuts were considered more an act of vanity rather than total dedication to God. Or perhaps, there is a mourning element involved: when we are in mourning, we don't get haircuts. It says in the midrash:

> Why does God command the *nazir* not to cut his hair? Because cutting his hair enhances his appearance ... while growing hair is a sign of sorrow and mourning. Therefore, God says, "Since this *nazir* has prohibited wine for himself in order to keep himself away from licentiousness, let him grow his hair long so that he will become untidy and will be pained by it; then, his evil inclination will not overcome him."[4]

---

1. Harold S. Kushner, *When Bad Things Happen to Good People: 20th Anniversary Edition, with a New Preface by the Author*. (New York: Schocken Books, 2001), p. 86.

2. While the cuticles and follicles are living cells receiving nutrients, the hard part of the nail and the hair above the scalp are keratin which is technically considered dead.

3. I heard from Rabbi Ami Silver that the *idra rabba*, one of the most significant sections of the Zohar, on Parshat Nasso deals with the Divine *partzufim* and focuses a lot on the hair of these various aspects of God. In introducing the *idra*, Rebbe Shimon relates it to the discussion of the Nazir's hair (Zohar vol.3 127b).

4. Bamidbar Rabba 10:10.

Rabbi Samson Raphael Hirsch explains: "Growing the hair un-impeded expresses isolation and introversion.... He seeks to be alone and to delve into himself.... He wants to do some spiritual, moral work of self-education."

The stories of two biblical personalities, one of whom was a *nazir*, reflect a perceived relationship between hair and an untamed nature. We're told that Esau was born covered in hair. The strife between him and his twin brother – Jacob – was epic. And Samson's hair was the source of his storied strength that he used to achieve conquests in the arenas of love (with Delilah, whose relationship with him was unsettled, at best) and of war (although his ultimate victory as a warrior brought about his own death). Perhaps Esau and Samson are able to remind us that the way to achieve true peace in our interpersonal relationships (and on a broader, international scale) is to look at each other on a level that is more than skin – or hair – deep.

The origin of the rule followed by some traditionally Jewish observant women to cover their hair comes from the idea that hair is *ervah* (nakedness).[5] Rabbi Sheshet says: "A woman's hair is a sexual incitement"[6] based on the idea, from the Torah itself, that it's humiliating to a woman to uncover her hair, since it is a private matter.[7] And it seems from the prophet Nehemia that pulling out hair is a sign of disrespect for both women and men:

> And I quarreled with them, and I cursed them, and I struck some of them, and I plucked out their hair, and I adjured them by God, "You shall not give your daughters to their sons nor take their daughters either for your sons or for yourselves."[8]

---

5. This was the prevalent view when and where all women, Jewish and gentile, customarily covered their hair. Today, since women in many societies no longer do so, it is perhaps no longer considered *ervah*. Other reasons for hair covering have been suggested.

6. BT, Brachot 24a.

7. Numbers 5:18.

8. Nehemia 13:25.

So then, hair is something to be guarded and protected. Consider the fear that was involved with allowing an idolater to cut a Jew's hair:

> We may allow them to heal us when the healing relates to money, but not personal healing; nor should we have our hair cut by them in any place. This is the opinion of R. Meir; but the Sages said, in a public place it is permitted, but not when the two persons are alone.[9]

When we comb the head, we are literally brushing over the brain, over the mind. The Baal Shem Tov taught that we are where our thoughts are. When we use the comb or brush, we can reflect on our thoughts. We can work on our *menuchat nefesh* (equanimity). For the Baal Shem Tov, we live by *Shiviti Hashem l'negdi tamid* ("I place God before me always"), and by keeping God in our consciousness, we make all that enters us equal, achieving spiritual equanimity. We realize that everything in the mind comes from one place and all is equal. Every thought in me is okay. If we attach to God our consciousness, it's all okay. Of course, not every thought should be spoken or acted upon. But the Hasidic tradition teaches us that, we can be gentle with ourselves around imperfect and impure thoughts. Hell is the place where one cannot find Godliness and can't find light. This is called *mochin b'katnut* (living with a constricted consciousness), where one's doubts and anxieties block an expanded consciousness. There is a block to the Divine light. Instead, living with equanimity, we can see that even in darkness there is light. When King David says he will not have fear as he walks through the valley of the shadow of death, it is not because God will remove the dark valley. That valley is life. Rather it is because "You are with me." When we are with God, everything can be okay, in our consciousness.

On Shabbat, we reflect on taking care of our hair, our appear-

---

9. Mishna, Avoda Zara, 2:2.

ance, our dignity, and the responsibility that comes with that gift. *Menapeitz* is the remedy we need to step away from the hectic circumstances of the workweek and truly take those precious moments to slow down and reflect. We need to be mindful of the notion that taking care of our bodies is akin to taking care of the world. How we interact with objects that manipulate our hair, or our teeth, or any other related part, is indicative of the way we perceive our obligations to ourselves and the broader world.

15.
Tzovei'a (Dyeing)

HERE, WE LOOK at the fifteenth *melacha*, which is *tzovei'a* (dyeing). The overarching concern of this series of *melachot* is working with wool, as the Israelites involved in the construction of the *Mishkan* dyed wool before spinning it into thread. This dyeing with various colored solutions was done to produce the coverings for the *Mishkan*. The *melacha* of *tzovei'a* specifically has to do with adding color to the wool. It has been extended to makeup and nail polish, painting, or coloring.[1] An interesting rule of this *melacha* is *ein tzevi'a b'ochel* ("there is no coloring by food"), meaning that coloring foods is permissible. One example: It is permitted to mix mayonnaise with ketchup in order to make a salad dressing even though a new color is produced. It is not about writing in general, that is the *melacha* of *koteiv* (writing); the purpose of that *melacha* is to create a symbol rather than to enhance with color.

Imagine a world without color, like the one that was experienced when television and photographs were primarily in black and white. We wish to live through a full existence, one that is colorful, vibrant and dynamic. The ability to interact with the full range of color is certainly an aspect of our encounter with the

---

1. Certain types of makeup are considered permissible, as the details of *tzovei'a* are very specific.

physical world, but spiritual color is a reality as well. Consider this explanation of prayer from Rabbi Joseph Soloveitchik:

> Prayer, which is like a mirror reflecting the image of the person who worships God with heart and soul, is shot through with perplexity, for worship itself is rooted in the human dialectical consciousness. Hence prayer is not marked by monotonous uniformity. It is multi-colored: it contains contradictory themes, expresses a variety of moods, conflicting experiences, and desires oscillating and opposing directions. Religious experience is a multi-directional movement, metaphysically infused. Prayer too does not proceed slowly along one straight path, but leaps and cascades from wondrous heights to terrifying depths, and back.[2]

Consider the reflection and radiance of light – indeed, the colorful visions – within prayer experiences:

> Whatever one implants firmly in the mind becomes the essential thing. So, if you pray and offer a blessing to God, or if you wish your intentions to be true, imagine you are light. All around you – in every corner and on every side – is light. Turn to your right, and you will find shining light. To your left, splendor, a radiant light. Between them, up above, the light of the Presence. Surrounding that, the light of life. Above it all, a crown of light – crowning the aspirations of thought, illuminating the paths of imagination, spreading the radiance of vision. The light is unfathomable and endless.[3]

At the beginning of the Book of Ezekiel, we learn of a profound prophetic experience:

---

2. Rabbi Joseph B. Soloveitchik, *Worship of the Heart: Essays on Jewish Prayer* (New York: KTAV, 2003), page 148.

3. Sha'ar HaKavanah, attributed to Azriel of Gerona (late 12th–13th century Spain).

The word of the Lord was [revealed] to Ezekiel the son of Buzi, the priest, in the land of the Chaldeans, by the river Chebar, and the hand of the Lord came upon him there. And I saw, and behold, a tempest was coming from the north, a huge cloud and a flaming fire with a brightness around it; and from its midst, it was like the color of the *chashmal* (electrum) from the midst of the fire. And from its midst was the likeness of four living beings, and this is their appearance: they had the likeness of a man. And [each] one had four faces, and [each] one had four wings. And their legs were a straight leg, and the soles of their feet were like a round foot, and they sparkled like the color of burnished copper.[4]

A whole field within kabbalah – *Merkavah* mysticism – is developed based on this opening passage in the Book of Ezekiel. The prophet's colorful vision is referred to as *Maaseh Merkavah* (Account of the Chariot); the kabbalistic literature based on it overlaps with *heichalot* (palaces) literature describing the throne of God.

Consider the idea, found in the Midrash, that humans are made from colors:

God gathered the dust [of the first human] from the four corners of the world – red, black, white, and green. Red is the blood, black is the innards, and green for the body.[5] Why from the four corners of the earth? So that if one comes from the east to the west and arrives at the end of their life as they near departing from the world, it will not be said to them, "This land is not the dust of your body, it's of mine. Go back to where you were created." Rather, every place that a person walks, from there they were created and from there they will return.[6]

---

4. Ezekiel 1:3–7.
5. The existing Hebrew versions of this midrash omit the significance and explanation of the color white as one of the four colors described here.
6. Yalkut Shimoni, Genesis 1:13.

This idea reminds us of the diversity of humanity and leads us to contemplate the significance of rights for those people who come from a diversity of backgrounds, especially those who leave their homelands because of oppression in order to find refuge elsewhere.

All people "belong" on the Earth because we are all made up from the same colors of earth. Following this ethical approach, we consider our responsibilities to the other. And we might contemplate the many-colored faces that represent the individuals to whom we hold those responsibilities. In this vein, consider the idea from the philosopher Emmanuel Levinas that, although we interact with different people with different facial features, to truly encounter them means to relate to the personal realities that are merely represented by those varied physical realities:

> To meet another, one must first welcome a face. This means more than looking at the features of the other face, or the color that characterizes the surface of his skin, or the iris of his eyes – as if in doing so one could perceive, grasp, know. Is not the face first of all expression and appeal, preceding that datum of knowledge? Is it not the nakedness of the other – destitution and misery beneath the adopted countenance?[7]

The Talmud suggests that the donkey upon which the Messiah will ride will be like a horse with a thousand colors.[8] The thousand-colored donkey is a good jumping-off point to understand the theology of Rav Abraham Isaac Kook and to explore what he terms the *tahalich hageulah* (the journey towards the ultimate redemption), a polychromatic or multi-colored, multi-layered redemptive phenomenon involving many different populations and many different conflicting processes. Each person, each group,

---

7. Jill Robbins, Ed., *Is it Righteous to Be? Interviews with Emmanuel Levinas*, (California: Stanford Univ. Press, 2001), 191.

8. BT Sanhedrin 98a.

each movement, has a crucial light, a vital element, that progresses toward an end, targeting the ultimate goal – redemption.

This point applies beyond the idea of Jewish diversity. Rambam (Maimonides) argued that Christianity and Islam[1] help to pave the path toward redemption. This is because of their scale and ability to spread monotheism.

In exploring the biblical mandate of *v'samachta b'chagecha* ("to be joyful on the holidays"), we see in the Talmud that there were already different customs around wearing colors:

> The Rabbis taught in a Baraita:[2] A person is obligated to gladden their children and members of their household on the festivals, as it is stated: "And you shall rejoice on your festival." With what does one gladden them? R. Yehuda says: "Men with what is suitable for them and women with what is suitable for them." Men with what is suitable for them, with wine. And with what does one gladden the women? R. Yosef taught a baraita: In Babylonia, with colored garments, and in Israel with pressed linen garments.[3]

For Jews living in the Babylonian diaspora, the women wore more colorful clothing, whereas in Israel they preferred pressed garments. Likewise, each of us experiences joy differently; for some, the women of the diaspora, it was through colorful clothing. For others, clothes can represent pure vanity, and still for others, a lofty spiritual ideal of one's religious service.

Rambam writes about the halachic problem of indelibly dyeing one's skin:

---

1. Indeed, Maimonides writes that Islam does not fall under the rubric of *avodah zarah* (idolatry).

2. The work of *Baraita* is considered a precursor to the Mishna, and records both many laws included in the Mishnah and many not included in the final redaction.

3. BT Pesachim 109a.

"Incising a mark" – The prohibition of tattooing that is biblically derived is making an incision in one's flesh and filling the
incision with eye paint, ink, or any dye that leaves an imprint.
This was the practice of idolaters who [permanently] marked
their bodies for the sake of their idol worship. Basically, [they
understood this to be] that they are likened to servants sold to
the idol and designated to serve it.

When one makes an imprint with one of the substances [listed
above], the punishment of lashes is carried out, whether it is a
man or a woman.

If one wrote but did not dye, or dyed but did not write [by
incising in the flesh] – this person is not liable, as it is written,[4]
"or incise any marks."[5]

While there is a general prohibition for a man to dye his hair to
look younger and more attractive[6] (aside from some exceptions
around job security),[7] there is also an idea inherent in the prohibition against idolatry relating to dyeing the face of a human:

> … And so is the halakha, that a face of a man is forbidden
> to seal with and forbidden to make. However, those faces of
> people that are dyed on the sheets with dyes and embroideries
> are permissible, since they do not have a full face, but rather
> half a face.[8]

What the Tosafot here seem to be doing in their enigmatic style
is distinguishing between painting a two-dimensional figure and

---

4. Leviticus 19:28.
5. *Mishneh Torah: Laws of Idolatry* 12:11.
6. *Lo Yilbash*: https://thehalacha.com/wp-content/uploads/Vol11Issue5.pdf.
7. This prohibition is related to *lo yilbash*, one wearing the clothing of the
other gender, which is extended to hair dyeing, as this was customary almost
exclusively among women. Today, when many men in general society dye their
hair and it is no longer exclusive to women, several halachic decisors permit it.
8. Tosafot, Avoda Zara, 43a, s.v., Lo.

fashioning a three-dimensional one. This distinction, in turn, appears to perceive some measure of false-god worship in an attempt to reproduce fully formed human reality in a full-bodied image, whereas simply depicting an aspect of human nature by using colors is fine.

Interestingly enough, those in the business of working with wool and dye were used as an example of how workers have the right to unionize to protect their job and wages:

> The wool workers and the dyers are permitted to say, "we will all be partners in any business that comes to the city."[9]

Some years ago, I found myself yearning for *techeilet* (blue tzitzit strings) one Shabbat morning, as this was the *parsha* (Torah reading portion) which mentions *techeilet*. I was sad that the dye needs to come from a *hilazon,* a snail-like creature understood to be the cuttlefish or hexaplex (murex) trunculus found on an Israeli coastal plain near Tel Shikmona. If the dye was traditionally considered valid if produced without living creatures, I would have been open to wearing it since the ideal is for that blue color to inspire lofty thoughts.

So, too, color engenders art, joy, and expression. But color can also be understood as something detrimental. Consider the phrase that we can't allow our past experiences, or our biases, to "color" our judgment. Here, "color" is meant as one's past skewing one's image of the present or the future. Why is it that sad or lonely music is called "the blues?" Consider the idea of a "litmus test," where one is tested (in a color metaphor) to see if they're worthy. But what results do we receive from such tests?

In philosophy, there is a concept called *verificationism.* The argument here is that for a claim to be cognitively meaningful it needs to be confirmed empirically. For example, an expression of a feeling cannot be categorized as true or false because we

---

9. Tosefta Bava Metzia 11:24–26.

would need verified evidence. But if unverified statements are to be viewed as problematic, are feelings truly meaningless? Is theology all meaningless? Is much of the field of ethics meaningless? After all, how can I verify the normative claim that murder is definitively wrong from an empirical perspective? Further, the principle of verification itself cannot survive the scrutiny of being verified. Life is more colorful than the black and white assessment of true or false. What is meaningful goes beyond what can be verified. Consider faith, love, and other deep internal life experiences.

Rather, we can see life through a prism, a kaleidoscope, with many vibrant, radiant colors, and appreciate the subjective realities that give so much meaning to our lives. And Shabbat, in particular, allows us to observe those aspects of life without needing to add color to the world, as we would do if we violated this *melacha*.

There are many colors to spiritual light. Rabbi Yitzchak Hutner (a 20th-century rabbinic scholar and halachic authority) taught[10] that there are fundamentally two different kinds of spiritual light. One is based on the *beracha, baruch hatov v'ha'meitiv* ("blessed Who is good and does good to others," meaning seeing the light in the good of everything). The other is based on *baruch dayan ha'emet*[11] ("blessed Who judges in truth," meaning seeing the light in the darkness). Indeed, on Shabbat and beyond, we can learn to see light, to see color, and become creators of dynamic vibrant visions.

---

10. Reported to have been a teaching given at a Purim seudah but never written.

11. This *beracha* is recited upon hearing of the death of one's immediate relative.

16.
Toveh (Spinning)

THE SIXTEENTH MELACHA is *toveh*, (spinning). Now that we have sheared, combed, and dyed the wool as featured in previous *melachot*, it is time for the wool to be spun into thread. This involves twisting the fibers together. It is instructive to note that several of the previous *melachot* involved separating an existing entity into its respective parts, and beginning with *toveh*, we move on to engaging in the opposite – combining separate entities into one new material.[1] A classic example would be to twist cotton into thread or to make rope or twine. Most of us aren't engaged with twisting wool during the week, let alone on Shabbat. But, then again, a lot of the *melachot* are not only about the specific actions they involve. Rather, the *melachot* also help us more broadly cultivate a consciousness that can be used toward repairing the world.

Let's review, and now add to, our broader philosophical approach here. Our proposal is that Shabbat does not need to be reduced to synagogue rituals and meals. Rather, the 39 *melachot* constitute the central foundation of the Shabbat experience. We can't bring Shabbat prayer and meals into the week, but we can

---

1. One of the Torah-based prohibitions (irrespective of Shabbat) is wearing wool and linen together in a garment. This wool-linen combination is referred to in the text as *sha'atneiz*. According to the Talmud (BT *Nidah* 61b) the derivation of the word *sha'atneiz* is three separate steps in the cloth making process: *shua, tavui, and nuz* (combing, spinning, and weaving).

bring a consciousness of the 39 *melachot* that we may refrain from on Shabbat into the six workdays. This is the *penimiyut haTorah* (the inner spiritual depths of the Torah). When we live with the 39 *melachot* in our collective consciousness during the week, the essence and beauty of Shabbat is revealed as we go about our working lives.

Conversely, when we refrain from those *melachot* on Shabbat, we remind ourselves of the spiritual meaning of those activities.

We can also view the weekday as a remnant of the last Shabbat, and equally anticipatory of the coming Shabbat. I'd suggest that each week we are, in a sense, reliving creation. On Shabbat we are alive! During the week, we are lifeless, or better still, in a way not born yet, not created yet, not yet conscious. With the consciousness of the 39 *melachot*, we are bringing ourselves to life, partnering with God in creation. It's not just humanity as such that is not yet created, not yet awake. More particularly, the Jewish people are spiritually asleep. We are alive but we are asleep. Our *ruach*, *nefesh*, and *neshamah* (different levels of our soul) are partially awake, by nature, although they yearn for deeper actualization. But our *yechidah* and *chaya* (basic, primary levels of our soul) are often just asleep even though we are alive as our consciousness is not consistently elevated. But Shabbat reminds us that we can tap into the deeper light of the soul. We can find the *or haganuz* (the spiritual light hidden at creation). We taste the light of the future in the present. All of our time is related to Shabbat. This is perhaps why, in the recitation of the *Shir shel Yom* (Psalm of the Day) upon the conclusion of the *Shacharit* service, the introductory verse refers to the days of the week as *rishon baShabbat, sheini baShabbat, etc.* ("the first day of the week," the second day of the week," etc.). An alternate reading of these references is "the first day towards Shabbat," "the second day towards Shabbat," displaying our anticipation of the coming Shabbat. We don't have separate, disconnected days; we only have days numbering towards Shabbat.

We mention spinning in our Friday night liturgy. In the singing of Eishet Chayil, we recite, "She sets her hand to the distaff; her fingers work the spindle. She gives generously to the poor; her hands are stretched out to the needy."[1] A spindle, and its working with it, is rather complex,[2] and so the process of spinning represents the virtue of a skilled and compassionate person.

Spinning is not, though, always a positive activity. When we speak colloquially about spinning a yarn, we are talking about telling a story that, for the most part, goes beyond the bounds of the literal truth. That can be highly destructive if the stories we tell are meant to misinform, to deceive, to misdirect. At the same time, we do well to remember that the process of concocting a fable can be used to entertain or even to educate. Indeed, when the ancient rabbis – and even some contemporary thinkers – engage in Midrash writing, they are at times spinning tales, but they are doing so *l'sheim shamayim* (for the sake of heaven), in order to elevate our thoughts and our actions by inviting us to consider the deepest mysteries of the Torah in terms of easy-to-digest stories that speak to our funny bones and our souls at the same time.[3]

Just as spinning can represent tale-telling, "spinning" also relates to conversation in general. We talk today about creating threads when we communicate electronically. The fact that spinning is a *melacha* that was necessary to build the *Mishkan* but that is prohibited on Shabbat reminds us of the differences between our conversations on Shabbat and those in which we engage during the week. In the weekday context, we either dash off notes quickly because we only have a moment, or craft them carefully so that we artfully – and sometimes with artifice – convey a thought in a carefully constructed manner. On Shabbat, we

---

1. Proverbs 31:10,11.

2. A spindle is translated as "a slender rounded rod with tapered ends used in hand spinning to twist and wind thread from a mass of wool or flax held on a distaff."

3. Rambam writes that those who take rabbinic *aggadah* literally are making fools out of the Sages.

create community with those with whom we communicate, taking advantage of the time that the day gives us, and the intimacy that avoiding twenty-first-century media demands, to interact in a spiritually meaningful way.

If we widen the angle of our consideration of the act of spinning a bit beyond the level of the spindle – that is, beyond the level at which individuals interrelate with other individuals – we can think about the use of spinning as a spiritual endeavor. We might think in this regard of whirling dervishes, Muslim mystics who spin to attain a spiritually elevated state. But we don't need to leave the Jewish tradition in order to see this sort of activity. Thus, the early medieval work known as Sefer Hasidim says that moving the entire body while praying is appropriate and in keeping with Psalms 35:1 that declares, "All my limbs will call out, 'God, who is like You?'"[4] Indeed, although many authoritative halachic sources frown upon the practice of *shuckling* (shaking or swaying) during prayer, today the practice of moving during davening is de rigueur in many synagogues.[5]

And if we zoom out still further, considering the matter at the level of the cosmos, we can reflect on how the planets have continued spinning because of their inertia. As we've known since the Copernican Revolution in the early 1500s,[6] planets are spinning

---

4. Sefer Chasidim 57.

5. It is interesting to note that Rabbi Yehudah Halevi (11th–12th century Spanish poet and philosopher) in his work Sefer Hakuzari, offers an entirely different, practical reason for the practice of *shuckling*. He takes us back to a time before the printing press when individuals did not own a *siddur* and thereby did not necessarily know the words of the prayers from memory. Rather, there was one central *siddur* held by the leader, and those surrounding him would bend over to see a few words or lines at a time, stand erect and recite those words, then bend over once again to see the following words, and so on. This swaying back and forth motion led to others mimicking it until it evolved into common practice.

6. Maimonides writes about planets (*galgalim*) much earlier, as did countless Jewish thinkers, but, of course, without the later knowledge that emerges in the 16th century and beyond. See the Moreh Nevuchim and the Mishneh Torah (Yesodei HaTorah chapter 3).

on their axes due to the law of physics known as conservation of angular momentum. In the vacuum of outer space, objects that are spinning maintain their direction and momentum, indeed their spin, since there are no external forces to slow them down or stop them. And so, even though plants that are rooted in the ground seem to be truly stationary, they keep spinning in our solar system.

The world is in motion.

Life is in motion.

Rav Saadia Gaon (9th–10th century) teaches that we live in a centripetal universe, to be understood according to Platonic ideas, where everything moves toward the center (toward the human). This is an anthropocentric approach (that is, one that sees humans as occupying the central position of existence, and that interprets everything according to its effect on humans). Rambam, however, taught that we live in a centrifugal universe that should be perceived in light of Aristotelian values. Rambam rejects anthropocentrism with the teleological position that God creates everything for its own purpose,[7] and thus the universe is centrifugal (everything moving away from the center), and the value of all increases as it goes outwards from humans and Earth, into the "active intellect" and beyond.

The science of both thinkers is known to be incorrect today, but there is still philosophical value to their approaches. In our own time, an important Jewish thinker and philosopher, Rabbi Norman Lamm, followed in the school of Rambam and wrote: "There is no need to exaggerate man's importance, and to exercise a kind of racial or global arrogance, in order to discover the sources of man's significance and uniqueness."

Although "there is no need to exaggerate man's importance" and there is a lot of value in expanding knowledge of the universe around us both for knowledge's sake and for the forward march

---

7. In biblical terms, as Proverbs 16:4 teaches, *l'maanehu* – for the sake of God as opposed to for the sake of humans.

of technology that advances the cause of human sustainability, on balance it is clear that the noble goal of reaching out into the cosmos must play second fiddle to the nobler goal of continued life on the only planet we call home. We must be invested in science, discovery, and long-term growth but we should use the long view to address today's human needs in the world we inhabit today.

This tension between the value of finely tuning our perspective so that we use the mechanisms we have available to us now to meet current concerns, on the one hand, and the development of broader and wider capabilities, on the other, calls to mind one more aspect of spinning. When wool is spun either with a spindle or even a spinning wheel, the end of the wool is attached to the tool with a piece of yarn.[8] Ironically, that means that one bit of wool cannot be made unless another one was spun into yarn earlier. Exhibiting comparable irony, one rabbinic view holds that as dusk was falling just before the first Shabbat after the creation of the world, God fashioned a primordial pair of tongs with which the first humanly made pair of tongs could be made.[9]

When we consider how hard it is to conceive of the point in time when humans had first amassed the basic devices that allowed them to meet the Divine command to exercise dominion over the world,[10] we realize that the means that help us exercise an appropriate level of control over our world have developed over eons such that we can maintain a laser-like focus on our parochial and contemporary needs, while also being aware that an ultimate conquest of the universe would require coming to grips with an aspect of infinity far beyond what humans could ever begin to understand.

When we contemplate the *melacha* of *toveh* and what it means

---

8. Spinning Yarn, https://www.instructables.com/spinning-yarn/; How to Set Up and Use a Spinning Wheel, http://www.raisingsheep.net/how-to-set-up -and-use-a-spinning-wheel.html.

9. Pirkei Avot (Ethics of Our Fathers) 5:6.

10. Genesis 1:28.

to spin, we see that it allows us to exercise the human creativity that we feel compelled to utilize all week, even as it brings us back to a spiritual center when we refrain from that activity on Shabbat. May we learn to spin beautiful tapestries that grant us *shleimut* (wholeness) and *menuchat hanefesh* (equanimity), and that can create *achdut* (oneness) and unite us.

17.

Meiseich (Stretching the threads of the warp)

W ITH THE SEVENTEENTH *melacha*, *meiseich* (stretching the threads of the warp), we encounter the first *melacha* involved with the weaving process itself.[1] Before one starts to weave, one must thread the woof and the warp. *Meiseich* is concerned with the crisscrossing of perpendicular threads. Weaving loops to make a potholder, for example, is forbidden on Shabbat. Playing a game that involves crisscrossing, however, is permitted, as long as the new structure will be dismantled shortly thereafter (on Shabbat itself). One may therefore play cat's cradle with their child on Shabbat.

To create fabric, one must weave together the warp and the woof. And with this ability, one has the freedom to create an infinite number of designs with different colors and patterns. The creative freedom inherent in the weaving process is a microcosm of all of human freedom, which in turn is represented in the thirty-nine *melachot* as a whole. When it comes to weekday creativity, the sky is the limit as to the material objects one can create.

But the fact that the *melachot* are permitted during the workweek but not on Shabbat does not divest Shabbat of its own

---

1. The horizontal threads in the loom are called the woof (or the weft) and the vertical threads are called the warp.

form of freedom. As Erich Fromm said in arguing that Shabbat
is indeed about freedom:

> [T]he Sabbath symbolizes a state of union between man and
> nature and between man and man. By not working – that is
> to say, by not participating in the process of natural and social
> change – man is free from the chains of time, although only for
> one day a week.[2]

Rabbi Abraham Joshua Heschel takes a similar philosophical
approach:

> He who wants to enter the holiness of the day must first lay
> down the profanity of clattering commerce, of being yoked to
> toil. He must go away from the screech of dissonant days, from
> the nervousness and fury of acquisitiveness and the betrayal in
> embezzling his own life. He must say farewell to manual work
> and learn to understand that the world has already been created
> and will survive without the help of man. Six days a week we
> wrestle with the world, wringing profit from the earth; on the
> Sabbath we especially care for the seed of eternity planted in
> the soul.[3]

Part of what this freedom inspires in us is the notion that each
of us strives to be our authentic selves. For example, PET scans
show that not all brains work the same way. (This is only a
medical evaluation, not a spiritual one.) And, although there are
economists and psychologists who would have us believe that
human behavior is entirely predictable, we know from experience that every human is unique and is empowered by choices

---

2. Erich Fromm. *You Shall Be as Gods: A Radical Interpretation of the Old Testament and its Tradition* (New York: Open Road Media, 2013).

3. Abraham Joshua Heschel. *The Sabbath: Its Meaning for Modern Man* (New York: Farrar, Straus & Giroux, 1995), p. 13.

of self-interest, altruism, or by something else on the spectrum entirely. What will we choose to weave together to create an interwoven fabric in our lives? We are the creators of our own respective tapestries.

Jean-Paul Sartre, arguably the most influential modern existentialist philosopher, argued that humans are radically responsible for who they are. He claimed that we create our own "essence" through how we live and that our "existence precedes our essence" since we are "terrifyingly free."[4] He probably overstated his case, nonetheless, the thought experiment is crucial. What would *I* choose to be – and how would *I* choose to act – if the choice were completely and entirely mine?

Of course, it is not entirely up to us. But what if it were?

Our creative capacity goes both ways. We impact the heavens, the Chassidic teachers suggest. Thus, just as we read at the beginning of the Torah about the Divine creation of the world in which humans live, the *melacha* of *meiseich* reminds us that we humans can be creative as well, and that human creativity extends to the imaginative ways in which we reach the highest spiritual heights to interact with the Divine. Through these interactions, we also develop our own selves.

One way to think about the human ability to create is to consider the creative impact of our interactions with other people. This aspect of our lives on Earth is embodied in a Talmudic teaching that prescribes a blessing to be recited if twelve months have passed since last seeing a particular friend: "*Baruch Atah, Hashem Elokeinu, Melech ha'olam, mechayeh hameitim*" – Blessed are You, God, our Lord, King of the universe, Who resurrects the dead."[5] This is rather strange since the person didn't actually die and become resurrected. Is it really so extreme if one hasn't seen a friend in a year? Rabbi Pinhas of Koretz, an eighteenth-century

---

4. Jean-Paul Sartre, *Being and Nothingness* (New York: Washington Square Press; Reprint edition 1993).
5. BT *Berakhot* 58b.

Hasidic master, teaches that we recite that blessing because the joy in seeing a friend (whom one hasn't seen for that long) creates an angel. This is related to the idea that angels can only survive a year on earth. If, however, two friends see each other again over the course of the year, the angel receives a one-year extension on life. But after a year, the angel is gone. So, indeed, when two friends reconnect after the lapse of a full year, a new angel must be created, and that is the resurrection we are blessing.

This discourse is mystical, of course, but it can be understood in more rational terms as well. The angel is the force, the energy, that exists in that space. A sacred Divine space between the self and the other whom we acknowledge has a greater sum than its parts (the two individuals). Similarly, our rabbis teach that whoever performs a mitzvah creates an angel.[6]

Our freedom, in a sense, creates angels above and below. This freedom, in turn, leads to gratitude to our Creator. In experiencing gratitude and in loving God, one comes to love God's act of creation and the totality of His creations. The Maharal of Prague writes:

> Love of all creatures is also love of God, for whoever loves the One, loves all the works that God has made. When one loves God, it is impossible not to love God's creatures. [Also, the converse is true.] If one hates the creatures, it is impossible to love God Who created them.[7]

There are, of course, different kinds of love. We should not love our spouse the way we love a stranger. We should not love a student the way we love our child. We should not love our enemy the way we love our friend. In some cases, we love the entirety of the person. In other cases, we may love the Divine light in a person

---

6. Pirkei Avot 4:13.
7. Netivot Olam, Ahavat HaRe'i, 1.

but not the individual person (which has become alienated from their internal Divine light due to their acts of evil).

God created and continues to create beautiful creatures, each one wholly unique and never to be replicated in history. To love God is to love the Divine creations.

Another Hasidic teacher, Rabbi Avraham Chaim of Zlatchov, seeks to reconcile human freedom with Divine omniscience:

> It is written, "God planted the garden in Eden from before."[1] [Our Sages comment that the Garden of Eden, or Paradise, was created before the universe.[2]]
>
> The holy Rabbi Dov Baer [the Magid of Mezrich] asked how was the Garden of Eden created before man? Is it not true that each person creates their own Garden of Eden through their good deeds?[3] This being so, where was this Garden of Eden before humans were created?
>
> He explained that for God, past and future are exactly the same – "God looks and sees until the end of all generations."[4]
>
> The delight that God has from the righteous who would do the Divine will, therefore, existed even before the righteous were created. This delight came before God, causing God to create the Garden of Eden. (Orach Lachaim, Bereshit)[5]

To give a sense of how uniquely creative humans are on the subjective level, and how free their minds are to develop creative thoughts, Deepak Chopra (a popular contemporary author and advocate of alternative medicine) writes:

---

1. Genesis 2:8.

2. BT Pesachim 54a. Cf. Bereshit Rabba 15:3.

3. See Recanti, beginning of BeChukotai; Avodah HaKodesh, Chelek HaAvodah 18, Sh'nei Luchot HaBrit, Beit Chokhmah (1:22a); Amud HaAvodah, Vikuach Shoal VeHaMeshiv 174 (45d); Nefesh HaChaim 1:12.

4. Zichronot in Musaf for Rosh HaShanah. See note 2:56.

5. Quoted in Torat HaMagid I, Bereshit (p.46).

Although everyone's brain can create countless thoughts – just to take a number, at ten thoughts a minute, a single brain would conjure up more than 14,000 thoughts a day, 5 million a year, and 350 million in a lifetime.

We *are* our thoughts. And each of us creates worlds in our minds. And this creative uniqueness gives rise to a well-known ethical truth:

> Adam was created alone in order to teach us that causing a single soul to perish is like destroying the entire world, and saving a single soul is like saving the entire world. Another teaching: Adam was created alone for the sake of peace, so that we cannot say to each other: "My ancestor was greater than yours." We are all created from the dust of the earth ... and none of us can claim that our ancestors were greater than anyone else's.[6]

Indeed, one vision of the "afterlife," when we return to the dust, is not about *our* afterlife but about others' lives after our life. Our "afterlife" is the world we leave behind better than we found it, the tapestries we wove during our lifetime. We return to the dust knowing we've made our best contribution and provided the fabric for the next generation.

Rabbi Dr. Yitz Greenberg builds much of his theology off much of the preceding passage. Here is one of his most acute accountings of how human dignity is bound up with human uniqueness:

> Human beings are beloved because they were created in the image of God. According to Tractate Sanhedrin 37a, anything created in the image of God is endowed with three intrinsic and inalienable dignities: infinite value (saving one life is equivalent to saving a whole world), equality, and uniqueness (images

---

6. BT Sanhedrin 37a.

created by human beings such as on currency or stamps can
be replicated or mass-produced, but each human being created
by God is like no other). The latter quality is the mark of being
created in God's image, for even identical twins are not completely identical. Uniqueness bespeaks human free will, which
enables individual, divergent responses from every person and
every situation. Honoring the quality and uniqueness implies
democracy. Respecting the dignity of uniqueness implies reject-
ing stereotypes and unfair generalizations.[7]

But a human being isn't created to be a finished product. The
world was created – is created – to be refined; it continues to be
refined. When the Torah says, "Which God created to do,"[8] it's
telling us that the world is full of imperfect things. As the Midrash states "Everything created during the six days of Creation
requires rectification."[9]

Consider an early refinement process by God based upon a
Talmudic understanding of the origins of the *"shnei hame'orot
hagedolim"* – the "two great sources of light" of creation.[10] This
story suggests that while the contents of the world face a constant
challenge to re-create themselves continually, even God can take
the process of re-creation too far. This Talmudic passage explains
the presence of the atonement offering among the sacrifices for
the New Moon, generally seen as a time of feasting. It tells a tale
about the sun and the moon, created as "the two great sources of
light," implying that they were originally of equal size, and why
God, as it were, needs to bring an atonement offering.

God then saw that sunlight needed to be stronger, to create the
bright light of day, while moonlight should be dim, to faintly

---

7. *Sage Advice*, page 148, Commentary on Pirkei Avot 3:14.
8. Genesis 2:3.
9. Pesikta Rabbati 23.
10. Genesis 1:16.

illumine the night. "Go diminish yourself," God said to the moon. When she protested, God had to force her to be smaller, and God made her light to wax and wane each month. But Divine justice understood that this was wrong, that God had sinned in retracting the moon's original equality. Life, as God created it, or as it emerged from within the One, is not fair. Therefore, God said that on each new moon day, among Israel's offerings, was the obligation to "bring an atonement for Me, because I diminished the moon."[11]

In this thread, we see that not all creations are good just because they are new or because they are the product of creativity. In the Torah, the first Divinely created weapon appears early,[12] followed soon after by the first humanly created weapons.[13] Weapons were a tragic, although perhaps necessary, form of progress in ancient society enabling the vulnerable to protect themselves. But it did not take long for violent abuse of these creations. Civilization continues to progress technologically as governments and societies must take increased responsibility for the violence for which the output of that progress is used. We collectively continue to face the complex Divine challenge that we mold the wonders of creation to the needs that they appropriately serve.

Indeed, one midrash imagines Satan in conversation with God. Satan thinks that as a creator, he is similar to God, missing the point of creation entirely:

> "For You created heaven, I created earth, You created firmaments, I created depths, You created animals, I created demons ... You created good things, I created bad things, You created the Garden of Eden, I created Gehenna ..." The Holy One be

---

11. BT, Hullin 60b.
12. Genesis 3:24.
13. Genesis 4:22.

blessed, said to him, "Fool who is in the world, you say to Me, 'I created Gehenna,' so pass into the midst of Gehenna."[14]

It is precisely our ability to create, indeed to do good acts in creative ways, that led Rabbi Joseph Soloveitchik to argue in favor of more concern with this world than the next one:

> The halakha is not at all concerned with a transcendent world. The World to Come is a tranquil, quiet world that is wholly good, wholly everlasting, and wholly eternal, wherein a man will receive the reward for the commandments which he performed in this world. However, the receiving of a reward is not a religious act; therefore, halakhic man prefers the real world to a transcendent existence because here, in this world, man is given the opportunity to create, act, accomplish, while there, in the World to Come, he is powerless to change anything.[15]

This is why we are not to wear mitzvah objects in an outward fashion in a cemetery. It can be perceived as mocking the deceased who are no longer able to exercise the deep living privilege to perform mitzvot.

So when we create fabric, what, or who, are we creating it for? Are we going to keep the poor warm from the cold? And *how* are we creating it? Are we using oppressed labor or are we creating the fabric in an enlightened manner? Are we weaving a beautiful tapestry to inspire acts of goodness? Or are we weaving out of ego, self-interest, merely to produce something new and different? What is it that we spend our lives toiling over in our warp and woof? The work is hard but it can have a deep purpose aligned with – indeed, woven into – our souls.

---

14. Midrash is quoted in Professor Marc B. Shapiro's book *Changing the Immutable*, page 79.

15. Joseph Dov Soloveitchik, *Halakhic Man* (Philadelphia, PA: Jewish Publication Society of America: 1991), p. 32.

By refraining from *meiseich* on Shabbat, we cross-stitch it perpendicularly to the other six days of the week. We are reshaping our relationship to time and space, offering a counterforce to the dominant momentum of society. We pause, reflect, and then move from woof to warp. We don't live a monolithic unidimensional life where all existence is parallel, but rather add layers to the tapestry (to hold it all together!), ensuring that the perpendicular can strengthen the whole.

18.

Oseh Shnei Batei Nirin
(Setting Two Heddles, Preparing to Weave)

I N THE EIGHTEENTH *melacha*, we continue to explore the theme of preparing to weave. Here, we look at *oseh shnei batei nirin*, the process of preparing to weave by setting two heddles. *Batei nirin* (the heddles), usually made from wire, are used to keep the warp threads separate from one another. By raising the warp threads, the weaver enables the woof threads to pass over and under them. After this *melacha* of preparing the loom, we will be ready for the next *melacha*, *oreig* (weaving).

It is interesting that the heading of this *melacha* mentions a specific number (two) of heddles that must be set (to be considered a biblical transgression). In fact, as we will see in future weeks, this is the first of several *melachot* in which two is the minimum required for culpability.[1] The reason is that two, as opposed to simply one, establishes permanence and staying power.

With regard to practical modern-day observance, what is this *melacha* about? According to most scholars, there are not any applications beyond actions that involve a loom. The one exception to this view, however, is that of Rambam (Maimonides). For Rambam, this *melacha* includes basket weaving and making

---

1. Two is also used regarding writing and erasing letters, and sewing and tearing out stitches.

sieves or strainers out of reeds. So this *melacha* can be seen as calling to mind the production and use of baskets.

What does the humble basket mean to us in Jewish tradition? Of course, there is the *teivah* (ark) that Noah was commanded to build, which was basket-like and made watertight by being covered inside and outside with pitch. More to scale is the *teivah*[2] (basket) that Yocheved – the mother of Moses – wove to save her son's life. Moses' basket was also covered on the outside with pitch, but on the inside, it was covered with a substance that had less of a stench. Rashi tells us that this substance is what saved the righteous Moses from the obnoxious odor of the pitch.

Sometimes a common word used to describe two items or events in the Torah draws our attention not only to their similarities but also to their differences. Such is the case here. Even though the construction of Noah's "basket" did not insulate him from the big bad world outside the ark, we are not told in the Torah of any attempt by Noah to try to convince God to save any human beings other than himself and his family. On the other hand, although Moses was protected from the discomforts of the outside world by means of the inner insulation of his basket, he grew up to have the inherent, and supremely human, understanding of his obligation to protect a Jewish slave being beaten by an Egyptian taskmaster, to save a person from harm at the hands of another person, to lead the Israelites through the desert for forty years, and even to defend the entire Israelite nation when God wanted to destroy it.

One *mussar* teacher, Rabbi Chaim Shmulevitz, shares an idea about human strength based upon the story of Moses' basket:

Our strengths are greater than we realize. A person really has the ability to reach much more than his natural [physical] strengths [we think we are limited to one level; we can move only this,

---

2. The word *teivah* simply means a box or container, hence the term used for both Noah's ark and a basket.

lift only that, only stay awake for so long, etc.]. It appears that this is the explanation that our Sages give on the sentence "The daughter of Pharoah sent forth her *amah* (arm) and took the basket that Moses was in." [According to the *midrash*,] her arm actually extended many *amot* (cubits).[1] It's not intended to be understood that her arm physically got longer and then her arm shrunk back to its original state. Rather, through the gathering of all her energy and her will to save this child, in the merit of that it was in her ability to achieve even the strength of Adam prior to the sin, even though the basket was far away. There is no measure to the strength of someone when they arm themself with *ometz* (fortitude) and *gevurah* (strength). If they do so, it's in their hand to reach much more than their natural strengths would dictate.[2]

Baskets represent work. They can be contrasted to soldiers carrying weapons of war. Work is generally constructive, while war, despite the many attempted justifications for it that are often offered, is destructive in form and divisive in content virtually by definition. At the same time, of course, not every bit of work leads to a noble end, and the "just war" theory is based on the idea that the concept of war is defendable as a sometimes-needed mechanism to pursue moral ends. In the Book of Nehemiah, we see the idea of engaging in both at once:

> From that day on, half my servants did work and half held lances and shields, bows and armor. And the officers stood behind the whole house of Judah, who were rebuilding the wall. The basket carriers were burdened, doing work with one hand

---

1. The word *amah* means both maidservant and arm. While there is disagreement as to the meaning in our verse, the *midrash* is utilizing the "arm" meaning. Furthermore, the measurement of *amah* derives from the arm (just as the modern measurement of foot derives from one's foot).

2. Rabbi Chaim Shmulevitz on "Yichud Lev" (Selections from Sichot Mussar).

while the other held a weapon. As for the builders, each had his sword girded at his side as he was building. The trumpeter stood beside me.[3]

What does this passage teach? Perhaps Nehemiah reminds us that finding the balance between carrying out the projects necessary for the world's development and resolving the challenging issues that divide us requires us to have the necessary tools at the ready.

Similarly, we learn about poverty as it relates to the breadbasket. Rashi writes:

> ["One who has bread in their basket is not comparable to] one who does not have bread in their basket" – This refers to one who has food today but worries about [food for] tomorrow.[4]

I recall, in various villages, around the global south, seeing hard-working women with babies on their backs and baskets on their heads out in the fields under the hot sun. Millions of laborers around the world are in such a predicament. Baskets upon their heads but empty baskets at home.

Part of the tragic reason that we have a global hunger crisis goes beyond apathy and indifference; division is often the culprit. We see ourselves as different, afraid of each other, in competition with each other, and rightfully fearful that if we don't get enough for ourselves then we will be left alone without anyone to care for us. We can continue to dream of a redeemed world, and that might indeed begin with religious pluralism made up, in a sense, of the many reeds that fit together to form a basket. As Rabbi Abraham Joshua Heschel wrote:[5]

---

3. Nehemiah 4:10–12.
4. Rashi, commentary on BT Yoma 74b.
5. Harold Kasimow et al., *No Religion is an Island: Abraham Joshua Heschel and Interreligious Dialogue* (Eugene, Oregon: Wipf & Stock Pub, 2009), p. 14.

Is it really our desire to build a monolithic society: one party, one view, one leader, and no opposition? Is religious uniformity desirable or even possible? Has it proved to be a blessing for a country when all its citizens belonged to one denomination? Or has any denomination attained a spiritual climax when it had the adherence of the entire population? Does not the task of preparing the kingdom of God require a diversity of talents, a variety of rituals, soul-searching as well as opposition?

Perhaps it is the will of God that in this eon there should be diversity in our forms of devotion and commitment to Him. In this eon diversity of religions is the will of God.

In the story of the building of the Tower of Babel we read: "The Lord said: They are one people, and they have all one language, and this is what they begin to do."[6] These words are interpreted by an ancient Rabbi to mean: What has caused them to rebel against me? The fact that they are one people and they have all one language.

"For from the rising of the sun to its setting My name is great among the nations, and in every place, incense is offered to My name, and a pure offering; for My name is great among the nations," says the Lord of hosts.[7]

This statement refers undoubtedly to the contemporaries of the prophet. But who were these worshippers of One God? At the time of Malachi there was hardly a large number of proselytes. Yet the statement declares: All those who worship their gods do not know it, but they are really worshipping Me.

Here we reflect on the power of religious pluralism and of diversity in general. What would our world look like it if everyone held the same political beliefs and religious practices? We could not reveal the full complexity of life and uncover the true beauties of

---

6. Genesis 11:6.
7. Malachi 1:11.

God's creation. There is one great tapestry of human life; there is one big breadbasket.

As we recite on Passover, the annual night when we celebrate liberation: "Let all who are hungry come and eat!" Freedom means *all* can eat. Freedom means all can feel satisfied. Freedom means that everyone can keep their dignity intact. It means we can reimagine the breadbasket. It means that today we prepare ourselves to weave our individual and collective lives so that they are ready for the messianic day when all can spend their time meeting their spiritual needs because their physical needs are already met.

Today, we tend to view problems as concrete and physical. But every spiritual tradition embraces, to one degree or another, a philosophy of idealism. Idealism suggests that fundamental reality is spiritual, not physical or material. Consciousness is central. There is a deeper reality beyond the senses. We can distinguish between matter and spirit. There is an absolute reality, and one is in bliss (in Eastern thought) if one can tap into it. For Hegel (18th–19th-century German philosopher), this is the absolute spirit where everything is a part of the infinite and nothing is (or can be) beyond. This doesn't have to be an embrace of dualism (mind vs. matter, physical vs. spiritual) but can follow an approach of monism, where there is one ultimate reality. Ethically, this moves us toward an understanding that nothing is actually mine. I am, after all, just part of the whole. The individual self is illusory. There is just one bread basket, not mine and yours. In *hasidut*, this concept is called *bitul hayeish* (nullification of self).

Within this commitment of interconnectivity and compassionate interdependence, we can still maintain our freedom. Jean-Paul Sartre writes, in *Being and Nothingness*, that it is in "bad faith" when one denies one's own radical freedom and assumes determinism. He is protesting against a withdrawal of selfhood. But we can maintain a commitment to both radical existentialism by deeply examining and experiencing our existence while also looking at a meta-existentialism at the collective level, one that is harmoniously whole made up of many parts with a meta-consciousness. In this way, we are, paradoxically, completely separate and free while also completely one and interwoven.

On Shabbat, we seek *menuchat Shabbat* (deep rest). This is to be found not through mindlessness but rather in mindfulness, where we are hyper-aware of what we're thinking, saying, and doing in a way that gives us rest by helping us to regain freedom and to expand consciousness. The Zohar refers to Shabbat as "The day of the soul, the day of Torah."[8] This is the day when we prepare to weave a new basket for a redeemed world. Each of us, alone and together, must prepare the loom.

The Book of Isaiah says: "The sun will no longer be for you the light of the day, and the shine of the moon will not illuminate for you; God will be an eternal light for you."[9] The *midrash* explains here that this will be the light that was concealed from the six days of creation that will enable one to see from one end of the world to the other.[10] Indeed, it appears as though we are weaving separately. But, in the spiritual light, we will see how our projects will come together.

When the first sin took place in the Garden of Eden, the garments that Adam and Eve wore turned from *ohr* (light, spelled with an *alef*) to *ohr* (leather, spelled with an *ayin*).[11] The Shelah HaKadosh (Rabbi Yeshayah HaLevi Horowitz, early 16th century) writes that while we still serve God with leather,[12] our actions in that regard will someday be changed to garments of light.[13] May our physical realities be transformed to spiritual realities. And may the spiritual truths hidden through the façade of the physical, be revealed.

The Jewish people are to be crazy "basket-cases," as it were,

---

8. Zohar (III, 95a). Also see Zohar (II 205a, 92a).
9. Isaiah 60:19.
10. Bereishit Rabbah 11:2.
11. Bereishit Rabbah 20:12, Zohar II 229b.
12. The *tefillin* are made of leather.
13. *Shnei Luchot HaBrit, Toldos Ha'Adam siman* 12.

always remembering that we emerged from both the *teivah* of Noah's ark and from the *teivah* of Moses' redemption as a baby. We are to play a socially subversive, non-conformist role in advocating for justice. The basket can remind us of this role to flow, at times, up the stream of the river and not just with the easy, popular current.

19.
Oreig (Weaving)

THE NINETEENTH *MELACHA* is *oreig* (weaving). Rambam (Maimonides) explains that this *melacha* is about *chibbur*, the act of compilation or bringing multiple entities together.[1] Specifically, *oreig* is the actual weaving of the cross-threads into one fabric, which follows on the heels of the previous two *melachot*, *toveh* and *oseh batei nirin*, both of which involve preparing the loom and the cross-threads for the weaving process. In turn, *oreig* sets the stage for taking these new pieces of fabric and using them to sew clothing, blankets, and the like.

Two of the most powerful moments of a Jewish wedding (which itself, of course, is an act of bringing together) have to do with clothes. Some people follow a custom of specifically the parents placing a *tallit* or *kittel* upon their child at the chuppah, marking the last time they dress their child as they hand over their partnership role to the incoming spouse. The other is the *bedeken,* covering the bride's face with a veil, yet another article of clothing.

Consider this teaching from Rav Shagar:[2]

> There is a kind of hiding one's face, a mature kind, that derives from the recognition that the deepest revelation appears *davka*

---

1. Commentary on the Mishnah 7:2.
2. Rav Shagar's name is an acronym for Rav Shimon Gershon Rosenberg (1949–2007, Jerusalem).

(precisely) through the coverings of one's face. As Rabbi Moshe Cordovero states, "The secret of revealing is through covering." This recognition that it is impossible to meet that which is inner directly; the essence will always succeed in escaping our regular understanding ... as Rabbi Pinchas of Koretz said, "Whatever it is that you want, don't chase after it."[3]

Clothing, besides its obvious practical qualities, represents covering and revealing. On the other hand, the covering aspect of clothes can represent deceit. Consider Jacob dressing up to deceive his father, Isaac. The Hebrew term for clothes is *begged*, while the Hebrew for betrayal is *begidah*; both share the same root letters. Likewise, the Hebrew word for overcoat is *me'il*, while the Hebrew for treachery is *me'ilah*. And finally, (we could do this for hours, so I will stop after this), the Hebrew for covering – like clothes – is *kesut*, while the Hebrew word for concealment is *kisui*.

Clothing has the potential to represent authority or power. How do we feel when we see someone in a police uniform, a military uniform, or medical clothes? What does such attire convey? Or religious garb like a priest's cloak or a turban or a *tallit* and *kippah*?

Power and authority are both exemplified by clothing, yet they are different qualities. In fact, power is more complicated than simple authority. In exploring this issue, Professor Steven Lukes (British political and social theorist) identifies three primary dimensions of power (in a social context, excluding power as the mere use of force):

1. Withholding from complying with another's desires (for example, not voting for them). On a collective level, this is about winning an observable conflict where there are observable preferences.

---

3. Shimon Gershon Rosenberg (Shagar), *Zikaron L'Yom Rishon*. Ed. Odiya Tzurieli (Jerusalem, Israel: Bet El Publishing Co, 2001), p. 43.

2. Setting an agenda, beginning with who decides what is decided; raising issues that become a part of the new discourse.
3. Shaping others' thinking.

As we explored earlier, Michel Foucault (20th-century philosopher and political activist) argued that power is everywhere in
our disciplinary society. But Lukes' approach suggests that social
power is unique and specific. We should work to attain awareness
of what influences we live under. And, so, clothes deceive us into
thinking that authority figures hold all the power. Or that the
roles symbolized by our respective garb represent a true reality
of ontological roles instead of constructed social status.

Ludwig Wittgenstein (20th-century Austrian philosopher)
wrote about the use of language as a mask. He compared the
idea of clothes hiding the true body, to language hiding the true
reality of thought:

> Language disguises the thought; so that from the external form
> of the clothes one cannot infer the form of the thought they
> clothe, because the external form of the clothes is constructed
> with quite another objective than to let the form of the body
> be recognized.[4]

Given today's experience in the time of pandemic and mask-wear-
ing, we can relate to the question of whether a mask is a disguise
or whether it's protection – or whether it's both! In any event,
thinking about the relationship between masks and language
brings us to a fascinating debate about the adequacy of language
to portray our true thoughts, our true reality. In modernity, there
was a lot of confidence in language. Consider Freud's notion of
talk therapy to reveal the hidden truths from childhood, which
depended upon speaking to the psychoanalyst. Yet, in post-mo-

---

4. Ludwig Wittgenstein, *Tractatus Logico Philosophicus*. (California: Har-
court, Brace, Inc., 1922), p. 63.

dernity, building off of Ludwig Wittgenstein (19th–20th-century Austrian-British philosopher), the idea has emerged that language is an utterly inadequate symbolism of deeper truths.

In the post-Holocaust era, we came to understand how utterly inadequate language is to truly explain suffering, to express the deepest emotions of trauma, or to respond to our deepest moral intuitions. On Yom Kippur, we take off "masks"[5] and engage in a day of words (prayers). On Purim, we put on masks and engage in celebration, more than prayer. They seem to be opposites. Yet, Yom Ha'Kippurim (another name for Yom Kippur) is a day "like" Purim.[6] They are similar in that on both days, we realize that we're always still wearing masks and need to learn how to remove them. And we reflect on the power of words even within their inadequacies.

Joseph Campbell (20th-century American professor) writes about how the hero has to go out and slay the dragon. But right after he has done so, he realizes that the dragon isn't gone. It is still inside him. Of course, sometimes one does have to go out and slay the dragon to save themselves, or to save others. But one must always know that they are still not defeating the dragon inside (the resentment, the anger, the psychological dimensions that generate the dragons). The clothes of the hero and the clothes of the enemy can give a sense that good and evil are clearly discernible. But either way, we still just see clothes covering up the deeper internal realities.

To understand moral conflicts, we need to go inwards and probe underneath the surface. Consider these three moral dilemmas:

1. In the first case, one is driving a trolley. If it continues straight, it will run over and kill five people. If the driver pulls a lever,

---

5. The custom is to wear white clothing on Yom Kippur and to refrain from wearing jewelry.

6. The word *kippurim* (the plural of *kippur*), means atonement. But a play on words led our Sages to reread the word as *ki-Purim* – the prefix "*ki*" meaning "like," hence it is a day "like Purim."

it will turn left and run over and kill one person. What should the driver do? Most think that actively pulling the lever and killing one is less bad than passively staying the course and killing five.

2. In the second case, the tension is still between five and one but this time one must push a "fat man" violently and aggressively off a bridge to fall on the track to prevent the train from running over and killing five people on the track. It is crucial, to the philosophers, that it is a "fat man," since he is abnormally large enough that he can actually stop the train, and one cannot consider throwing their thinner self off the bridge since they will not be large enough to stop the train. In this scenario, even though it is still one vs. five, most are not willing to actively throw the man off the bridge.

3. In the third case, one does not need to physically push the "fat man" off the bridge but merely pull a switch that will pick him up and drop him onto the tracks. While more are willing to do this than in scenario two, it is not so many more. Essentially, still, most are not willing to actively put the man on the track.

Here, we try to understand why we prefer some moral approaches to others even though the results are ultimately the same. Some have explained this phenomenon based on Thomas Aquinas' doctrine of double effect. Essentially, even though there is a foreseen consequence, it is not intended. While each case has a clear consequence that will emerge, how active our intention is, remains crucial. For many religious groups, this resolves some end-of-life conflicts as well, specifically for one who is unwilling to intentionally euthanize another but also wants to reduce suffering. Based on the doctrine of double effect, one can offer end-of-life pain management where one foresees death but does not actually intend it.

On the surface, moral dilemmas are clear. Saving five lives is better than saving one. But, once we dig into complicated facts and realities, we see that moral dilemmas are rarely so clear and simple. They are often clothed or covered to represent ideologies, and it is quite easy to just follow an ideology. Liberal or conservative, Reform or Orthodox, capitalist or socialist, ideologies, etc., prescribe solutions, so we think that we need not think. However, when we strip off the ideological clothes, we see a more complex reality that must be addressed and struggled with.

After having looked at the many steps necessary to prepare for the *melacha* of *oreig*, we now conclude our examination of the weaving process. In a broken, imperfect world, there can be something deeply satisfying to complete a basket, garment, or tapestry. Indeed, such completion can fill us with a sense of wholeness. This is the feeling we strive for on Shabbat as well. We look at an incomplete, broken world, with the goal of weaving together a perfect *mishkan* of time within the storm.

So, on Shabbat, we reflect on the weaving of garments and tapestries and the notion of coverings. This encourages us to reflect on the processes of revealing and concealing, elucidating and deceiving, complicating and over-simplifying. Further, connected to weaving clothing is the notion that God clothes the naked. We must emulate this beautiful Divine attribute. May we weave "garments of kindness."

20.

Potzei'a
(Separating, Removing Threads; Unweaving)

W E ARE NOW halfway through our series exploring the
melachot. The twentieth *melacha*, *potzei'a*, deals with
removing loose threads from the finished garment
once the weaving process is complete.[1] For Rashi,[2] the halachic
concern leading to categorizing this activity as a *melacha* is that
by unweaving threads or separating them, they will perhaps, in
turn, be used for a constructive purpose,[3] such as re-weaving
torn material. In that sense, this *melacha* could be described as
perfecting a woven cloth.

There is a trend among some people (primarily, but not exclusively, young people) to wear garments that look used: hats that
are torn on the brim, ripped jeans, and clothes that are clearly
secondhand. This aesthetic can appear rather strange to the significant majority of people who prefer to wear clothes that look

---

1. The word *potzei'a* also means to wound; the noun form is *petza*. Like a
loose thread in a garment, a wound on the skin is an imperfection, an undoing,
so to speak, of the otherwise perfect skin.

2. BT Shabbat 73a.

3. A general rule regarding the *melachot* is that they are all used for a
constructive, and not destructive, purpose. Therefore, the undoing of an entity
(i.e., the opposite of weaving, of writing, of sewing) are a *melacha* insofar as
they themselves are a constructive activity or lead to a constructive activity.

well-kept and new. For most, if a garment has a loose thread, they would cut it off, and if there was a rip, they would get rid of the garment or mend it. Ripped clothes are viewed by many as unprofessional and sloppy. Of course, in Jewish thought, torn garments represent mourning. One rips their shirt, for example, upon seeing the *Kotel* or upon hearing of the death of one's family member or teacher. One thus undoes the wholeness. One shows externally the grief they feel internally.

On Shabbat, as we have said, we want to pretend as though the world is whole and perfect, so that our vision of utopia carries us through the other six days of the week, when we stare at the brokenness in the face and do all we can to fix it. So why wouldn't we want to pull that final thread out on Shabbat so that our shirt can look perfect too?

Here, we are reminded to live in that gray paradox that confronts us with a world that is imperfect yet totally perfect at the same time; whole, yet broken. We are wearing a garment and we see a final imperfection. It reminds us to return to that spiritual paradox where, like our shirt, the whole is complete and good but there is work to do. On Shabbat we look at the thread and just let it be, as we remember that this is not our time to work but to reflect on the work, to step back and be renewed.

We can lose focus of the goal; we can take our eyes off the prize. At a wedding, we know why we married someone. On day one of a job, we know why we accepted it. At the start of a campaign, our energy is fresh. And then we lose focus. We forget. The Jewish people stood at Sinai and knew what was at stake for the future. But then we drifted away. In the lead-up to and right after the Six-Day War in 1967, the Jewish people knew what it was like to suffer a Holocaust and to look national destruction of war in the eyes. The existence of Israel itself was on the brink. But decades later, we forget those risks and those miracles.

So how can we return consistently to those moments of clarity? Rav Shagar writes:

This is how God created man: Redemption comes upon him from the outside, and imprints inside him powerful experiences that he longs to return to. The experiences give him a feel for what he is capable of attaining in his life; they place before him a summit that he will always aspire to return to and reach. The longing for these experiences turns into a force that motivates one to move forward, and ... through the power of his inner work, he will be able to attain these experiences again.[4]

Consider the celebration of one's anniversary or our Jewish holidays. We wish to return our consciousness to the past and celebrate the connection of our current relationship to that past and the concomitant continuity.

We have to work hard to return to Sinai, to return to our wedding day, to return to those moments of great clarity. This work becomes all the more challenging where one's "self" is not merely one's personal belongings, one's personal memories, or one's own narrative. When someone reflects upon a more enlightened sense of self, that individual expands into a collective. Rabbi Shimon Shkop (19th–20th-century Talmudic scholar) writes:

We must try to clarify [for] ourselves the quality of one's "self," because through this each man's worth is measured, each according to their own level. One who is crude and unrefined, for one's "self" is restricted to material things and to his body. Above this is someone who feels that one's "self" is comprised of both body and soul. Above this is someone who includes the members of their household as a part of their "self." And [for] the one who follows the path of Torah, one's "self" includes all the people of Israel, because really each Jew is like an organ that is part of the body of the people of Israel. And [for] a complete person, it is

---

4. Rav Shagar, *Zeman shel Cherut*, p. 102. Translated by David Lester in *Jewish Marriage: The Ceremony, the First Year, and the Journey that Follows*, Page 57.

good to embed in his soul and feel that all the worlds are one's "self." And one is only a small organ inside all of creation. And then one's love of oneself also helps one to love all the people of Israel and entire creation.[5]

But how can one hold the consciousness of such an expanded sense of self? How does one work to renew and recharge one's memory of total connectedness? This is not easy. But we live in the middle spaces – between remembering and forgetting, perfection and brokenness, connectedness and separation, woven and torn, agreeable unity and disagreement.

We need the disagreements and the separation. Rebbe Nachman of Breslov writes:

> There is a quality to disagreement that relates to the creation of the world. The essence of the creation of the world comes about through the "empty space." Without this empty space everything would be one, endless unity. There would be no room for the creation of the world. Therefore, the light was withdrawn to the sides creating an empty space. Out of this empty space all creation happens....[6]

Unity doesn't allow for creation. There needs to be tension, disagreement, and difference. In the space that is created between the self and the other, the thesis and the antithesis, the argument and the counter-argument, there can be real creation. There is the perfect garment and the garment that has a dangling thread. There is the perfect life one dreams of and the life with that dangling thread that unravels the dream.

---

5. Rabbi Shkop, *Sha'arei Yosher*, Vol. 1, second page of the introduction. Translated by David Lester *in Jewish Marriage: The Ceremony, the First Year, and the Journey that Follows*, Page 130.
6. *Lekutei Moharan* 1:64:4.

Practicing this spiritual approach involves listening closely. The late Rabbi Lord Jonathan Sacks writes:

> Until Israelis and Palestinians are able to listen to each other, hear each other's anguish and anger and make cognitive space for one another's hopes, there is no way forward.[7]

It is hard to be patient or tolerant when confronted with pain or injustice. But the Hebrew terms for both patience (*savlanut*) and tolerance (*sovlanut*) are almost identical and share the same root, which also means to suffer. To be tolerant of another with a different view and patient for reconciliation means that the full truth is not within me. And it can be painful to realize that the whole truth is not within any one of us and that peace isn't possible at the moment. We suffer in our patience and tolerance, but it can be suffering of fruitful optimism in a sense.

Sometimes the best and worst, the true and the false, the joyful and the painful, are not far apart. Sometimes, they are right next to each other. Consider this *midrash*:

> Why did the Holy One create both the hell of Gehenna and the heaven of the Garden of Eden? In order that one may borrow room from the other. And how much space is there separating them? ... The rabbis said that they are right next to one another.[8]

We think of opposites as far apart but sometimes they are right next to each other. Israeli Jews and Palestinian Arabs can live right next to each other and sit next to each other on the bus. Republicans and Democrats are found in the same family and next to each other at Thanksgiving, or perhaps every Shabbat meal. The rich and the poor pass each other on the street. Simi-

---

7. Rabbi Jonathan Sacks, *The Dignity of Difference: How to Avoid the Clash of Civilizations* (New York: Continuum, revised edition, 2003), 189–190.
8. *Pesikta de Kahanah* (Shemini Atzeret 30).

larly, some of our own internal truths or personal narratives are wrapped with little, or big, lies. What stories do we tell ourselves about ourselves? Which parts are crystal clear in truth? Which are completely nonsensical stories destroyed upon true self-examination, only created as defense mechanisms?

We walk the streets wearing garments to look our best. We hide bodily imperfections with garments that are themselves imperfect. On Shabbat, we stop and say: It's satisfactory. My body is not perfect. My clothes are not perfect. None of it is. We live in an *olam hasheker* (a world of lies) with a *lev nishbar* (broken heart). Starting to see that reality can be empowering. When we apply both humility and courage, we can emerge into a state of being comfortable with imperfection.

So, on Shabbat, we refrain from *potzei'a* and the tablecloth has a loose thread. It's okay. Let's meditate on that loose thread and welcome it to our table.

21.
Kosheir (Tying a Knot)

THE TWENTY-FIRST *MELACHA* is *kosheir* (tying a knot). One is biblically culpable only if he/she ties a knot that is both a *kesher shel kayama* (a knot that will endure) and a *ma'aseh uman* (a craftsman's knot). Tying one's shoelaces or necktie, for example, is permissible, since one ties them with the intent of untying them later in the day. A sailor or a young American boy involved in the Boy Scouts is frequently taught about the importance of learning to tie a knot. But is it important to know how to tie a knot in the Jewish tradition? The Talmud records:

> Rav Yehuda quoted Rav: A scholar must learn three things: scribal arts, slaughter, and circumcision.
>
> Rav Hanania bar Shelemia quoted Rav: Also, the *tefillin* knot, the wedding blessings, and the knots of *tzitzit*.
>
> And [why does] the other one [Rav Yehudah disagree]? These are common [knowledge].[1]

Rashi explains that the *gematria* (numerical value) of the word *tzitzit* is six hundred. Six hundred, plus the five knots and the eight strands, equals 613, which is the number of the *mitzvot*. The knots are essential in helping us to understand all the *mitzvot*.

This is about conscious life in our awake state. Rav Kook,

---

1. BT Hulin 9a.

teaching about the value of dreams, argues that our dream state is like "a secure knot to life as a whole."

> As for dreams: From a clear perspective of the knowledge of God, we are led to conclude that our inner world is conducted in ways no less accurate and precise than the external world. Therefore, it is impossible that the state of dreaming, which takes up a considerable part of life, is not bound in a secure knot to life as a whole, both materially and ethically. And since it is a general rule, it is impossible for a person to correctly perceive their inner state – their true relation to the Divine ideas, which are the basis for happiness and ethics; one's inclination towards happiness and good as such, not as the result of any external cause – and [to know] according to this, the value of his powers in regard to their use and needs. Such an inner inclination is therefore better recognized in an instinctive way, so that not only the rational mind recognizes it. The power of free imagination, together with rational analysis, puts the matters in their [proper] place, and clarifies the impressions that flow from the innermost content of the self-conscious. These impressions are the most reliable; this is the content of dream analysis and the soul's inner emotions as a whole.[2]

We may talk about the difference between seeing God's face and seeing God's back.[3] But there is another paradigm that equates God's back with the Divine *tefillin* knot:

> 'I will remove My hand and you will see My back' (Ex. 23). R. Hannah bar Bizna said in the name of R. Shimon Hasida: 'This teaches that God showed Moshe the knot of God's *tefillin*.'[4]

---

2. *Iggrot Ha'R'ayah*, 85.

3. When Moshe asked God to please show him God's glory, God responded: "You will see my back, but my face shall not be seen." As God is incorporeal, this is understood to be a euphemism, in turn lending itself to several interpretations.

4. BT Brachot 7a.

What do we learn from seeing the Divine *tefillin* knot?[5] It seems that God's face and back may represent something universalistic about the human relationship to the Divine (theodicy). But the *tefillin* knot signifies the God of Sinai, a particularistic manifestation, the aspect of God that illustrates most directly and specifically the Jewish relationship to God, indeed, the partnership with the Divine.

Another suggestion is that seeing God's *tefillin* is akin to seeing the Divine light, since the word *ohr* (meaning leather, spelled with the letter *ayin*)[6] is the same as the word *ohr* (meaning light, spelled with an *aleph*)[7]. This is based on the idea that God made *kotnot ohr* (garments of leather) for Adam and Eve when they realized they were naked (after eating the fruit in the Garden of Eden); at the same time, these garments enabled them to "see the light." But the simple reading of this image is that God creates a lasting knot (connection, relationship, covenant) with the Jewish people symbolized by this particularistic knot. Another way to think of this, however, is that God has agreed to bind Himself to the *mitzvot*, not only those that are between man and God, but also those that are between man and man (i.e., the same ethical commitments in which mankind is obligated). Thus, we can expect God to be merciful and act justly. This is why Avraham can challenge God at Sodom to act justly.

It's interesting to note that the Rashbi (Rabbi Shimon bar Yochai) places the two "knotty" *mitzvot* next to classical ethical *mitzvot*:

Rabbi Shimon bar Yochai says: "It says, Honor God with your wealth"[8] – With what should you honor God? With that which

---

5. See footnote 3. God's wearing of *tefillin*, too, is clearly a metaphor, intended to convey a certain imagery.

6. *Tefillin* must be constructed of leather.

7. Reishit Chochmah, *Shaar Ha'kedushah*, 77, written by Rabbi Eliyahu de Vidas, 16th-century Hebron.

8. Proverbs 3:9.

God graciously gives to you. Separate your gleanings, your forgotten sheaves, the leftover corners of your fields. Separate *terumah*, give the first tithe, the second tithe, the poor person's tithe, and dedicate the *challah* (set-aside piece of dough given to the *kohein*) of the loaf. Make a *sukkah* [booth], a *lulav* [branch], a *shofar* [horn], *tefillin* [phylacteries] and *tzizit* [knotted fringes]. Feed the poor and hungry, and give drink to the thirsty.[9]

Tzitzit and *tefillin*, if one chooses to wear them or not, remind us of the big picture. Through engaging in these rituals, we zoom out to the bigger ethical and spiritual picture: We can remember that everything matters.

On the contrary, from the perspective of nihilism, nothing matters. So too, someone in midlife might begin to perceive the futility of his or her life, that they didn't achieve the goals that their young selves had hoped to achieve. Things may still have importance, nonetheless, as one moves closer to the end of life, many people become filled with feelings of pointlessness. Arthur Schopenhauer (18th–19th-century Germany) – arguably the philosopher who was most famous for pessimism – teaches about the intersection of futility and hopelessness. According to some readings of Ecclesiastes, that book also investigates the meaning of life and suggests that it comes up empty.

How might we respond to anxiety in the face of our mortality? When we take on projects and goals that have a hard endpoint, psychologists say, we might feel a deeper sense of futility. But we can respond by engaging in what matters, by undertaking activities that do not have a measurement or an endpoint. This is equivalent to doing something *lishmah* (for its own sake). In the morning liturgy, we recite a list of "*devarim she'ain la'hem shiur*" (virtuous activities that have no measure).

This is a great role that religion can play for us. There is no end to learning, to serving, to prayer. We engage in ritual not to

9. JT Peah 1:1, 15d.

complete a task or project but for its own sake. Indeed, as the Talmudic sage Rabbi Tarfon reminds us, even though we must live up to our responsibilities, we are not obligated to finish the work that faces us.[10] The challenge that all humans face – to leave the world better than we found it – ties us together.

At times, we feel that our life is becoming untied. It is in those times that we engage in *kosheir* and re-tie our knots, solidifying our sense of self, our soul-power, and our deepest way of being, by doubling down on activities that are ends in and of themselves. On Shabbat, we still wear *tzitzit* (without actually tying them) but we do not wear *tefillin*.[11] We reflect on the act of tying to see how tied together reality can be: the conscious and the unconscious, the physical and the spiritual, the ritual and the ethical, the Divine face and the Divine *tefillin* knot.

10. Pirkei Avot, 2:21.

11. The reason for not wearing *tefillin* on Shabbat is that in the Torah, both *tefillin* and Shabbat are referred to as an *ot* (sign). We take care that the *ot* of Shabbat does not take a backseat to the *ot* of tefillin.

22.

Matir (Untying a Knot)

THE TWENTY-SECOND *MELACHA* is *matir* (untying a knot). The overall theme of the *melachot* is the concern with creation. Just as God created on the first six days of the week and refrained from creating on Shabbat, so do we. However, *matir* is a rather strange and confusing *melacha* because it's not about creating anything. Rather, it is about *undoing* something that *was* created.[1] The Talmud, therefore, informs us that *matir* applied in the *Mishkan* in the act of untying and tying knots for the nets used to trap the *chilazon* (the animal from which the bluish *techeilet* thread was derived).[2] By extension, it has been suggested that *matir* also includes untying a knot in order to tie a better knot! Through this lens, we understand that, indeed, ultimately there is a creative action intended.

In the *Mishkan*, knots were used to tie together stitches at the end of fabric. On the Biblical level today, we are only concerned

---

1. Until this point, the only *melacha* which dealt with undoing rather than doing was *potzei'a* (removing threads from a garment or cloth). But there, the removing of these threads is a form of perfecting the whole. Here, regarding *matir*, there doesn't seem to be even an indirect creative process involved.

Furthermore, regarding later *melachot* of undoing, such as *mocheik* (erasing) and *korei'a* (tearing), the Mishnah states explicitly (BT Shabbat 73a) that they are considered a biblical *melachah* only when done with the intention of redoing, i.e., erasing with the intent of rewriting and tearing with the intent of resewing. No such condition is stated regarding *matir*.

2. BT Shabbat 73a.

with knots that are intended to be a *kesher shel kayama* (a knot of permanence) and therefore must be tight, such that they are unlikely to become undone.[3] Of course, there are hundreds of different variations of knots. Knots have been crucial to various forms of work throughout history for sailors, farmers, and so on.

In our daily life, what does it mean to untie? What does it mean for something to become unraveled? Let's start with the self, more specifically with the mind. What is the mind? And could we argue for an "extended mind" (i.e., a mind that doesn't end at the skin and skull)? Perhaps our "mind" includes our larger enhanced system of data collection and knowledge. Perhaps my iPhone data or my laptop documents are not merely tools but an extension of my mind since they are reliably accessible. My brain (internally) and what readily accessible knowledge I have (externally) are tied together. Yes, they could be untied, but it would take a lot of creative energy.

Perhaps, the skin is not the boundary of the self. That which has availability and/or portability could be part of the self. Certainly, something may be within the brain but be inaccessible (such as forgotten data). Is that still part of the self if it is not reliably retrievable? Now, with external data being considered part of the mind, we may have questions of ownership when there is shared data; this can raise interesting moral questions.

What happens when a mind starts to unravel? When our laptop breaks and our documents are inaccessible? When our phone is lost along with all ability to retrieve access to contacts? That which used to be stored in the mind (an idea or a phone number) is now expected to exist in technology.

What happens when something else tied tightly together, such as a family, unravels? A family is tied together tightly by bonds of obligation. Consider this Talmudic passage about responsibility:

---

3. See our discussion of the previous *melacha, kosheir* (tying).

Whoever is able to protest against the wrongdoings of their family and fails to do so is punished for the family's wrongdoings. Whoever is able to protest against the wrongdoings of their fellow citizens and does not do so is punished for the wrongdoings of the people of their city. Whoever is able to protest against the wrongdoings for the world and does not do so is punished for the wrongdoings of the world.[4]

We are tied together in families, in communities, and globally. This means we have rights as well as obligations. When those relationships unravel, life becomes complicated and messy. Consider a divorce and how two people divide up the many things that tied them together and to which they are tied: their property and the children in their custody.

Indeed, the institution of the family is at risk in contemporary times. The late sociologist Peter Berger writes:

One influential line of modern thought has argued that the family is in need not of change but of abolition. Karl Marx suggested that the bourgeois family lay at the heart of the capitalist economy. Radical post-Freudians argued that it was a source of the psychological distress, schizophrenia especially. Feminists like Shulamit Firestone saw it as the perpetuation of patriarchy. Sir Edmund Leach, in a famous sentence in his Reith Lectures, summed it up when he said that "Far from being the basis of the good society, the family, with its narrow privacy and tawdry secrets, is the source of all discontents."[5]

While families can always be improved, the foundational basis of the Torah is the family. Our Torah is the story of a people, of a family, of many families making up one family. Consider that the

---

4. Babylonian Talmud, Shabbat 54b.
5. Peter L. Berger, *A Rumor of Angels: Modern Society and the Rediscovery of the Supernatural* (Garden City, New York: Anchor Books, 1970), p. 70.

first commandment in the Torah is *peru urvu* (to have children).[6]
The family is an institution for us to defend, even as it evolves.
The knots can become untied, but we must tie them again. How
will we make the knot tight? A tight knot may feel suffocating
and confining. How can we allow for freedom and individuality
while keeping the knot tight?

Of course, in community, family extends further. Princeton
sociologist Robert Wuthnow reports that in answer to the question – "If someone in your family became seriously ill, who could
you count on for help?" – 86 percent of regular attendees of
religious services replied that it would be someone in their con-
gregation; 50 percent said someone at work; 35 percent referred
to public agencies. The religiously committed were more likely
to have a neighbor they could count on, voted in local elections,
attended neighborhood meetings, contributed to charitable ap-
peals, and performed voluntary work.

I would humbly submit that the *Shema* prayer includes the
phrase *b'chol levavecha* ("with all of your heart") and not just
bilevavecha ("with your heart") with regard to loving God because "*chol*" – *all* – suggests that my heart transcends myself. This
is to say, my heart, my essence, includes what is outside of me.
My heart is divided into so many pieces (e.g., a piece reaching to
God, one to Torah, others to my spouse, children, broader family,
Clal Yisrael, humanity, animals), and through these relationships,
we can move toward love for God. To say "in my heart" would
limit love to my own life of affect (reserved for my personal
emotional, subjective experience). As the Baal Shem Tov taught,
one can't say *Shema* until one feels love for others in the room.
Once our hearts begin to transcend ourselves, each heart has
the permission and ability to reach the heavens. This is about
spiritual development leading toward the capacity for empathy.
By expanding the heart, we truly feel others' joys and sorrows.

---

6. The words *peru urvu* literally mean "be fruitful and multiply." This commandment was first given to Adam and Eve, and later to Noah (after the flood).

We are not only obligated to love and be there for each other; we are also to learn to forgive each other. Rav Kook writes:

> One who grieves constantly for their sins and the sins of the world must constantly forgive and absolve themself and the whole world, and in so doing draw forgiveness and a light of loving-kindness onto all of being, and bring joy to God and to God's creatures. One must first forgive oneself, and afterward cast a broad forgiveness over all, the nearest to them first, on the branches of the roots of the soul, and on their family, their loved ones, their generation, and their world, and all worlds.... And thus is revealed all the good that is hidden away in everything, and one attains the blessing of Abraham, since there is no generation in which his likeness does not emerge.

We learn how to untie the pain and resentment in us and let go of the tight grip. Indeed, some knots we wish to never untie. Other knots, we can learn to untie and release. This is why the word *matir* means both permit and untie. We release one, thereby "untying" them, of an obligation. In a divorce, one is *mutar* (permitted to meet others, released from the knot of marriage).[7] Our society works not only because we have tight knots but also because we can have the freedom to release certain obligations and grant others autonomy.

This dichotomy of knots – perhaps we can even call it a "knotty" dialectic – is reflected in the blessing we say each morning ending with the words *matir asurim*,[8] literally meaning "Who unties the tied." The standard translation of these words recognizes the Divine power to free those in captivity,[9] but it might also be understood to mean the Divinely granted freedom

---

7. So too, in leaving a job or other formal relationship, one is *matir*.
8. *Matir asurim* can also, in a legal sense, mean to permit the forbidden.
9. Another understanding of the words *matir asurim* is that God gives the power to those awake to move about freely, thereby "releasing" them from their motionless (or semi-motionless) state.

to those who are bound in place by stultified thinking. On one level, we all yearn for that sort of freedom. One learns how to make spiritual life more inclusive and accessible in ways it may have been blocked in the past. We need to remind ourselves that what seems unattainable, or "tied," is most often actually attainable; we should make our own effort to untie the knots that hold us back rather than simply waiting passively to be freed.

On Shabbat, we reflect: Which knots must I keep tight? Which knots must I be *matir,* in turn allowing me to choose a new type of knot? After all, there are hundreds of different kinds of knots to choose from, so which ones are the best to pull tight and which ones to let loose? Only experience, patience, and the ability to look inwards will allow us to appropriately be *kosheir* and *matir,* and to know for sure.

23.
Tofeir (Sewing)

THE TWENTY-THIRD *MELACHA* is *tofeir* (sewing). In the twenty-first *melacha*, *kosheir* (tying a knot), we looked at connecting two substances. The *melacha* of *tofeir*, however, looks at connecting two substances via a third substance to make them one. Sewing was done in the *Mishkan* to combine woven cloths, using thread to connect one piece of cloth to another. On a practical level today, *tofeir* goes beyond just sewing and includes acts like stapling, gluing, or taping. It would not, however, include buttoning since items do not become fused when buttoned together. Safety pins and Velcro, too, are not problematic unless one's intent is to leave the two materials attached permanently or for a lengthy period of time.[1] Therefore, it doesn't apply to temporary items like disposable diapers. Just as *kosheir* (tying a knot) has a polar-opposite partner *melacha* of *matir* (untying a knot), so too our *melacha* this week of *tofeir* has a partner *melacha* which we'll be discussing in the next *melacha*: *korei'a* (tearing or unsewing). As in several other *melachot*, one is only biblically culpable if he/she sews two stitches, as two indicates permanence.

Tofeir, in a broader sense, relates to the process of cognition. One of the many reasons that every individual thought that we

---

1. Just as we learned previously that tying shoelaces is not problematic, shoes fastened by Velcro are equally a non-issue for the same reason.

have matters is because our thoughts are fixed together; they are sewn together. This is why, through new experiences and new thoughts, our memories are not verbatim replicas of the experiences we remember. Rather, our memories represent thoughts as they developed and evolved in our memory. Rav Abraham Isaac Kook writes:

> Each body of thought has its own logic, and all ideas are tied to each other by a systematic relatedness.... There is no such thing as a vain or useless thought ... since each emanates from the same source in the Divine wisdom. If there are thoughts that appear futile or empty, the futility and the emptiness are only in the outer garb in which these thoughts are enwrapped. But if we probe into all their inwardness, we shall find that they, too, offer us the sustenance of life.... And as a person grows in the scale of perfection, they draw upon all ideas of his own and those of others, for the kernel of abiding truth. They are made more perfect through them, and they through them.[1]

It's also true that we have the ability to allow some thoughts to unfortunately suppress the fullness of the rest of our being, rather than allowing the interconnectedness of experience and thought to evolve naturally. Rabbi Irwin Kula (a contemporary author and thinker) explains this notion well:

> Our ideas about life often act as a protective coating. We "know" what life is like and so we do not have to experience its myriad nuances. We sentence life to exile. Life doesn't change its way; we too often refuse what life offers. We deplete experience in different ways. One can be too realistic, one can be too fantastic, one can be scientistic, one can be overly fanatical and zealous ...[R]ather than have a war between these different dimensions

---

1. Abraham Isaac Kook and David Cohen, *Orot Ha-Kodesh*, Vol. I (Jerusalem, Israel: Mosad HaRav Kook, 1985), p. 17.

of experience, it's much more fruitful to keep open the possibility that each have a voice, that each have a say in the play of voices and to see what happens.

Seeing the bigger picture, the full tapestry sewn together, is one way we might think of the value of the study of religion and of comparative religion, from a perspective of theological pluralism. The late American scholar of religious studies, Huston Smith writes:

> From a purely human standpoint, the wisdom traditions are the species' most prolonged and serious attempts to infer from the maze on this side of the tapestry the pattern which, on its right side, gives meaning to the whole. As the beauty and the harmony of the design derive from the way its parts are related, the design confers on those parts a significance that we, seeing only scraps of the design, do not normally perceive. We could almost say that this belonging to the whole, in something of the way the arts of a painting suggest, is what religion is all about.[2]

Going from global religion closer to home to American culture, consider these words from former President Barack Obama's book *The Audacity of Hope*:

> If we Americans are individualistic at heart, if we instinctively chafe against a past of tribal allegiances, traditions, customs, and cases, it would be a mistake to assume that this is all we are. Our individualism has always been bound by a set of communal values, the glue upon which every healthy society depends. We value the imperatives of family and the cross-generational obligations that family implies. We value community, the neighborliness that expresses itself through raising the barn

---

2. Huston Smith, *The World's Religions* (New York, New York: Harper One, 2009), p. 387.

or coaching the soccer team. We value patriotism and the obligations of citizenship, a sense of duty, and sacrifice on behalf of our nation. We value a faith in something bigger than ourselves, whether that something expresses itself in formal religion or ethical precepts. And we value the constellation of behaviors that express our mutual regard for another: honesty, fairness, humility, kindness, courtesy, and compassion. In every society (and in every individual), these twin strands – the individualistic and the communal, autonomy and solidarity – are in tension, and it has been one of the blessings of America that the circumstances of our nation's birth allowed us to negotiate these tensions better than most.[3]

We sew together a nation by sewing together the individualistic desires with the collectivist impulse. We are a mélange that honors diversity but also honors the collective space of tolerance and collaboration that we inhabit together. Within that culture, we must ensure that while individuals have the freedom to pursue their dreams, we also maintain a collective responsibility for those whose entry has been blocked.

In his work *Discourse on the Origin of Inequality*, Jean-Jacques Rousseau (18th-century philosopher, Geneva) was quite critical of socialization, arguing that it leads to *amour propre* (self-love), a force driving people to constantly compare themselves to one another and to seek happiness through dominating one another. Mass exploitation inevitably emerges where the rich, by and large, deceive the poor to believe that they truly have access to equality. In his work *The Social Contract*, Rousseau further argues: "Men are born free, yet everywhere are in chains." It's often argued among philosophers, that he offered the foundation for modern human rights and for democratic principles as we know them today.

One of the questions that emerges regarding justice and free-

3. Barack Obama, *The Audacity of Hope* (New York: Crown, 2006), p. 55.

dom, is how we can punish others who aren't free. For example, if one is a hard determinist, how can anyone be punished at all? It isn't their fault that they committed a crime. It's because of their traumatic upbringing, or their DNA, or the situation they found themselves in, or because of their fundamentalist indoctrination, or due to their deep poverty and desperation, etc. Indeed, according to the "just deserts" retributivist approach, they don't deserve any punishment at all. A consequentialist, on the other hand, can argue that, even if they don't "deserve" it, the punishment keeps society safe by excluding the one who can harm others. But can the utilitarian go too far? What if they argue that we should grossly torture an individual or punish them excessively for the good of broader society to deter others? So, a third possible approach, to ensure we avoid excessive punishment, could be a model of self-defense. We require someone with COVID-19 or other highly contagious viruses to quarantine not because they deserve punishment and not to deter others but, rather, to defend ourselves collectively from their potential harm.

One who has various serious mitigating factors as to why they harmed another still must be punished but not necessarily because they deserve it nor to deter others, but because we must defend ourselves. Of course, the mass incarceration system in America is tragically broken. Wealthy people derive profit (financial or otherwise) through the incarceration of others, minorities in particular. To give one statistic to demonstrate one dimension of the problem: America consists of only 5% of the world's population yet has 25% of the world's incarcerated population. The extremely high recidivism rate shows that our harsh approach is not working.

In the three primary realms of justice (criminal justice, distributive justice, and social justice), we reflect on how our philosophy of freedom versus determinism affects the ideals we strive for. And, so, as former President Obama points out, we must figure out how to keep the individual's rights and freedoms intact while honoring the needs of the collective. It's quite complicated, and so we sew and then unsew. It's not one garment but an ever-evolving sewing and unsewing of many different garments.

Just as we work to build our community and society, we can imagine God, above, sewing together this world in partnership with us. Consider this teaching from the great twentieth-century *mussar* teacher, Rabbi Shlomo Wolbe:

> The Sages relate that (the Biblical figure) Hanoch was a shoe-maker. "Over every stitch that he sewed in a pair of shoes, he would perform unifications of the heavenly realms." Rabbi Yisrael Salanter explained what form these unifications took: Hanoch invested careful thought and intent into each stitch – his intention was that each stitch go[es] toward creating a comfortable and sturdy shoe so that the owner would be able to get the maximum benefit out of it.... When an individual infuses loving-kindness and love of other human beings into his work, this is the greatest form of "unifications!"[4]

This idea that each stitch can be sewn with deep intentionality and a spirit of loving-kindness is a very powerful one. Whether others might think that a given occupation, such as that of a shoemaker, is too lowly for their tastes, any action done with the proper mindset can elevate the actor to the heavens. In the words of Dr. Martin Luther King, Jr.,

> ... even if it falls your lot to be a street sweeper, go on out and sweep streets like Michelangelo painted pictures; sweep streets like Handel and Beethoven composed music; sweep streets like Shakespeare wrote poetry; sweep streets so well that all the host[s] of heaven and earth will have to pause and say, "Here lived a great street sweeper who swept his job well."[5]

---

4. Rabbi Shlomo Wolbe, *Alei Shur*, Vol. I (Jerusalem, Israel: Bais Hamussar, 17th edition, January 1, 1967), p. 269.

5. Excerpts from "The Street Sweepers Speech," https://www.eternitynews .com.au/archive/street-sweepers-speech-celebrate-mlk-day/.

With such a mindset, we can infuse a deep sense of purpose into all we do to foster the creativity that was Divinely modeled for us with the primordial creation. Consider this teaching from Rabbi Eliyahu Dessler (twentieth-century Lithuanian Torah scholar):

> Every moment in the life of every creature facilitates a unique revelation of Godliness ... This is the idea behind the concept mentioned in our daily prayers, that God "each day, constantly, renews Creation." For each moment is a self-contained universe [i.e., the creation of each moment is the creation of a new world.][6]

Indeed, in knowing our purpose well, we avoid comparison with others. This helps us to sew together a society where everyone's talents are actualized, without jealousy. Consider this teaching from Rabbi Shlomo Wolbe:

> An individual who knows themselves and is aware of their nature, and who knows that whatever God has given them is a wondrous gift – if they will only take advantage of their talents and strengths, they will attain all desirable traits. Such an individual does not suffer from jealousy or envy another person's lot in life! ... Do not compare yourself to others. Have faith in your Creator that God has given you all of your spiritual needs!

This is indeed a high level of achievement, but it's what we're striving for together: to be our best and to love others being their best. That will enable us not only to engage in *tofeir*, to sew together a societal fabric by bringing together our fates and destinies, but to be that merged fabric as we allow our unique individualities to act and come together.

---

6. Rabbi Eliyahu Dessler, *Michtav M'Eliyahu*, Vol. I, p. 313.

24.

Korei'a (Tearing)

I N THE TWENTY-FOURTH *melacha*, we look at *korei'a*, the process of tearing, unsewing, ripping. The coverings of the *Mishkan* were fabricated by sewing different panels together. To repair a covering, one would have to tear damaged areas to fix and resew it. This *melacha* is the converse of the previous one, *tofeir*, uniting disparate articles together through sewing. Since all of the *melachot* are constructive in nature, the type of tearing that would biblically fall under the heading of this *melacha* would include only tearing that is done for the purpose of resewing. On a rabbinic level, however, tearing without the intent of resewing or repairing would be problematic.

A third category of *korei'a*, also rabbinic in nature, is tearing while at the same time creating a new item or repurposing it, even if it would not involve actually resewing or repairing. An example of the latter would be tearing open an envelope, as it can now be used as a "new" container. In addition, *Korei'a* doesn't apply to food.[1] For example, ripping off a piece of challah for Shabbat dinner is perfectly acceptable.

The notion that we're confronted by the broken and the repaired, the ripped and the sewn, embraces a certain dichotomy or duality as to how the world should appear. Such ideas about

---

1. We previously learned that the same is true regarding *tzovei'a*, coloring or dying.

order and perfection may be helpful at times and destructive at other times.

We address the question of duality as it relates to our perceptions of what is positive and what is negative on an emotional level and in our relationship with the physical world. We have the power to use these questions to navigate our relationship with the concept of perception: What is a perfect home? What is a perfect face? Which breaks in a home need to be repaired and which breaks need not be? Which body imperfections need to be fixed and which embraced?

Dualism provides a matrix for philosophical analysis. In modern philosophy, there are three different types of dualism:

1. Substance Dualism – This distinguishes between the mental realm and the material realm; the two never overlap.
2. Property Dualism – This posits that the body and the mind are both parts of one material substance. Consciousness is organized as it is precisely because of the material world.
3. Predicate Dualism – This theory holds that mental predicates can't be reduced to physical predicates. An example: "God is good" might be a concept that we can think about, but one in which we cannot reduce the act of "being good" into a physical thing (predicate).

In contrast, there are three different types of monism:

1. Idealistic Monism – Only the mental realm exists (we call this consciousness).
2. Materialistic Monism – There is only the physical realm.
3. Neutral Monism – There is only one substance, but it is neither mental nor physical (although those emerge from that third – or maybe first – substance).

In both monism and dualism, from the perspective of Complex Systems Theory, all is interconnected. It can be viewed as one

interconnected tapestry or as disparate parts that are interconnected. The paradigm of separation and unity becomes quite
complex.

So what does this mean on a metaphysical level (or if we were
to consider supernal realities beyond the material world)? If all is
God, then we embrace a perspective of monism (as in pantheism
or panentheism) that considers God to be absolutely immanent
and where the world is entirely contained within God and God
within the world. If there is body and soul, or God and world,
then we embrace a dualism that describes God as having both
immanent and transcendent characteristics. Some have described
Jewish thought as pseudo-dualistic in that we are always trying to
repair the world and unify God's name during the week – dualism
– and yet on Shabbat, we seek a monastic experience of *deveikut*
(clinging, and thereby releasing separateness).

The distinction between dualism and monism is related to
differentiation, the process of recognizing distinctions between
items, concepts, facts. So, considering the *melacha* of *korei'a* –
taking one thing and making it two – raises the question of what
we can truly know beyond the one, in this case, beyond the
singularity of oneself – one's mind.

In Kant's renowned work, *Critique of Pure Reason*, he discusses how the mind organizes experiences in two different ways:
1. The way the world appears to oneself, and 2. The way one
thinks about how the world appears. The "noumena" are the
things that exist regardless of how our minds interpret them.
The "phenomena" are the realities that are interpreted from our
minds. Kant's suggestion, radical in his time, was that nothing
objective can truly be known (the noumenal material world).
The only knowledge we can ever truly hold is that which is
presented from our minds (the phenomenal mental world). All
data is contextualized as it passes through the subjective filters
in the mind. The "true" external reality is always limited as it
passes through the mind and is never truly known.

Here we discuss notions about idealism, the idea that the world is truly composed of mental ideas and not of physical things. It's a fundamentally different way to conceive reality from what is most common. Kant, in his transcendental idealism, never assumes that external reality does not exist nor that it is not important but rather just that we will never be able to transcend our mental limitations. Kant further distinguishes epistemologically between two other crucial categories: (1) *A priori* propositions which don't require experience to know $(2+2=4)$, and (2) *A posteriori* propositions, such as claims like "all dogs are happy," which require experiential justifications to be true.

What does it mean to "know" something or someone? We mean something different when we say we know how to *do* something practical than when we say we know a certain fact (such as a place, a person, or a feeling). In French, this is *sauvoir vs. connaitre*. In Hebrew, we say *ani yodeah vs. ani makir*. Interpersonal knowledge is different from factual knowledge.

When the Torah says someone knows someone else, it refers to intimate knowledge, i.e., sexual relations. In Genesis 4:1, for example, it says *V'ha'adam yada et Chava*, "Adam knew Eve," and she gave birth to Cain.

What does it mean to say "I know *celebrity X* but I don't know him or her?" Or "I know about him but I don't actually know him?" Truly knowing each other requires a relationship, some symmetry, some mental connection. I can't say "President Obama and I 'know' each other" if all we did was meet briefly in a way that I'll always remember and that he'll immediately forget.

What does it mean to say that we know our parent(s)? Or know our child? How did we know them but not know them now? A consequence of knowing someone might mean that we have access to predicting their behavior or their disposition.

What does it mean to say that we "knew" someone twenty years ago? How did we know them then but not know them now? What does it mean to say that we know our parents? Or that we know our child? Perhaps a consequence of knowing someone might mean that we have access to predicting or intuiting their behavior or disposition.

Here, we are exploring the dynamics of intersubjectivity but not one that is totally cognitive (also emotional and social). The assumption here is that there is an "other" and a "self" (dualism once again). But what happens in "care work?" Indeed, there are unique ethical entanglements that can be found in care work (for a parent, child, spouse, strangers, etc.). In dependency work, new questions emerge about the boundaries and limits of responsibility. One often must put the dependent's needs before their own and not have the luxury of thinking of one's own rights. This sort of intersubjectivity calls to mind Martin Buber's conception of the *I* relating to the *Thou*: an approach to meaningful human relationships that depends on each partner in the relationship understanding and relating to the other on a deep level.

Here we can also reflect on Levinas' notion of "Response Ethics," namely, that my existence comes into being in response to the other. This philosophy is about radical alterity, that the other is infinitely other, and how it would be impossible to exhaust one's knowledge of the other. We can also reflect on "Care Ethics" as developed by thinkers such as the psychologist Carol Gilligan. Here we see how care, relationships, and responsibilities carry more weight than abstract rights and concrete principles. In evolutionary psychology, we know that part of our own survival is tied up with the survival of our tribes and our families. But ethically, we care for each other not only due to survival but due to love and responsibility. If it were only for survival, we would leave the old and weak behind. They cannot strengthen themselves against the risks. But, from a religious worldview, our *raison d'être* is found in securing the most vulnerable.

How can I decide to spend more time, resources, and energy caring for a parent when I know I can save a hundred human lives (or 10,000 animals) for the same amount of money? We may not have a good moral justification for doing so, yet we trust our moral intuition. On the far extreme, moral intuitions are infallible; they are the voice of God. On the other extreme, moral intuitions that can't stand up to the critique of moral reason are worthless. In Judaism, we embrace a middle spot that moral intuitions are neither everything nor nothing but are somewhere in between. For example, we suspect it may be speciesism to engage in violent medical testing on smart non-human mammals that would suffer greatly (as would their families) instead of on a severely cognitively impaired orphan, who no one would mourn for. And yet, our deep moral intuitions tell us that the human being, even if less cognitively capable, has human dignity that we should prioritize. In that sense, we can think about the significance of human relationships in terms of how they focus on the individuality of each person – and therefore how we distinguish between one person and another, just as we distinguish between two pieces of material when we rip them apart.

Perhaps for that reason, we symbolize our grief when a parent or other close relative dies by performing *keriah* (from the same root as *korei'a*), ripping our clothing.[1] Conversely, though, we can consider that when a baby is born through a Cesarean birth, a type of tearing apart brings forth life. And with that new life, we have a new opportunity to form a new relationship with a new individual.

The world has been ripped and torn apart by disasters and violence. Our job is to engage in *korei'a*, to rip out the destruction and repair it. This repair should take place within the self, the family, the community, society, and the world at large. It becomes even more complicated, and yet powerful at the same time, given how interwoven and interconnected all the beauty and all the destruction are. We can embrace the paradox that within our

---

1. It is interesting to note that for a parent only, one tears *keriah* on the left side, closer to the heart, yet for all other relatives it is performed on the right side, indicating the uniqueness of the parent-child relationship. Only a parent brings a child into this world; only a parent's death, then, upends and reverses that act of creation.

work to repair, we have our own unique piece that is separate from the rest (dualism) and that this piece is our unique work and sacred responsibility. And yet, we can also embrace the oneness of it all and how we must collaboratively unite to see how we can repair through allyship and partnership. On Shabbat, we reflect on this holy work and on the duality – and unity – of all existence. It is not just us sewing and unsewing. Our tapestries are interwoven.

Once again, through the *melacha* of *korei'a,* we see how what seems to be a destructive activity can actually be a positive, constructive one, and how the microcosm experienced in life on Shabbat can inform us about the macrocosm of the universe and our responsibility to it within this world.

25.
Tzad (Trapping)

I N THIS NEXT set of seven *melachot*, we will look at and discuss the hides used in the coverings of the *Mishkan*. These
melachot will introduce us to deep questions regarding the
human relationship with animals and the dignity of animal life
(and animal souls). The natural first step in producing these hides
is to hunt and then trap the animal, and so the twenty-fifth *melacha* is *tzad* (trapping). The act of using a trap is a challenging
melacha to codify into rules since it can be quite subjective. For
example, closing a door on a bird that is loose could be considered trapping it, whereas closing a house door on a worm may
not be, as it is free to move around.

Here is a question that applies to many people today: What
about closing the door to a room where there is a dog or cat? It
turns out that trapping only applies to wild or untamed animals.
So a tamed dog can be brought inside by its owner, and can even
be penned up in a specific room in the house, but closing a door
on a wild, stray dog is problematic unless it is to protect others,
of course.[1] On the Torah level, we're dealing with trapping when
it's an animal that is traditionally hunted, such as a deer. The

---

1. This is so because a wild, untamed animal will feel and recognize that
they are trapped, whereas a house pet has been accustomed to being in a
specific location in the home. It is instructive to note that *tzad*, then, is in a sense
subjective, as it takes into account the perception of the animal being trapped.

Talmudic rabbis extended this *melacha* also to animals that historically one does not try to hunt (unless one's life is potentially in danger). One may for example place a cup over a bee if one fears being stung,[2] and most obviously, one may trap an animal that may be life-threatening, like a poisonous snake.

Even when we wish to protect ourselves, we can do so more compassionately. Rabbi Moshe Feinstein, arguably the most highly regarded *poseik* (halachic authority) of the 20th century, argued that, although it is permitted to kill insects, even on a weekday, it is better to kill them (or rodents) by indirect means – such as setting a trap – rather than directly killing them with our own hands.[3] He suggests this approach, based on character development, lest we become used to acts of cruelty.[4]

Human beings can become entrapped psychologically as well. In this connection, Eckhart Tolle (contemporary American spiritual teacher and author) offers a new interpretation on an idea emerging from Jean-Paul Sartre:

> He [Sartre] looked at Descartes's statement "I think, therefore I am" very deeply and suddenly realized, in his own words, "The consciousness that says 'I am' is not the consciousness that thinks." What did he mean by that? When you are aware that you are thinking, that awareness is not part of thinking. It is a different dimension of consciousness. And it is that awareness that says "I am." If there were nothing but thought in you, you wouldn't even know you are thinking. You would be like a dreamer who doesn't know he is dreaming. You would be as

---

2. This question arises when sitting in the *sukkah*. There is, however, a rule that *hamitzta'eir patur min hasukkah* – one who is in distress is exempt from the mitzvah of sitting in a *sukkah*. Therefore, the generally accepted ruling is that if one is bothered by or afraid of bees that are in the *sukkah,* better that they leave the *sukkah* and eat the meal inside their home rather than trapping the bees.

3. *Iggerot Moshe, Choshen Mishpat* Vol. 2, no. 47. Also see: http://www.ravaviner.com/2009/09/killing-mosquitoes.html.

4. Rav Moshe Feinstein was recognized, among other things, for his outstanding compassion for all creatures. This is but one example.

identified with every thought as the dreamer is with every image in the dream. Many people still live like that, like sleepwalkers, trapped in old dysfunctional mindsets that continuously re-create the same nightmarish reality. When you know you are dreaming, you are awake within the dream. Another dimension of consciousness had come in.[5]

Tolle continues:

> At the core of all utopian visions lies one of the main structural dysfunctions of the old consciousness: looking to the future for salvation. The only existence the future actually has is a thought form in your mind, so when you look to the future for salvation, you are unconsciously looking to your own mind for salvation. You are trapped in form, and that is ego.[6]

It is frightening to be trapped physically, scary to be trapped psychologically, and frustrating to be trapped spiritually. Sometimes the most comforting thing (aside from being liberated, of course) is having someone else with us in the entrapment; the only thing worse than suffering with others is suffering alone.

Animal behavior has much to tell us in this regard also. In 2010, scientists conducted an unusual, and touching, rat experiment. They locked a rat in a tiny cage, placed the cage within a much larger cell, and allowed another rat to roam freely through that cell. The caged rat gave out distress signals, which caused the free rat also to exhibit signs of anxiety and stress. In most cases, the free rat proceeded to help her trapped companion, and after several attempts usually succeeded in opening the cage and liberating the prisoner. The researchers then repeated the experiment, this time placing chocolate in the cell. The free rat

5. Eckhart Tolle, *A New Earth: Awakening to Your Life's Purpose* (NY: Penguin Books, 2005), p. 55.
6. Ibid, p. 308.

now had to choose between either liberating the prisoner or enjoying the chocolate all by herself. Many rats preferred to first free their companion and then shared the chocolate (though quite a few behaved more selfishly, proving perhaps that some rats are meaner than others). How amazing that liberating those who are trapped may be a phenomenon built into the DNA of animals.

Yet, why do we trap others at all? By observing the phenomenon of mass incarceration, we see that we even trap human beings. We also know that through factory farming, animals themselves are often born entrapped. Then we have the phenomenon of hunting, indeed a sport for some. Let's examine some of the history of this sport and the Jewish legal perspectives of trapping innocent animals to kill them for sport.

American history illustrates the destructiveness of indiscriminate hunting.[1] Until the twentieth century, there were no laws concerning hunting. However, after the extinction of once numerous species such as the passenger pigeon, and the near extinction of the American buffalo (mostly due to a military strategy to starve American Indians, along with hundreds of thousands of buffalo slaughtered by passengers riding in trains[2] set aside for hunting), there was a rising sense that some wildlife needed protection, and eventually the federal government joined states in taking action. The Lacey Act of 1900 prohibited interstate commerce involving illegally seized wildlife.[3] President Theodore Roosevelt established the first wildlife refuge in 1903, and in 1905 the Game and Bird Preserves Act laid the foundation for many wildlife preserves and refuges where animals were protected from hunting. Then, in 1913, the Migratory Bird Law began to protect migratory birds on a federal level, and over time hunters had to have a hunting license or "stamp" to hunt waterfowl and

1. https://www.animallaw.info/article/federal-wildlife-law–20th-century.
2. https://www.smithsonianmag.com/history/where-the-buffalo-no-longer-roamed-3067904/.
3. https://training.fws.gov/history/TimelinesLawEnforcement.html.

endangered species. Until recently, protection has been at the core of federal policy on hunting. Now even this modicum of respect for the natural world appears to be in jeopardy. Sadly, hunting remains a popular sport in America with 15,202,669 paid hunting license holders, per U.S. Fish and Wildlife Service in 2021.[4] The blood sport enjoyed long ago by the pagan Pharaohs and in the Roman Colosseum continues to offend our humanity.

Jewish law is quite clear on this issue. Rabbi Yechezkel Landau (18th-century halachic authority), forbids recreational hunting, which he considers to be cruel in light of the Torah prohibition against causing pain to animals. Among other considerations, he argues that it is a waste of time.[5] Rabbi Landau explains that, in the Tanach,[6] we find recreational hunting as an activity that people of poor character, such as Nimrod[7] and Esau,[8] found pleasure in. The more virtuous leaders in the Torah – including all three patriarchs, Moses, and King David – tended to be shepherds rather than hunters. In fact, the Midrash teaches that Moses was chosen as the great leader precisely because of the compassion he showed to his flock.[9]

Furthermore, the Rema (16th-century Polish Talmudist) writes that one who hunts with dogs will not participate in the great feast upon the arrival of the Messiah.[10] In addition, the Talmud teaches that we should not walk in the cruel ways of idolaters by attending gladiator events or circuses and the like that use animals as fodder for entertainment.[11] Rashi adds that included here is "the hunting of animals by means of dogs, all for the

---

4. National Hunting License Data. www.fws.gov/wsfrprograms/subpages /licenseinfo/Natl%20Hunting%20License%20Report%202021.pdf.

5. *Teshuvot Noda BiYehuda*, Yoreh Deah 2:10.

6. *Tanach* is an acronym for the three sections of the Hebrew bible: *Torah, Nevi'im* (Prophets), and *Ketuvim* (Writings).

7. Genesis 10.

8. Genesis 25.

9. Shemot Rabbah 2:2.

10. *Darchei Moshe Orach Chaim* 316:2.

11. Avodah Zarah 18b.

sake of merriness and frivolity." The Rema[12] teaches that hunting might be forbidden on weekdays as well as on Shabbat because of the ways of frivolity; the Or HaChaim (Rabbi Chaim ben Atar, 17th–18th-century Jerusalem biblical commentator and thinker) explains that humanity was only given permission to kill animals when necessary for food but not for other reasons;[13] Rabbi Shaul Mortira (17th-century Amsterdam)[14] argued that hunting was forbidden due to the cruelty involved;[15] Rabbi Shimshon Morfogro (18th-century Italy) argued similarly that hunting is forbidden and that we should not follow the cruel ways of Esau.[16]

Although the Torah specifically seems to condone hunting wild animals, or to at least appreciate the desire to do so, it also stipulates that the blood must be covered.[17] Commentators take a number of different approaches to explain the reason for this mitzvah. Maimonides argues that this ritual is meant to distance Jewish practice from pagan blood rites. He suggests that pagans would collect the blood after slaughter and eat the animal's meat while sitting around the blood; for Maimonides, we pour out and cover the blood to distance ourselves from these pagan practices of using the blood to connect with spirits:

> ... they imagined that in this manner the spirits would come to partake of the blood which was their food, while the idolaters were eating the flesh; that love, brotherhood and friendship with the spirits were established, because they dined with the latter at one place and at the same time.[18]

---

12. Shulchan Aruch, Orach Chaim 316:2.
13. Commentary on Leviticus 17:11.
14. Among Rabbi Mortira's famed students was Baruch Spinoza, who was eventually excommunicated by a *beit din* which included Rabbi Mortira himself!
15. Givat Shaul, Vayeishev, 44a.
16. *Shemesh Tzedakah*, Yoreh De'ah 57.
17. Leviticus 17:13.
18. Maimonides, *Guide for the Perplexed* 3:46.

The Sefer HaChinuch suggests that we cover the blood in order to refine our innate human character.[19] The author of the Chinuch[20] argues that if one were to become accustomed to merely slaughtering animals and immediately consuming them while their blood still lies before them on the ground, they might become even more insensitive to the world, numbed to quotidian violence. Thus, the mitzvah is present as an instruction to cultivate compassionate virtue.

Rabbi Samson Raphael Hirsch (19th-century German scholar and community leader) takes a different approach to this mitzvah. He suggests that we cover the blood in order to distance ourselves from the animalistic essence of human beings. Animals kill other animals without thought, but, as humans, we must be more elevated. According to Hirsch, we refrain from consuming the blood to demonstrate that we are not mere animals, and to prevent the life force of the animal (the blood) from entering into our life force.

Each of these approaches acknowledges that killing animals reflects an aspect of our humanity. There seems to be a traditional discomfort with the reckless way other societies have handled this. Even further, there is an implicit demand that one be connected with one's food source. Thus, Jewish law, and its underlying values, completely rejects the norms of the factory farming industry as it exists today.

Some may see these rules around covering the blood as a basic manner of food preservation since it was evident even in ancient times that bloody meat spoiled quickly, whereas meat drained of blood and salted could be preserved. Other cultures follow parallel principles, such as the Muslim halal rule of draining blood, and the old European, and then American, culinary custom of smoking and salting meat. Similarly, blood-borne diseases such as rabies, malaria, hepatitis B and HIV, lead modern healthcare

19. Rambam's *Sefer HaMitzvot*, mitzvah 187.
20. The Sefer HaChinuch's author remains anonymous.

workers to be careful; relevant knowledge is a modern development. As we saw from the COVID-19 pandemic, cruelty to animals is deeply connected to the creation of viruses and to the spread of pandemics. However, as explained above, Jewish sages over the centuries obviously had more in mind than a simple meat inspection code.

This mitzvah is perhaps yet another attempt from the Torah to move us toward vegetarianism. The Torah did everything possible, short of prohibiting the consumption of meat, to make it very difficult to eat meat and to distance ourselves from death. While those who are not yet vegetarians are no longer engaging in the traditional ritual of shame – pouring out the blood before consuming meat[21] – to be reminded of the death that has been caused and of our own mortality, we might all take more steps to learn about the harsh realities of mass production of food today and how it is harming human health, animal welfare, and the environment.

I suggest that the primary reason that Jewish tradition tells us to cover the blood is to arouse in us a feeling of shame. In fact, the Talmud teaches that this mitzvah is from where the very concept of *bizui mitzvah*, "shaming a commandment," is derived.[22] We look at the blood of the animal, glistening on the ground or dripping down our hands and filling a pool upon the earth, and we become aware of our own mortality and the fragility of our existence. All we can do at that moment is to rush to cover it up.

Shame is not something that many politicians, apathetic to such matters, understand. The abject cruelty reflects a certain nihilism that permeates the ethos of self-interested politics. In their quest to roll back even the most modest protections for animals, they display their ignorance and disturbing lack of

---

21. The pouring out of the blood, as well as much of the preparation of meat for consumption, is primarily done today in the slaughterhouses, not seen and therefore not paid attention to by the average consumer.
22. BT Shabbat 22a.

compassion. We can only pray that, with time and grit, the easy access to kill innocent creatures is stopped by the election of sensible individuals in government who respect and care for the welfare of animals.

By thinking about the *melacha* of *tzad* and not trapping animals on Shabbat, we can reflect on ways that we ourselves are trapped, the way other human beings may be trapped, and how non-human animals may be trapped as well. We can emulate the Divine in working for liberation for all. Of course, we may argue that confinement may be necessary at times. But there is still far more confinement of humans and animals than can ever possibly be needed. It is in our hands to change that.

26.
Shocheit (Slaughtering)

WHEN THE *MISHKAN* was built, hides needed to be pre-pared. The first step, as we saw in *melacha* 25, was *tzad* (trapping). Now, in *melacha* 26, the second step is *shocheit*, the slaughtering of the animal that was trapped. This *melacha*, like its predecessor, challenges us to wrestle with our ethical responsibilities as compassionate people: killing creatures in the name of sanctifying holy spaces.

As is the case with trapping, if one's life is at risk, one may kill an animal to protect themselves. Few of us are ever presented with the possibility of killing a chicken or cow on Shabbat, but the Talmud says that killing a tiny insect is forbidden just like killing a camel.[1] Furthermore, with the *melacha* of *shocheit*, we're not only concerned with killing but also with causing an animal – including a human being – to bleed.[2] Thus, for example, some people will refrain from brushing or flossing their teeth if they are concerned that it will lead to bleeding.

Since eating meat involves *shechita,* killing the animal, let us define five distinct eras regarding its consumption, four biblical and the last post-biblical:

---

1. BT Shabbat 107b.

2. The reason *shocheit* includes causing bleeding is that when one kills, they are removing the *nefesh* (soul) of the animal. Elsewhere we are told that "the blood is the soul" (Deuteronomy 12:23), and thus when one causes bleeding they are, as it were, removing a bit of the soul.

1. The Garden of Eden (the ideal) – a vegan diet[1]
2. Post-Flood – eating meat becomes permissible[2]
3. Post-construction of the *Mishkan*[3] – For *Benei Yisrael*,[4] eating meat is restricted to that which has been offered as a *korban* (sacrifice).[5]
4. Post-entry into *Eretz Yisrael*[6] – eating domesticated animals outside a sacrificial context is once again permitted for *Benei Yisrael*.[7]
5. Factory Farming – the oppressive torturing of animals presented as *kashrut*, like all mass-produced meat for consumption, becomes immersed in capitalism, prioritizing profits and meat accessibility over the local humane treatment of animals.[8]

Rabbi Abraham Isaac HaCohen Kook taught that, in the messianic era, humanity would return to the Garden of Eden model,

---

1. While eating meat is not discussed in the Garden of Eden story, the direct permission to eat meat is not mentioned until after the flood, implying that until that time it was forbidden.

2. The permission to eat meat (Genesis 9:3) is immediately followed by the prohibition of eating blood, which in turn is followed by a prohibition of, and punishment for, killing human beings. Implicit here is a warning that allowing oneself to eat meat can, when not guarded, lead to "animalistic" behavior, even to the extreme of cannibalism. This is true regarding all permissible activity; we must be careful not to take our actions too far, lest we enter forbidden territory.

3. Leviticus 17:3,4: "If anyone of the house of Israel slaughters an ox or sheep or goat in the camp, or does so outside the camp, but does not bring it to the entrance of the Tent of Meeting to present it as an offering to God, before God's Tabernacle, bloodguilt shall be imputed to that man: he has shed blood; that man shall be cut off from among his people."

4. This restriction does not apply, of course, to Noahides (gentiles).

5. This is the view of Ramban (Nachmanides), based on his understanding of the verses in question.

6. Deuteronomy 12:21.

7. This permission is granted because, as the verse states, the *Beit Hamikdash* (Temple), where all *korbanot* must be offered, will have one central location in Jerusalem, far from most of the Israelites (as opposed to the *Mishkan* which traveled with them).

8. Putting it another way, this outcome was clearly not the Torah's intention in allowing one to eat meat.

with even the Temple service including the flour offering, but not allowing animal offerings in the Third Temple.[9] As he explained:

> It is impossible to imagine the Master of all things, who has mercy on all creation, making it impossible for the human race to survive except by shedding blood, even the blood of animals.[10]

We know that when the Torah teaches the concept "Do not stand idly by the blood of your neighbor" it is referring to humans.[11] And when we think of "bloodshed," we tend to think of humans. But the Sefer HaChinuch condemns the indiscriminate killing of animals, as well, calling it "bloodshed":

> But to kill them [that is, animals] without any benefit involves wanton destruction and is called bloodshed. And even though it is not like the bloodshed of a person, due to the superiority of a human and the inferiority of an animal, it is called bloodshed ..."[12]

Consider this poem, "The Market," from Shmuel HaNaggid (10th–11th-century Spanish scholar and poet):

> I crossed through a souk where the butchers
> hung oxen and sheep at their sides,
> there were birds and herds of fatlings like squid,
> their terror loud
> as blood congealed over blood

---

9. While it is rumored that Rav Kook himself was a vegetarian, this is not the case, as he himself writes that he ate a small piece of chicken on Shabbat. His eminent disciple, Rabbi David Cohen (known as "the Nazir," as he was a Nazzarite), was indeed a vegetarian.

10. Rabbi Avraham Yitzhak HaCohen Kook, *A Vision of Vegetarianism and Peace*, sec. 1.

11. Leviticus 19:16. See more in the Babylonian Talmud on Sanhedrin 73a.

12. Sefer HaChinuch, commandment 186.

and slaughterers' knives opened veins.
In booths alongside them the fishmongers,
and fish in heaps, and tackle like sand;
and beside them the Street of the Bakers
– whose ovens are fired through dawn.
They bake, they eat, they lead their prey;
they split what's left to bring home.
And my heart understood how they did it and asked:
Who are you to survive?
What separates you from these beasts,
which were born and knew waking and labor and rest?
If they hadn't been given by God for your meals,
they'd be free.
If He wanted this instant
He'd easily put you in their place.
They've breath, like you, and hearts,
which scatter them over the earth;
there was never a time when the living didn't die,
nor the young that they bear not give birth.
Pay attention to this, you pure ones,
and princes so calm in your fame,
know if you'd fathom the worlds of the hidden:
THIS IS THE LAW OF MAN[13]

Not only should we recoil from the shedding of animal blood as
we do from human blood, we should consider bloodshed to be
an assault on the Divine creation as well. By definition, shedding
human blood is an attack on the Divine image:

> A king of flesh and blood entered a province and the people set
> up portraits of him, made images of him, and struck coins in
> his honor. Later on, they upset his portraits, broke his images,
> and defaced his coins, thus diminishing the likeness of the king.

---

13. "The Market," from The Poems of Shmuel HaNaggid.

So also, if one shed blood, it is accounted to him as though he had diminished the Divine image. For it is said: The shedder of human blood ... for human beings were made in the image of God.[14]

We are not only told not to shed blood, but we are instructed that if we have the capacity to save life, we must do all we can to save it:

The Torah gave permission to the physicians to heal;[15] moreover, this is a religious requirement and is included in the category of saving a life, and if the physician withholds services, it is considered as if they were shedding blood.[16]

Rebbe Nachman teaches a spiritual lesson based on the idea of humans having blood. He teaches that we uphold the "Divine honor" by not responding to attacks.[17] He writes that *dam* (human blood) represents the *yeitzer* (the human desire for instant gratification). When someone critiques or attacks us, our "blood rises," and our natural inclination is to want to lash out and criticize and attack back. He offers us the chance for meditation when we move *dam* (blood) to *dom* (silence or stillness). In this way, we gain control of our impulses by moving our hot blood to slow stillness.

We can learn a different, but sensitive, lesson when we read about blood from the Exodus story. The first plague turned the Nile River to blood. "God said to Moses, 'Say to Aaron: Take

---

14. This is a well-known parable told in many different ways. To read more on this, see David Flusser, *Judaism of the Second Temple Period: Sages and Literature* (Jerusalem: The Hebrew University Magnes Press, 2009), pg. 160. Also see Genesis 9:6, M'chilta D'Rabbi Yishmael, BaChodesh.

15. Exodus 21:19 states: *V'rapo yerapei*, ("He shall heal") referring to one hitting and wounding another, implying that a doctor may engage in healing and conversely that one in need of medical services must seek it.

16. Shulchan Aruch, Yoreh De'ah 336:1.

17. Likutei Moharan 6:2.

your staff and stretch out your hand over the waters of Egypt and they shall become blood.[18]" The commentators wonder here as to why Moses didn't just do it himself. Why did he need his brother Aaron to accompany him? Rashi writes that Moses couldn't do the deed himself due to his gratitude of having been saved in the river as an infant. From this teaching, we learn how gratitude can be channeled into personal responsibility. How can we ever harm something that has assisted us?

Blood is sacred. It is our source of life. It is not short of astounding that today we can donate blood to save the lives of others. It is equally amazing that one can engage in the process of dialysis to prolong the life of one with kidney failure.[19] The sanctity of blood is true for all blood, not just our own. This understanding can prevent us from moving into tribalism. The rabbis taught:

> One came before Raba and said to him: "The governor of my town has ordered me: go and kill so-and-so; if not, I will slay you. What shall I do?" He answered him: "Let him rather slay you than you should commit murder; who knows that your blood is redder? Perhaps his blood is redder."[20]

Blood serves a deep purpose. It courses through a body with the beating of the heart, finding its way with the powerful constriction and relaxation of the arteries, moving along through progressively smaller vessels until it reaches the tiny capillaries where it nourishes the cells. With its ebb and flow, it reminds us of our fragility, of our mortality. For this reason, Job cries: "O' earth, do not conceal my blood! Let there not be a place for my screams!"[21]

---

18. Exodus 7:19.

19. Of course, dialysis is a huge inconvenience not to mention physically uncomfortable, at best. Nonetheless, having this modern technology, until further medical advancements can move us beyond, is itself remarkable.

20. Babylonian Talmud, Sanhedrin 74a.

21. Job 16:18.

When a woman or girl sees the blood of menstruation on Shabbat, this can be a spiritual reminder as well. It can be a sign of fertility,[22] a sign of the sanctity of blood,[23] and it can be a reminder of the blood lineage where one shares the same DNA with one's ancestors.[24]

Six days of the week we see blood being spilled along the road and we dare not stand idly by. On Shabbat, we don't look at the blood. As we experience *mei'ein olam haba*, a day which resembles the World to Come, we imagine ourselves striving to be eternal and angelic, not mere frail, mortal human beings. Further, we imagine that all blood is equal, representing the life source gifted from God to all beings who need it down on Earth. A human, a camel, and even a fly, with blood that's called hemolymph, all share this gift. We dare not draw blood from anywhere. After Shabbat, we return to a broken hierarchical world where we protect our "own" humans before our enemies: humans before animals, and land animals before insects. May the *melacha* of refraining from *shechitah* on Shabbat sensitize us to the sanctity of all blood. May the consciousness of *dam* (blood) bring us *dom* (stillness).

---

22. Although, tragically, it is not always a sign as such.

23. Like a *korban* (offering) as one offers up one's own body in service to God.

24. This can also be a sign of Jewish continuity for those born Jewish. For those who have converted into Judaism, only in a spiritual sense.

27.
Mafshit (Skinning)

ONCE AN ANIMAL is trapped, what is its use? Regarding the construction of the *Mishkan*, after an animal was trapped and slaughtered, its hide was removed in preparation for the curtains and coverings. This is the twenty-seventh *melacha*, that of *mafshit* (skinning). Insofar as this being a *melacha*, *mafshit* applies to all types of species: mammals, birds, and even fish; any animal that has skin that can be removed. If one's own skin is peeling, they may not peel it further on Shabbat. This *melacha* doesn't apply to cooked animals that one eats as food, i.e., removing the skin on one's plate at a meal is not *mafshit*. Rather it only applies to a raw, uncooked animal.

Doesn't it seem excessive to need hides in a humble house of God? The Talmudic rabbis discussed, in various ways, the limits of what hides could be needed, and why:

> Rabbi Aha son of Ya'akov said: "There should be no poverty in a place of wealth."[1] Why, then, does God need goat's wool, from which sacks are made? We could instead have used three covers of scarlet wool, and over them another thirty processed hides.[2]

---

1. While this rule is invoked several times throughout the Talmud, it is not an actual biblical verse and its source is unclear.
2. BT Shabbat 102b.

Indeed, there could always be more added to the utility and design of the *Mishkan*. The detailed recording could be seen as a form of moral accountability to ensure nothing more elaborate was done. It's also worth noting how early in Jewish history, there is already some progress in the move away from using animal-based materials. The Shem MiShmuel (Rabbi Shmuel Bornsztain, 20th-century Hasidic thinker) argues that the fact that the *Mishkan* had more animal-based materials than the *Mikdash* (Temple) demonstrates this progress. Moving from animals to inanimate objects in building a holy place embodies the concept of *ma'alin bakodesh* (we ascend toward holiness): it's appropriate to aim high in trying to achieve holiness.

Hides, of course, have a much earlier and holier role in Jewish thought. The Talmud records:

> The Torah begins with an act of righteousness and ends with an act of righteousness. It begins with an act of righteousness, as it is written, "Unto Adam also and to his wife did the Lord God make coats of skins, and clothed them" (Genesis 3:21). And it ends with an act of righteousness, as it is written, "And God buried him (i.e., Moses) in a valley." (Deuteronomy 154:6).[3]

This pairing and juxtaposing of an aspect of the Torah's opening narrative and its finale puts into relief the progression from the use of the animate – animal hides used – to the inanimate. But it also provides a source for the essence of Jewish ethics: *v'halachta bidrachav* (*imitatio Dei*)[4]:

> Rabbi Hama son of Rabbi Hanina said: "What does the text mean: 'Walk after the Eternal your God?' It means to walk after the attributes of the Holy One of Blessing. Just as God clothes the naked, so should you clothe the naked, as it is written: 'And

---

3. BT Sotah 14a.
4. Emulating the Divine.

the Eternal God made garments of skins for Adam and his wife and clothed them' (Genesis 3:21). Just as the Holy One of Blessing visited the sick, so should you also visit the sick, as it is written: 'And the Eternal appeared to him by the terebinths of Mamre [after Abraham's circumcision]' (Genesis 18:1). Just as the Holy One of Blessing comforted mourners, so should you also comfort mourners, as it is written 'After the death of Abraham, God blessed his son Isaac' (Genesis 25:11). Just as the Holy One of Blessing buried the dead, so should you also bury the dead, as it is written: 'God buried him [Moses] in the valley' (Deuteronomy 34:6)."[1]

Let's move our attention from the notion of animal skin as a utilitarian item to human skin as a boundary. Human skin is also a holy tool that helps to elevate us toward the Divine. Rabbi Lawrence Kushner offers a powerful thought:

> Could not several people be members of a single living organic unity? If one person can in sickness or sin be fragmented, cannot several people in holiness be one?
>
> Where does a person end and begin? Is it really at the outer border of one's skin? As if to say everything that is inside is person, everything outside, non-person. Is this not saying that our least subtle sense, the sense of touch, defines a person? And what if our ability to see were as fine as that of the electron microscope? When we came to the skin line there would still be spaces. Or if we were, as we probably are, able to see infra-red energy patterns, a person's shape would so change again. Or what of the influence a person has? Does a respected person's boundary end with his or her outer skin?
>
> Where does anything begin and another thing end? If all the cells in a body are replaced many times during a single lifetime, then what makes a person the "same" person? Why have we

---

1. Ibid.

so ruthlessly superimposed borders on things? Fragmented the cosmos. Maybe there are no "objects." Maybe we have only invented them! Agreed to pretend they are, so we can exploit, use and control. Hoping thereby somehow to outwit death. But we do not realize that the very means which we have chosen to keep ourselves alive is what fragments us from ourselves, from one another, from our source of life, and it is this choice that ultimately kills us.

The fragmenting, controlling, separating, saying that one thing ends here and another begins there. I own this. Control that. Extend my boundaries to there. Over yours. Will have more. Be more. Live longer. But surely this is death. Suppose instead that we are all of one piece.[2]

Indeed, skin represents the self. But it also represents moral responsibility, defining where the self ends and the new person begins. In fact, the opening verses of the Torah suggest that skin, which represents the human body, should be united: "Therefore shall a man leave his father and his mother, and shall cleave to his wife; and they shall be one flesh."[3] Rashi suggests here:

> One Flesh: The child is formed through the two of them and there [in the child] their flesh becomes one.

For Rashi, becoming one flesh is about the creation of a new flesh (a child). Ramban (Nachmanides) offers a contrasting view:

> And they shall be One Flesh: The child is formed through the two of them and there [in the child] their flesh becomes one. Thus, the words of Rashi. But there is no point to this since in beast and cattle ... their flesh is united into one in their offspring.

---

2. Lawrence Kushner, *Honey from the Rock: An Introduction to Jewish Mysticism* (Vermont: Jewish Lights Publishing, 1977), chapter 91.
3. Genesis 2:24.

The correct interpretation appears to me to be that in cattle and beast the males have no attachment to their females. Rather, the male mates with any female he finds, and then they go their separate ways. It is for this reason that Scripture states that because the female of man was bone of his bones and flesh of his flesh, he therefore cleaves to her and she nestles in his bosom as his own flesh, and he desires to be with her always. And just as it was with Adam, so was his nature transmitted to his offspring that the males among them should cleave to their women, leaving their fathers and their mothers, and considering their wives as if they are one flesh with them. A similar sense is found in the verse: "For he is our brother, our flesh; to any that is near of his flesh (Gen. 37:27)." Those who are close members of the family are called *sh'eir basar* (near of flesh). Thus, man will leave "the flesh" of his father and his mother and their kin and will see that his wife is nearer to him than they.

For Ramban, the goal is a relationship, the intimacy of marriage itself, a relationship that includes, but goes well beyond, the physical.

But we know the tragic history (and current reality) that emerges regarding skin: bias. Rabbi Jonathan Sacks writes:

> If we think less of a person because of the color of his or her skin, we are repeating the sin of Aaron and Miriam – "Miriam and Aaron spoke against Moses because of the Cushite woman."[4] There are midrashic interpretations that read this passage differently but the plain sense is that they looked down on Moses' wife because, like Cushite women generally, she had dark skin, making this one of the first recorded instances of color prejudices. For this sin, Miriam was struck with leprosy.
>
> Instead, we should remember the lovely line from Song of Songs: "I am black but beautiful, O daughters of Jerusalem, like

---

4. Numbers 12:1.

the tents of Kedar, like the curtains of Solomon. Do not stare at me because I am dark, because the sun has looked upon me."[5]

Jews cannot complain that others have racist attitudes towards them if they hold racist attitudes towards others. "First correct yourself; then [seek to] correct others," says the Talmud.[6] The Tanakh contains negative evaluations of some other nations, but always and only because of moral failures, never because of ethnicity or skin color.[7]

Rabbi Lord Jonathan Sacks writes here about the sin of racism. Indeed, oppressing others due to their skin color is as absurd as it is cruel. But, here, we must search among intellectual roots to consider how we might transcend baseless ideas. There are many different angles to take. Empiricism emerged to challenge rationalism, the notion that humans have innate knowledge. There are three different types of empiricism:

1. Classical Empiricism – As seen in the thinking of John Locke (17th-century England), one is born *tabula rasa* (with a blank slate) knowing nothing at birth. The idea of innate knowledge is totally rejected.
2. Radical Empiricism – Here William James (19th–20th-century American psychologist) famously argued that all knowledge comes from the senses. Rather than reason, it is experience that enables us to know anything at all.
3. Moderate Empiricism – While this approach still suggests that most knowledge emerges from experience, it also allows for some types of knowledge (such as mathematics) to be understood without direct experience but purely from reason.

---

5. Song 1:5.
6. BT, Bava Metzia 107b.
7. Rabbi Lord Jonathan Sacks, *Lessons in Leadership* (Jerusalem: Maggid Books, 2015), p. 270.

Indeed, one can sit in an ivory tower and determine that what is "reasonable" is X, Y, or Z. Instead, we must experience the world and study those experiences. Reason is not valueless but it must be scrutinized and tested. For too long, women, people of color, blue-collar workers, and the like were considered to be inferior. Some assumed, like Plato, that people had essences that determined what they were. Does skin reveal the essence of a person? Does it hide the essence of a person? Or do people not have an essence at all? What we know for sure is that the skin is not an accurate representation of what is inside. It is part of the story but only a small part.

On Shabbat, we take the time to look at our skin in the mirror. It may look old or young. It may look brown, white, or black. It may look familiar or foreign even to the person whose skin it is. It may look scarred or healed. It might have been used as a space to write a message – perhaps a voluntarily written message, chosen during a visit to a tattoo parlor[8] to celebrate a person's self-perception, or perhaps in the course of the tattooing suffered by a victim of the Holocaust. But then we must transcend our skin and realize that it is hardly the complete and true self.

On Shabbat, we don't "skin." This is to say that for six days of the week, we can care about how we look (our clothes, our weight, the softness of our skin, the whiteness of our teeth, etc.). It's acceptable. We are human and humans have always cared and will always care about how we look. Indeed, in keeping with the social aspect of ourselves, we should. But on this day of the week, even as we still take care of our appearances, we forget about our skins. It doesn't mean we just eat cake in our pajamas all day. We are able to look good and take care of our bodies. It means that we meditate and pray in ways that tap into our deeper selves, reminding us that as mere mortals, we are just flesh and

---

8. Tattooing is used here merely as an example; a permanent tattoo is of course biblically forbidden.

blood, but as eternal sparks we hold a holy flame that must be tended to, to ensure that it never burns out.

Even as we transcend our own skin, may we learn "to be happy in our own skin." Humans are plagued with inadequacies (many of which are about physical experience). Disengaging from *mafshit* on Shabbat allows us to see that we are created in the Image of God, and that we are to love our own skin as being one manifestation of God's unique image.

28.
Me'abeid (Tanning, Salting)

IN THE PREVIOUS *melacha*, we discussed the utility of animal hides in the *Mishkan*. Now that we have the hides, what exactly do we do with them? The *melacha of me'abeid* is about that process.[1] Once the skin has been removed from the animal, the hides must be preserved through salting[2] to remove moisture as well as adding oils, and to be transformed into leather by tanning and by stretching the hides to flatten them. We continue to do this today to produce a Torah scroll or other holy ritual scrolls. Consider also how kosher meat needs to be salted in order to remove the blood. We also dip our challah in salt on Shabbat to remind us of the salt which accompanied the *korbanot* (sacrifices) in the *Mishkan*. Most famously, we dip our parsley in saltwater on Pesach to remind us of the bitterness of slavery. Salt can be useful but also humbling and painful, as with Lot's wife, as we shall see.

Regarding *me'abeid*, the biblical prohibition of this salting

---

1. The word "*me'abeid*" literally means "working with." In the case of animal hide, working with it entails the processes of tanning and salting as discussed here.

2. While the mishnah lists *me'abeid* (tanning) and *molei'ach* (salting) as two separate *melachot*, the gemara treats them as two parts of the same *melacha* (of *me'abeid*). In order to maintain the total number of thirty-nine *melachot*, the gemara adds *mesarteit* (scoring the leather) to the list (as opposed to it being subsumed in another *melacha*).

and/or adding oil activity on Shabbat doesn't apply to processes involving the preservation of food. For example, an act such as pickling would only be rabbinically proscribed,[3] not disallowed on a Torah basis. On a practical level related to the *melacha*, we should be concerned with an act like oiling a leather shoe in order to preserve it.

We should ask: When an object is transformed, up until what point is it still the original product as opposed to something new? At what point does a cake become a cake rather than a mixture of its ingredients? At what point does a meeting of sperm and egg become a fetus? At what point does a child become an adult? At what point do individuals working together become a team? At what point does a hide become leather? In identity studies, we might consider change from three different approaches using the perspective of a tree:

1. **Perdurantism** – The tree undergoes a series of stages in its life based on the temporal changing of its parts.
2. **Endurantism** – The tree is always the same and is whole throughout its life. Even as a tree loses leaves (or the like) it remains the same tree.
3. **Mereological Essentialism** – The tree's parts are essential to the whole and as the parts change, the whole changes. So when a tree loses its leaves, it is no longer the same tree. The parts changed and now the whole is something fundamentally different.

In considering our own life journeys, we might wonder, am I as an 80-year-old the same person as when I was 40, or when I was 20, or when I was 5? Sure, I changed a lot, but those iterations of myself were still me. But were those (or will those) versions

---

3. Pickling or brining on Shabbat with the intention of consuming the food only sometime after Shabbat is problematic due to a separate rabbinic proscription of *hachanah*, i.e., preparation on Shabbat for the weekdays ahead.

of myself be fundamentally different so that only in the loosest sense can I say they are or were *all* me?

In issues of identity, we often return to "the first philosophy," that of metaphysics. There are three primary branches to metaphysics:

1. **Ontology** – the study of existence and being (and change that may emerge in states of being)
2. **Universal Science** – the study of reasoning and logic ("first principles")
3. **Natural Theology** – the study of God and creation

Here too, we can ask: When does "nothing" become "something" or, vice versa, when does something become nothing? What does it mean for something, or someone, to exist in the first place? What does it fundamentally mean for someone (or for God) to exist? And from a zoomed-out perspective of history, what does it mean for something or someone to exist temporally but not eternally?

The Sefer Yetzirah[1] says that there are three parts to the creation of the world:[2] 1. Space (*olam*) 2. Time (*shanah* [year]) and 3. Soul (*nefesh*). While space can be tangible, time and soul are completely intangible.[3] And time is a reality – or maybe a fiction? – that can be studied scientifically, while the soul can be the object of consideration but is neither tangible nor observable. Thus, while we might perceive the created world, creation itself is ethereal and elusive. So, too, revelation happens through these

---

1. *Sefer Yetzirah* is the earliest existing work on *kabbalah*, or Jewish mysticism. Its authorship is unknown, and it is fascinating that it is ascribed by some to Rabbi Akiva, and to others as far back as Abraham!

2. *Sefer Yetzirah* 3:4.

3. What happens when there is a clash? This is what the Bnei Yissascher says (ma'amar 9:5) happened when the Israelites started their conquer of Yericho on Shabbat (Joshua 6:15. See the commentary of Rashi there too). He argues that the soul (*Clal Yisrael*) needed to enter the world (the land) and accept the time (Shabbat).

three channels: a space for revelation, a unique time of revelation, and a spiritual dimension of revelation. When a human being is created, is this something physical or metaphysical? Yes, there is a body. But, also, the boundaries of time help to define the person's existence, and the person's existence has a spiritual dimension as well. What does it mean for this human to exist at all?

Are philosophical problems real? Ludwig Wittgenstein (20th-century Austrian-British philosopher) believed that all philosophical problems were linguistic puzzles and could be solved with grammar. Karl Popper (Austrian-British contemporary of Wittgenstein) believed that philosophical problems were real problems to solve. Wittgenstein and Popper had a fierce disagreement but they only came together face-to-face one time. It was such an intense and disputed encounter (albeit lasting only ten minutes) that a whole book was written about it: *Wittgenstein's Poker*.[4] We can begin to understand how significant this disagreement can be when we consider theodicy. Is the problem of Divine justice to be resolved through language or to be solved with logic?

We can ask a similar question about the President of the United States. When does a mere citizen become President? When they win the election? When the election is officially certified as valid? After an inauguration? After the people accept an inauguration? Is "President" an ontological status or merely a societal agreement? Thomas Hobbes (17th-century England) was a staunch monarchist who defended King Charles I. During the English

---

4. *Wittgenstein's Poker* was written by David Edmonds and John Eidinow to describe the various accounts of the October 25th, 1946 brief encounter. Bertrand Russell, a colleague of Popper who was himself another philosopher with ideas in tension with Wittgenstein's, was also present.

Part of the importance of the book is found in its exploration of how we cannot understand philosophers merely from the books they have written. We also need to understand their lives and conversations. This is also true in Jewish thought. This idea is reified when we use Aggadic literature to help us understand halacha.

Civil War,[5] however, he fled to France where he authored his most famous work: *Leviathan*.[6] Hobbes was pessimistic about human nature and believed that people were primarily self-interested. He argued that the goal of government is to respond to that fear and self-interest of individuals. For Hobbes, governments could ultimately only be sustained if they maintain order (reducing the fear of war for the people) and by instilling fear in the people (that there will be punishment if there is disorder). When the government grants rights, the people, in turn, grant power to the government; this mutual interaction maintains a "social contract." When this trust falls apart, historically, we often see that there is a revolution.

But nothing ever truly remains the same. Just as people are growing, the zeitgeist is evolving, and society is changing. Some are pushing progress. Some are pushing conservation. Some have no clue that anything at all is going on. How are people (like a President or King, or a citizen without rank or title) to stay on top of the changing times?

Prochaska and Nocross (2001) identified six stages of change:

- Precontemplation (no awareness of a problem)
- Contemplation (awareness of the problem, not yet committed to change)
- Preparation (intending to change)
- Action (working on change)
- Maintenance (working to prevent relapse)
- Termination (change process complete, not likely to relapse)[7]

Perhaps the most important factor in working for change is to believe it's possible. Carol Dweck (contemporary American psy-

---

5. These wars took place from 1641 to 1651.

6. He was ultimately banned by the king's court not for disloyalty to the monarchy but for disloyalty to the church. He did not believe that God granted the king the right to rule but rather the people did.

7. These stages are described in Dr. Mona Fishbane's *Loving with the Brain in Mind* (New York: W.W. Norton & Co., 2013), p. 213.

chologist) identifies two different orientations toward change: a fixed mindset and a growth mindset.[8] For parents and teachers, more important than helping a child become good at something is helping them to realize that it is their effort that enables their growth.

And as we mentioned earlier, why did Lot's wife turn into a pillar of salt[9] after looking back[10] at the destruction of Sodom?[11] Two possible explanations might be given for why she turned to salt:

- Lot's wife must have had a secret longing for that way of life[12]
- Lot's wife sinned with salt (asking neighbors for salt in an effort to alert them to the guests that they then came to abuse)[13]

The process of salting is, therefore, about transforming an object. Thinking about it gives us the opportunity to reflect on how we change. One suggestion from the Talmudic rabbis, related to salt, is that we might embrace a mode of change embodied in asceticism:[14]

> This is the way of Torah: Eat bread with salt, drink water in small measure, sleep on the ground, live a life of deprivation –

---

8. She posited this notion in 2006.

9. Near the Dead Sea, at Mount Sodom, today there is a pillar of salt named for Lot's wife.

10. The language of the verse describing Lot's wife turning into salt is obscure. The verse states: *Vatabeit ishto mei'acharav*, **vatehi** *netziv melach* ("His wife looked behind him, and **she became** a pillar of salt"). The word *vatehi* can also be translated as "**it became**," referring to the city itself and not necessarily Lot's wife.

11. Genesis 19:26.

12. Scharfstein, Sol (2008). *Torah and Commentary: The Five Books of Moses: Translation, Rabbinic and Contemporary Commentary* (Jersey City, NJ: KTAV Publishing), p. 71, #26.

13. Schwartz, Howard *Tree of Souls: The Mythology of Judaism* (NY: Oxford University Press, 2004).

14. Pirkei Avot (Ethics of the Fathers) 6:4.

but toil in Torah! If you do this, "You are praiseworthy, and all is well with you." You are praiseworthy – in this world; and all is well with you – in the world to come.[15]

Rashi's commentary on this Mishnah argues that this perspective isn't anti-wealth:

> This Mishnah is not telling a wealthy person to live a life of deprivation in order to learn Torah, but rather it should read like this: EVEN if a person only has bread and salt to eat, nor a pillow or blanket to sleep with, but lies on the floor, nevertheless [he should] not desist from learning Torah, for in the end they will learn in wealth.

Here, "wealth" is not the goal, but rather a means for enablement of noble pursuits. Salt is either necessary or at least appropriate, for one who is seeking growth. One can live and learn modestly yet still achieve great things. But once one has "wealth" or status, will they remember the floor and the salt? When one has been transformed, is their past recognizable? Is their early stage of life retrievable?

A bloody, smelly hide of a killed animal becomes a beautiful decoration in a sacred place. Does this part of the *Mishkan* in any way resemble its origins? How can we evolve and grow yet remember that from dust we came and to dust we return? Any noble stature in this world can be understood to be a façade. We are mortal and we will be forgotten. We can salt the hide all we want. We can dress ourselves in fancy clothes and drive fancy cars and return to fancy homes. In the end, we are mere flesh and bones.

Humility is not only a crucial character trait. It may actually be the root trait of all others. Rabbi Bachya ibn Pakuda (11th–12th-century Spanish Jewish philosopher) writes:

---

15. Also see the Rambam on salt and learning in Hilchot Talmud Torah 3:6.

Is humility dependent upon other virtues, or are the other virtues dependent on humility? My answer is as follows ...

... Consequently, it is not possible for people to serve God unless they assume all the attributes of service – namely humility and lowliness before God – and divest themselves of all the attributes of mastership – namely, grandeur, honor, majesty, glory, pride, and the like ...

and a prerequisite to their attainment. For this reason, it also follows that no virtue can be predicated of someone whose heart is devoid of humility before God and contains even the slightest trace of pride or haughtiness.[16]

Indeed, our honor is not found in our wealth, our degrees, or our social status. It is in honoring others that we find our own honor. Ben Zoma famously teaches: "Who is honored? One who honors others."[17] Indeed, our humility can be about seeing that so much of our accomplishments are based on our privilege. We can take up no more and no less space than we deserve in the world given that all people are equal and yet all people are unique. Our humility can be rooted in seeing that we are not in control of the world. We prostrate ourselves before God knowing that we have responsibility but not control.

On Shabbat, as we contemplate the *melacha* of *me'abeid* and what it means to change and evolve, we have the opportunity to reflect on humility – not a humility that dismisses our accomplishments, breaks down our self-esteem, or dismisses our own nobility, but rather a humility that embraces where we are now, where we have come from, and where we will ultimately go.

---

16. Rabbeinu Bachya ibn Pekuda, *Duties of the Heart, The Gate of Dedication of Purpose, Humility and Repentance* (Yeshivath Beth Moshe, 1998), Chapter 8, p. 589.
17. Pirkei Avot 4:1.

29.

Mesarteit (Scoring lines)

As we continue to explore the topic of hides and their use in the *Mishkan*, what once seemed esoteric becomes more and more realized as the foundation for spiritual renewal. The previous *melacha, me'abeid,* discusses the use of salting hides once they are removed from the animal. So now, the hides need to be cut to the appropriate size and shape. One aspect of preparing hides to be cut constitutes the 29th *melacha: mesarteit.*[1] One needs to score the hides, to scratch lines on their surface that will show where they are to be cut. In a more modern context, this *melacha* would perhaps also apply to folding a paper to show where to cut later.[2] This does not, though, apply to using a knife to trace on food. The requisite scoring of lines when writing a Torah scroll is referred to as *sirtut* (from the same root).

Life unanalyzed is a chaotic mess. One of the goals of religion is to take that mess and make meaning out of it. We decide how and where to be *mesarteit,* to draw lines and cut things

---

1. As mentioned in the footnotes to the previous *melacha, mesarteit* is not listed in the mishnah as one of the *melachot;* rather, *me'abeid* and *molei'ach* (tanning and salting) are listed as two separate *melachot.* The gemara, however, concludes that *me'abeid* and *molei'ach* are part of the same *melacha* (and both falling under the heading of *me'abeid).* To keep the total number of *melachot* at 39, *mesarteit* is added to the list.

2. Folding without making a crease is permitted, e.g., folding a cloth napkin or even loosely folding a paper napkin. Folding laundry falls under a separate category and presents issues unrelated to *mesarteit.*

as we determine what is in and what is out. We take a formless mass and shape it; we interpret that which is raw. One can be a radical relativist and say that those cuts are in vain and that life truly has no meaning. One can, in the opposite extreme, be a fundamentalist and say that the shape and meaning of everything is pre-determined, clear, and absolute. But Judaism, I propose, offers an alternative view. Judaism informs us that we must be alive, responsive, and ever-evolving in our meaning-making process.

Friedrich Nietzsche was one of the most significant philosophers of the late 19th century. In the 1870s–1880s his health severely declined (dysentery, syphilis, and diphtheria). In 1889, he suffered a nervous breakdown and he never regained his sanity, spending the last eleven years of his life in a vegetative state until his death in 1900. What happened at that moment of nervous breakdown? Nietzsche saw a man whipping a horse on the street. Nietzsche ran in between the whip and the horse, yelling for the beating to stop, hugging the horse. He then collapsed crying, never to recover again.

It's such a tragic story and yet it points to Nietzsche's core humanity. We cannot keep our humanity intact and fail to be emotionally and spiritually shaken by brutal violence and pointless suffering. We need not throw ourselves under the whip. We don't need to collapse in illness, futility, and exhaustion. We must take care of our physical health and our mental health and protect ourselves. But we also cannot stand silent if we wish to keep the inner light of our moral essence alive.

For Nietzsche, "humanity" is not enough. The difference between a human and an animal is the project of self-mastery, and the difference between a human and an *ubermensch* (stellar human being) is living by good conscience. One must truly be morally alive, radically awake.[3] Nietzsche wanted to uncover how we might escape nihilism (the rejection of all, concluding

---

3. This state is referred to as the Eternal Recurrence (affirming each life choice as if we'd have to relive that choice eternally).

that life is meaningless) through an affirmation of life, but his illness didn't give him the chance to finish his grand project.

Of course, one aspect of affirming the dignity of life consists of recognizing the flexibility that individuals have to decide for themselves the boundaries that define when a life begins and when it ends according to the mores that govern their lives, whether they are moral, religious, communal, or other types of considerations.

When we see hate, cruelty, a world that is burning, there are many different ways to act (or to refrain from acting). Each of us chooses our moral pursuits based on our own spiritual authenticity. What is not an option is to fail to feel, to look at the whip and merely to turn away and gleefully take the next bite of our sandwich. What is not an option is just to hide in religious doctrine or to immerse ourselves in political ideology and social media bandwagoning, where we believe that we need not think or feel but rather only need to do no more than just shout what everyone else is shouting.

We must wake up! In seeing the horse whipped, we see that *we* are being whipped. To suffer is a collective trauma, not merely personal. We are all interconnected. To take care of one another, we must take care of ourselves. To take care of ourselves, we must take care of one another.

I suggest that, as Jews, our primary response in a complex world should not be to philosophize, but rather to express gratitude for all that is good and all that is possible. The Talmud[4] says that Leah was the first human to thank God.[5] Earlier generations offered *shevach* (praise) to God,[6] but she is the first to introduce *hoda'ah* (thankfulness).[7]

---

4. BT, Brachot 7b.

5. Genesis 29:35.

6. Genesis 9:26, 14:20.

7. She thanks God for the birth of Yehudah. Her gratitude, translated from the language of emotion to the language of Hebrew, provides the meaning of his name. Rabbi Shmuel Yitzhak Weinbaum suggests that what Leah truly

Sometimes it takes a long time to learn to appreciate what we have. Consider this Talmudic passage:

> *Because ... not caused it to rain*: Because there was no man to work the soil, and no one recognized the benefit of rain, but when man came and understood that they were essential to the world, he prayed for them, and they fell, and the trees and the herbs sprouted.[8]

Making meaning of life doesn't just mean interpreting the hard parts, but is also about expressing gratitude for the good parts. In every moment of our existence, we are unconsciously engaged in an expression of prayer in which our souls are yearning (crying! longing!) to unite with the compassionate interconnectivity of all things, all life, and the Oneness of all being. If we can just be silent and still for a moment and witness this intense energy, we can be transformed through radical gratitude for the gift of life, the gift of spiritual attunement.

This gratitude must be not just to God but also to humans. Rebbe Nachman writes: "It is forbidden to show ingratitude, whether to a Jew or a non-Jew."[9]

Similarly, Ernest Becker (20th-century American anthropologist) writes:

> Now that we see what we might call the ontological or creature tragedy that is so peculiar to man: If he gives in to Agape, he risks failing to develop himself, his active contribution to the rest of life. If he expands Eros too much, he risks cutting himself off from natural dependency, from duty to a larger creation; he pulls away from the healing power of gratitude and humility

---

wanted was to be loved by Jacob with the same kind of love with which he loved Rachel. Her gratitude to God is for the child that will help her husband love her even more.

8. BT, Hulin 60b.
9. *Sefer Hamidot*, Tefilah 62.

that he must naturally feel for having been created, for having been given the opportunity of life experience.

Man, thus, has the absolute tension of dualism. Individuation means that the human creature has to oppose itself to the rest of nature. It creates precisely the isolation that one can't stand and yet needs in order to develop distinctively. It creates the difference that becomes such a burden; it accents the smallness of oneself and the sticking-outness at the same time. This is natural guilt. The person experiences this as "unworthiness" or "badness" and dumb inner dissatisfaction. And the reason is realistic. Compared to the rest of nature man is not a very satisfactory creation. He is riddled with fear and powerlessness.[1]

We want to be a part of the whole but also to be singular. The pathway to balancing humility and courage, the subjective and the objective, responsibility of the self and obligation to the other, is to be immersed in gratitude. This thankfulness gives birth to a sacred mandate to transcend the self in service of others. Here is how two contemporary thinkers describe this phenomenon:

> There are two sides to gratitude: the first is appreciation, where you're valuing something that has happened, and the second is attribution, where you're recognizing the role of someone or something else in bringing it about. Even when you're grateful to yourself, it is likely that others played a role in your development for the skill, strength, or quality you used. Gratitude is a social emotion. It points our warmth and goodwill out toward others.
>
> When gratitude levels are high, not only are we more inclined to return favors, but we're also more likely to assist complete strangers. In the 1970s, American psychologist Alice Isen demonstrated this in an experiment in which coins were left in public phone booths so that the next person using them

---

1. Ernest Becker, *The Denial of Death* (New York: Free Press, 1973), page 153.

would get a free call.[2] When the person had finished and was leaving the phone booth, one of the experimenters appeared to accidentally drop a file of papers just in front of the subject. The process was repeated near phone boxes that hadn't been primed with coins. People receiving the unexpected lucky gift of a free phone call were much more likely to help the experimenter pick up her papers. This experiment, and a host of others like it, suggests that our willingness to act on behalf of others isn't just attributable to some people being good-natured and others less so. Our readiness to help others is influenced by the level of gratitude we experience.[3]

One Midrash tells a profound story of the expression of gratitude in the life of the Talmudic sage Rabbi Shimon ben Shetah:[4]

It is related of Rabbi Shimon ben Shetah that he once bought a donkey from an Ishmaelite. His disciples came and found a precious stone suspended from its neck. They said to him: "Master, The blessing of the Lord will bring riches."[5] R. Shimon b. Shetah replied: "I purchased a donkey, but I have not purchased a precious stone." So he went and returned the gem to the Ishmaelite who exclaimed, "Blessed is the Lord, the God of Shimon ben Shetah!"[6]

The Ishmaelite felt despair that he would never receive his valuable stone again and so, naturally, he would feel gratitude toward Rabbi Shimon ben Shetach for returning it. But the Ishmaelite

2. Alice Isen and Paul Levin, "Effect of Feeling Good on Helping: Cookies and Kindness," Journal of Personality and Social Psychology 21, no. 3 (1972): 384–388.

3. Joanna Macy & Chris Johnstone, *Active Hope: How to Face the Mess We're in without Going Crazy* (Novato, CA: New World Library, 2012), page 45.

4. 1st century BCE.

5. Proverbs 10:22.

6. Deuteronomy Rabbah 3:3.

goes further than just expressing gratitude to the Rabbi. Rather, he expresses gratitude to the God of the Rabbi. That is a way of thanking both by honoring the Rabbi's belief and God by extension. Gratitude, indeed, can bring us closer not only to God but also to religious pluralism. Kindness, and justice, can inspire it all.

In 2015, Pope Francis addressed our ecological crisis in *Laduato Si': On Care for Our Common Home.* Here, the Pope connected our inner spiritual lives with the planet's health. He noted that to address the climate change crisis, we need a spiritual revolution toward the virtues of humility, gratitude, and sobriety, and away from the vices of greed and overconsumption due to a fear of scarcity.

Indeed, gratitude is not just spiritually and morally meaningful. It is a virtue that can change our behaviors and the way we respond to various moral issues. In this spirit of changing the world by first changing ourselves, Rabbi Shlomo Wolbe[7] shares an insight on how to cultivate more gratitude:

If one appreciates that all the needs one has fulfilled [for others] are truly goodness and kindness, one most certainly increases love and friendship in the world and comes to realize that one exists in a world of kindness. When one hides from this recognition, the world is grey. [One's perception is that] every person is only doing their job, each merchant only wants to profit, the doctor only wants the payment, the educator only the salary – there is no goodness, no kindness, and no friendship. The world is sucked dry. No! We want to live in a bright world, a world full of goodness and kindness, love and friendship! This illuminated world is built through showing gratitude to all.[8]

---

7. 1914–2005.
8. Rabbi Shlomo Wolbe, *Alei Shur* Vol. 2 (Jerusalem, Israel: Bais Hamussar, 1967), p. 280–281.

He further writes:

> Gratitude is intellectually compelling and it is a very good trait –
> so why are we so often ungrateful? There are two reasons for
> this. The first is that a person's first impression is that everything
> comes by itself, and that it is all coming to him. The other reason
> is: When I receive good from someone and I recognize that good,
> I become indebted to him.

It is said that when the Kotzker Rebbe (Rabbi Menachem Mendel
Of Kotzk, 18th–19th-century Poland) was ready to throw away
his old shoes he would first wrap them in newspaper to show his
gratitude before putting them in the trash. We express gratitude
not only to God and to people but to all that we have benefited
from.

But let's consider the messy side of gratitude as well. What
about the person who has suffered so much and feels more tension than gratitude? We cannot judge them. Consider the words
of Rabbi Yehuda Amital (20th–21st-century Israeli Rosh Yeshiva
and thinker):

> On my first Yom Kippur after being liberated from a Nazi labor
> camp, I prayed with other survivors in a cramped cellar. I cannot
> fully describe the storm of emotion that I felt then, but I will try
> to reconstruct some of that feeling.
>
> I was young then. I had no children. My parents had been
> murdered, along with most of the population of our town.
> Amongst the survivors in that small room, there were people
> who had lost their children, parents, spouses, and siblings. They
> prayed, and I with them. Was their worship of God based on
> gratitude? Can a Jew who has lost a wife and children possibly
> serve God on the basis of His kindness? Can a Jew whose job
> was the removal of the charred remains of corpses from the
> crematoria of Auschwitz be capable of serving God on the basis

of gratitude? No, not in any way, shape, or form! But where, then, does that leave us?[9]

Rabbi Amital quotes the Talmudic statement that after seeing the destruction of the holy Temple, the prophets Daniel and Jeremiah could no longer refer to God as "awesome" and "mighty" for "since they knew that God was truthful, they would not lie to God."[10] Rabbi Amital teaches that serving God "must be built on truth, not on falsehood or flattery (*hanifa*)."[11]

Indeed, perhaps we should not express gratitude for that which we don't feel grateful. We must bring our emotion and cognition together, and bring our honesty and integrity in prayer and expressions of thanks.

Sometimes those who have so little can be our teachers of gratitude.

Not too long ago, I spent the morning in a border detention center talking with a woman named Florence. She opened her heart so deeply. She was serving as a pastor of a small church in Africa but recently had to flee her home country of Cameroon after the government tortured her and shot and killed her husband and now was coming after her. She got a flight to Ecuador and had to flee to Colombia, was hiding in the jungles of Panama, sought safety in Costa Rica, fled rape in Nicaragua and Honduras, was starving in Guatemala, was robbed in Mexico and finally raised her arms as she approached the US border seeking asylum.

Instead of receiving a hug, a hospital, and healing therapy, she has been locked away as a criminal for many months now waiting for court trials to determine her destiny. Looking at her

---

9. Mosheh Mayah, *A World Built, Destroyed and Rebuilt: Rabbi Yehudah Amital's Confrontation with the Memory of the Holocaust*, Appendix: "Confronting the Holocaust as Religious and a Historical Phenomenon" (KTAV, 2005), page 146.

10. BT Yoma 69b.

11. JT (Jerusalem Talmud) Megillah 3:7.

burns on her body from being tortured, I felt that this should be someone deeply angry, and yet she only radiated faith and light. She has no family with her, no money or property, no home, no country, and no plan or control over any plans, but said the only thing that has enabled her to keep going is her faith in God and a trust in the path forward.

I wish I could share with you a picture of her deep eyes that didn't leave my mind all morning. So much pain and fear in those eyes. So much faith, light, and Godliness in those eyes. One might think she'd be full of hate for America for criminalizing her when she was seeking nothing more than asylum, survival, and reunification with her sons, but she only expressed gratitude that she has food (although she said she can't really eat it due to her African eating norms) and a roof over her head (albeit a jail cell). She said through all this pain and loss, she continues to experience revelations from God that she is seeking to understand (I'll maintain her privacy about her spiritual visions).

Florence traced together her story and through all the struggles and hardship she traced it into a meaningful story of survival and gratitude. We have this choice every day in our lives. When we are feeling down or frustrated, we can cling to gratitude. We can just keep re-focusing our mind and spirit toward all the good in life and in our particular life! If we will it, light can prevail over darkness!

When a *sofer* (scribe) prepares parchment for writing a Torah, a *mezuzah*, or *tefillin*, as we mentioned at the opening of this chapter, the *sofer* traces *sirtutim*, lines that are used to keep the writing evenly spaced. When we remember the Shabbat prohibition of *mesarteit*, we can bear in mind that Torah concepts allow us to make our own *sirtutim* to mark the boundaries between the dark experiences that all of us encounter in the world and those many aspects of our lives for which we must – indeed, we desire to – express gratitude, and which are lit with the light of Shabbat.

30.

Memacheik (Smoothing, Scraping)

AS IN THE previous *melachot* on the theme, we are still concentrated on hides in this *melacha* of *memacheik*. The hides in the *Mishkan* needed to be scraped to remove any hair and to be smoothed out. Consequently, activities to accomplish a smoothing of any kind, fall within the scope of this *melacha*. A modern example of such an activity would be sanding. According to some authorities, using a bar of soap,[1] creams, ointments,[2] or even toothpaste[3] fall under this *melacha*. As typical, the *melacha* doesn't apply to actions taken in connection with eating food like smoothing peanut butter or margarine onto bread; however, it may apply to how one is preparing food to be presented.

Why do we want things smooth? Smooth objects are pleasant to touch and touching is such a profound human sense. While it would seem that touching would be a major locus for *mitzvot* observance since we interact with objects daily, a good portion

---

1. When using a bar of soap, one smoothens the surface anew.

2. Aside from smoothing the skin, one changes the texture of ointments and creams when applying them, presenting another halachic consideration. Anointing with oils and liquids, such as applying cologne and perfume, is therefore not problematic.

3. Rav Moshe Feinstein, *Igrot Moshe, Orach Chaim* 1:112 forbids using toothpaste, while Rav Ovadia Yosef, *Yabia Omer* 4:30, permits it. It is reported that Rabbi Joseph B. Soloveitchik brushed his teeth with toothpaste on Shabbat. It should be noted that using mouthwash is permitted (see footnote 2).

of the *mitzvot* are connected to the sense of hearing, such as prayer or listening to the Torah reading. Consider that the most central Jewish prayer is called "Hear!" (*Shema*). Some *mitzvot* have to do with the sense of sight (like the mitzvah to make an *etrog* beautiful). Regarding sight, Isaiah prophesied: "Your eyes will see your Master."[4] Some have to do with the sense of smell (like smelling spices at *havdalah*). The human spiritual potential, regarding smell, is made clear right at the beginning of the Torah: "God breathed into Adam's nostrils the soul of life."[5] And the rabbis taught that smell was maintained as a particularly pure and spiritual sense because it was the only one that didn't benefit from the sin of the Garden of Eden.[6] Some *mitzvot* deal totally with the sense of taste (such as eating matzah on Passover, for example).

But what *mitzvot* are involved with the sense of touch?[7] There are not many. Most obviously would be the mitzvah of *peru urvu* and *onaah* (regarding marital intimacy), but perhaps all *mitzvot* relate in some way to the sense of touch because in order to perform every mitzvah we must appreciate the smooth and seamless relationship between our intention to perform that mitzvah and the real world that we must inhabit in order to perform any mitzvah.

Consider how the *havdalah* service, the weekly transition from Shabbat, emphasizes reawakening our senses to serve God. *Havdalah* inspires us to be spiritually actualized in this physical world. The blessings progress from the most physical to the most sublime.[8] First, we start with the sense of taste with the blessing

---

4. Isaiah 30:21.

5. Genesis 2:7.

6. Bnei Yissaschar, Chodesh Adar 1:9.

7. While wearing *tefillin*, for example, involves touching it in order to put it on, the mitzvah is wearing it and not the touching. We do have the custom of touching the *tefillin* and *tzitzit* (and perhaps kissing them), but this is custom, not part of the mitzvah per se. Kissing a mezuzah, too, is merely a custom.

8. See this idea fleshed out further by the Rashbatz (quoted in the Kaf Hahayim 296:3).

over wine, requiring the wine to touch the mouth. The second blessing on the spices, regarding the sense of smell, doesn't necessitate physical touch, only proximity. The third blessing, over the sight of the light, is even more subtle and can be experienced from a distance. Lastly, the fourth blessing of *ha'mavdil* is about the intellectual capacity of discernment, the most abstract of all, which does not seem to involve touch at all, although we can only discern the world and its meaning if we are "in touch" with it.

But just because touch is so physical, is it necessarily superficial? Deepak Chopra writes:

> More than anything, love is a deep sense of spiritual connection, of being touched, moved and inspired to heights beyond our normal limits. It is a connection with a deep, fundamental truth that runs through all of life and connects us together. Love makes the mundane sacred – so that it is cared for and protected. When we lose our sense of connection with all life, we have lost the sacred, and we no longer care for and protect that which nourishes us.[9]

The late poet Amos Oz[10] wrote a touching poem about what it means to touch and to be touched, to change and to be changed:

> The Land of Israel is not a museum of God.
> No place is a museum of God,
> no person and no inanimate object is a thing of worship.
> It is permissible to both touch and change these things
> on the condition that you yourself are prepared
> to be touched and changed.
> The condition is love.
> I know: It is impossible to 'educate to love' –

9. Anodea Judith, *Wheels of Life: A User's Guide to the Chakra System* (Minnesota: Llewellyn Publications, 1987).
10. 1939–2018.

you cannot 'educate someone to love the land,'
nor can you 'educate someone to love the scenery.'
With love, you can "infect" someone else.
Sometimes love can be awakened,
sometimes, but not with a strong hand,
not with an outstretched arm, and not with burning anger –
rather through an approach of mutuality.
You come to a place – a hill, the desert, a spring, a house ...
You change it and make your mark upon it,
but it is also to be open
and give it the opportunity to leave its mark on you.[11]

Ravindra Kumar Karnani (a contemporary Indian poet), trans-
lating a moving old Hindu poem, shares how we long to be physically touched by God but know not what that would feel like:

> The child whispered, "God, speak to me"
> And a meadowlark sang.
> The child did not hear.
>
> So the child yelled, "God, speak to me!"
> And the thunder rolled across the sky
> But the child did not listen.
>
> The child looked around and said,
> "God let me see you" and a star shone brightly
> But the child did not notice.
>
> And the child shouted,
> "God show me a miracle!"
> And a life was born but the child did not know.

---

11. A booklet which contains this poem identifies it as being from an article
titled "Loving the Land," while a website has the name of the Poem as "Leaving
a Mark."

> So the child cried out in despair,
> "Touch me God, and let me know you are here!"
> Whereupon God reached down
> And touched the child.
> But the child brushed the butterfly away
> And walked away unknowingly.[12]

Would we even know if we were touched by God? Heinz Kohut, the developer of the field of self-psychology, wrote:

> The inner world cannot be observed with the aid of our sensory organs. Our thoughts, wishes, feelings, and fantasies cannot be seen, smelled, heard, or touched. They have no existence in physical space, and yet they are real, and we can observe them as they occur in time: through introspection in ourselves, and through empathy (i.e., vicarious introspection) in others.[13]

We are physical beings gifted with powerful senses, but we also transcend our physicality. To understand ourselves and others, we must go beyond the sensory level.

Touch is a human need. Babies want to nurse. Seniors need hugs. Every person, and animal, needs touch to feel a connection and to feel loved, albeit in different ways. It can provide a basic sense of security, even beyond affection and warmth. Of course, we also must be sensitive to the ethical boundaries of even basic casual touch, especially where there are dynamics of power at play.

The *melacha* of *memacheik* reminds us of how much we value the physical experience of touch, and "smooth touch" in particular. And yet, we are reminded that the physical senses can open the soul. And, at the same time, we recognize that the most sublime dimensions of human experience are indeed not sensory at all.

---

12. See Leonard W. Heflich, *Live as Long as You Dare! A Journey to Gain Healthy, Vibrant Years* (Bloomington, ID: iUniverse, 2008).

13. Heinz Kohut (ed. Paul H. Ornstein), *The Search for the Self: Selected Writings of Heinz Kohut 1950–1978* (New York: Routledge, 2011), 205–206.

31.
Mechateich (Cutting into strips)

THE THIRTY-FIRST MELACHA is *mechateich*, the cutting of an item to a specific desired size. In the *Mishkan*, one engaged in *mechateich* when cutting the animal skins to desired sizes to sew them into the coverings for the *Mishkan*'s structure. This *melacha* applies to all items with the exception of, as usual, food that will be eaten on Shabbat. This type of cutting involves using a tool in a normal manner. Cutting a piece of paper with scissors is problematic, as is cutting foil or plastic wrap on the built-in serrated blade. It is not about using one's hand.[1]

During the Exodus narrative, God is the primary actor and the Israelites are, in many ways, passive recipients of Divine directives. But with the construction of the *Mishkan*, there is a significant shift in agency and the Divine-human relationship. The Torah tells us that God appointed Betzalel as the architect – or maybe the general contractor? – of the *Mishkan* project. Bezalel was not simply to follow a Divine plan for its construction. Rather, the verse reads that Bezalel is *lachshov machashavot* – to think thoughts.[2] That is to say, while Bezalel was to follow a pre-designed plan, he was given license, even a mandate, to decide how to go about accomplishing this. The building of the *Mish-*

---

1. Cutting with one's hand, e.g., tearing, is the separate *melacha* of *korei'a* (the 24th *melacha*).
2. Exodus 35:22.

234

kan was to be a collaborative effort between Bezalel and God. Human beings are given license to consider how to accomplish the mission of representing the Divine on earth. Rabbi Jonathan Sacks writes:

> The *Mishkan* was the first thing the Israelites made in the wilderness, and it marks a turning point in the Exodus narrative. Until now God had done all the work. He had struck Egypt with plagues ... taken the people out to freedom ... divided the sea.... Now God instructed Moses ... to make something for Him. (But) this wasn't about God.... This was about humans and their dignity.... God gave the Israelites the chance to make something with their own hands, something they would value because ... *they had made it.*... For the first time God was asking them ... to be active: to become builders and creators....[3]

It's interesting to note the shift from brutal, monotonous slave labor to using those same skills to create beautiful things. Consider that an enslaved Hebrew might have to endure brutal, monotonous labor while creating beautiful things such as the Egyptian pyramids (or, as was the case for a French-trained chef, owned by Thomas Jefferson, culinary delights). A slave laborer – brutally beaten for the slightest mishap or perceived laxity – is much less likely to create the desired, beautiful product than one given the encouraging environment and space to do so.

The philosophical field of aesthetics emerged in the eighteenth century, and currently involves two major approaches: the philosophy of beauty and the philosophy of taste.

Initially, "taste" was something taken for granted as resolved through reason. One can objectively, perhaps rationally, determine what is aesthetically *good*. But then came "The Immediacy Thesis" which states that it is not through reason that something

---

3. Rabbi Jonathan Sacks, Covenant & Conversation, "Why We Value What We Make (Terumah 5778)," February 13, 2018.

is determined beautiful but rather through "taste" itself. Ratio-
nalists objected! They conceded that a meal would be "good"
based upon taste and not merely about reason. But not so a play
or a symphony. Whether a play is good is not merely about taste,
they said, but is also about higher rational judgments based on
reason. That is because a meal can be tasted and judged "immediately" whereas a play requires a process of reasoning that is not
accessible immediately. The Scottish philosopher David Hume
argued that "taste" in aesthetics is unlike the five external senses.
He explained that since it was an internal sense, it relied upon
existing operations in order for beauty to be seen, embraced,
and understood.

When experiencing art, should we experience it intellectually
or sensually? A brief review of modern art history reminds us
of how different thinkers have thought of this question. In the
eighteenth and nineteenth centuries, Romanticism grew, and art
shifted away from classical representation toward expression.
Moving into the twentieth century, there was a shift from expression toward abstraction and deeper appreciation of the form.
Further into the twentieth century, there was yet another shift
where abstraction was abandoned, and more philosophers agreed
that art should have no tight definition at all. This "de-definition"
of art, as suggested by philosopher Morris Weitz, was built off
earlier understandings of the philosophy of art and language
developed by the Austrian-British philosopher Ludwig Wittgenstein.

Let's look toward Indian philosophy, too often ignored in the
West. There is more to learn from Indian philosophy beyond
the most commonly quoted idea: *ahimsa* (the philosophy of
satyagraha, nonviolent resistance, popularized by Mahatma
Gandhi). Many different philosophies emerged from India – called
darshanas in Sanskrit – which include both Hindu philosophies
(from the orthodox schools[4]) and non-Hindu philosophies (from

---

4. Samkhya is the oldest of the orthodox philosophical schools suggesting

the heterodox schools). The Hindu schools draw philosophical principles from the ancient Hindu sacred text, the *Vedas*. One of the six *Astika* (orthodox) schools of Indian philosophical traditions is Yoga. In the second century, the Yoga sutras set the goal of Yoga to be the quieting of the mind in order to attain a detachment (*kaivalya*).[5] Another one of the schools was Nyaya which suggests a philosophy that learning knowledge (a system of logic) will lead to liberation from suffering. Other orthodox schools in Hinduism include *Vaisheshika*,[6] *Purva Mimamsa*, and *Vedanta*. Aside from the orthodox Hindu schools of Indian philosophy, four heterodox non-Hindu schools emerged such as *Carvaka* (developed on materialism, skepticism, and atheism).

We have often looked toward Western philosophy for Judaism's understanding and expansion, perhaps because influential Jewish thinkers lived in Europe, or were themselves influenced by non-Jewish Western thinkers. But the *Mishkan* was built in a desert on the border between the Western and Eastern worlds. Monotheism spread west with Christianity and Islam. Eastern spiritual traditions (of various theologies) continued to spread east. The study of aesthetics would be a great place to begin learning how to integrate from both hemispheres.

On our aesthetics-related theme of cutting, as it relates to historical traditions, consider this from American historian David Nirenberg's magisterial historical survey, *Anti-Judaism*:

My three-thousand-year history will perhaps offend most against the current conviction, as Michel Foucault famously

---

a dualistic philosophy that everything in reality emerges from *prakiti* (energy or matter) and from *purusha* (the soul). But unlike the typical Western versions of dualism of mind and matter, this is based on soul and energy, although there are certainly some similarities. Here one's total liberation is achieved once one knows the differences between the soul dispositions and matter.

5. The Yoga school draws upon the metaphysics and psychology of Samkhya.

6. 6th century BCE.

put in the late 1960s, "history is for cutting." That conviction is strong among historians of ideas, some of who go so far as to suggest that to guard against false continuities, we should treat texts and ideas – especially the most classical and seemingly enduring – as "speech-acts," their meaning to be interpreted only within the immediate historical context of their utterance.

Certainly, the task of cutting is critical: the mid-twentieth century, for example, experienced the depth of horror that can be produced when nations fantasize [about] their ancestry in the past. But no amount of cutting can eliminate the historian's need to generalize, that is, to create connections and continuities between non-identical things. And cutting also has its risks. In the sixteenth century, Montaigne mocked a similar tendency in his age, citing words of the ancient Roman philosopher Seneca: "Cut anything into tiny pieces and it all becomes a mass of confusion."[7] Nor are the risks only epistemological, for fantasies of freedom from the past can be as dangerous as fantasies of continuity with it.[8]

So how will we choose to "cut" and tape and glue, if you will, to construct a Jewish intellectual history? Who are the Jews? Who are *we* as Jews? And what are the sources of continuity? We have to ask that question because we must wonder who the Jews were 3,000 years ago, 2,000 years ago, 1,000 years ago, and even 100 years ago and today! How can we speak with authority about any ideas being uniquely Jewish, given how ideas evolve, and how they were, and are, so deeply influenced by surrounding cultures? And how many Jews, at every given time, had alternative perspectives and philosophies to the ideas that "won out" in the history books?

7. Seneca, Epistulae Morales 89.3, cited by Michel de Montaigne in "On Experience," in *The Essays: A Selection*, trans. M.A. Screech (London: Penguin Books, 2004), 3.13, 366.

8. David Nirenberg, *Anti-Judaism: The Western Tradition* (New York: W.W. Norton & Company, 2013), page 9.

There is an often-told story regarding cutting. Three men were employed as stone cutters. They were asked what they were doing: One said he was "cutting stone," one answered that he was "doing his job and earning a living," and the third responded that he was "building a palace."

The first two, we might imagine, were not so pleased with their monotonous, grueling work. The third, on the other hand, we can suspect was more invested and prouder, having zoomed out to perceive a great vision. So too with our own lives. Whether in any given context we function as leaders, as followers, or as observers, in order to imbue what we do or what we see with the meaning that it deserves, we must zoom out and tell the full grand story of who we are, from where we have come, and where we are headed. Yet, at the same time, that story must be honest, accessible, and engaging, and must at the same time account for our relationship with the collective.

When one is "cutting," some parts of the history, some dissenting voices, and some versions will inevitably need to be cut out. The actors must make hard choices to cultivate a collective vision. And historians must struggle with understanding it all.

How did Jews engage with Canaanites, Romans, Zoroastrians, Greeks, Indians, Spaniards, Poles, and Americans in the past? The story is, of course, complicated. But we will need to weave together a narrative and then cut some versions out. Just as important as *that* story, though, is the story of the future! Will it be filled with despair and cynicism? Will it be taught as a cyclical repeat of our past?

Or can we inspire a new chapter?

On Shabbat, we reflect on *mechateich*, on cutting and shaping. What parts of our personal narratives shape our respective current consciousnesses? What parts of our collective narrative (both national and Jewish) shape our future? On Shabbat, we learn to let go of what is holding us back and to re-commit to our most true principles, making them manifest in this fragile world with beauty and fortitude.

32.

Koteiv (Writing)

THE 32ND *MELACHA* is *koteiv* (writing). More specifically, according to the Talmudic rabbis, one only involves this *melacha* if they write two or more letters.[1] In the construction of the *Mishkan*, writing (and specifically writing two letters or numbers) was used to match corresponding planks and boards with one another. We might further say that one letter by itself is perhaps merely a squiggle, but two letters can form a word and have meaning. (It is worth noting that Hebrew has no one-letter words, whereas English and other languages do have words that contain one letter, such as "a" or "I.") On a rabbinic level, even writing one letter would be *koteiv*. Writing with foods (such as ketchup or icing) is not *koteiv*, as long as one intends to eat that food on Shabbat itself.

Language has always been complicated. We learn in the Torah about the power of language from the story of the Tower of Babel.[2] God seeks human unity but also wants diversity. But diversity without collaboration and respect leads to moral chaos. On the other hand, unity without diversity leads to tyranny – sometimes the tyranny of an individual tyrant and sometimes the tyranny of the majority – and the oppression of difference.

---

1. We've learned regarding previous *melachot*, e.g., *tofeir* (sewing), that two or more constitutes permanence.
2. Genesis 11:1–9.

In the story, this is symbolized through language. God wants us to work together but also to be different. The passage begins by informing us that all spoke only one language with few words. So, in response to the oppressive unity of the people of Babel, God "mixes up" their language, (Rashi understands this to be the origin of many different languages), and spreads humanity across the globe.[3] The Midrash asks the question: Why did God destroy the society of Sodom but only scattered the society building the Tower of Babel?[4] The answer given is that the people involved with the Tower of Babel demonstrated that they loved each other by speaking one language, so God didn't want to rid the world of them entirely and therefore God only scattered them. But the people of Sodom hated each other so God wanted to eliminate them from the world.

Indeed, it stands to reason that understanding each other can lead to love. And failing to understand one another can lead to fear and hate. Rabbi Jonathan Sacks explains the challenge of how different languages block us from communicating with one another:

> We often miss the significance of this word [*Shema*/listen] because of what I call the fallacy of translatability: the assumption that one language is fully translatable into another. We hear a word translated from one language to another and assume that it has the same meaning in both. But often it does not. Languages are only partially translatable into one another. The key terms of one civilization are often not fully reproducible in another. The Greek word megalopsychos, for example, Aristotle's "great-souled man" who is great and knows he is, carries himself with aristocratic pride, [and] is untranslatable into a moral system

---

3. The Torah itself informs us that the name "Babel" comes from the Hebrew root *bet-lamed-lamed*, meaning stirring and mixing up.
4. *Avot d'Rebbe Natan* 12:6.

like Judaism in which humility is a virtue. The English word "tact" has no precise equivalent in Hebrew. And so on.[5]

Famously and controversially, Rabbi Sacks also once wrote: "In the course of history, God has spoken to mankind in many languages: through Judaism to Jews, Christianity to Christians, Islam to Muslims."[6] One of the most complex dimensions of language is an attempt to explain Divinity or prove that there is a God.

There are three classical philosophical approaches to proving the existence of God:

1. Ontological Arguments – *a priori* abstract reasoning suggesting the necessity of a perfect Being
2. Cosmological Arguments – reasoning that there must be a First Mover
3. Teleological Arguments – reasoning that the order of the world and universe demonstrates that life (and all creation) was designated with a purpose by the Creator

Today, rather than offering proof, many speak of beauty and gratitude; they express their feeling that the world is just so beautiful and wonderful and that they need an address for their gratitude. Others talk about how they've experienced miraculous Divine help. A belief in God can also lead to optimism about the future and to a sense that life is sacred. But how is one to explain that in tangible terms? How can that be expressed in words? For some, the entire matter can't be discussed through a prism of objectivity but rather only through the human realm of subjectivity. This is to say that the realm of consciousness is

---

5. Jonathan Sacks, *Lessons in Leadership: A Weekly Reading of the Jewish Bible* (New Milford, Connecticut: Maggid Books, 2015), p. 251–252.

6. Rabbi Sacks was later pressured to retract this statement of religious pluralism.

far deeper and further reaching than the realm of language and cognition. According to Rambam (Maimonides) and his negative theology, we can't really say anything specific about God; Rather, we can only describe what God *is not*, i.e., God is not mortal and has no physical features. Rambam states expressly that any description of God's physicality, e.g., God's taking the Israelites out of Egypt with a strong hand, is strictly a metaphor.

While we can't find adequate language to prove the existence of God, perhaps more important than the question of whether we can believe in God is whether God can believe in us. More than focusing on any theological and philosophical concerns, we should be spiritually focused on the moral concern of how we are doing. In keeping with the need to move the question back to personal responsibility, the Kotzker Rebbe famously answered the question "Where is God?" with "Wherever we let God in!"

To the sages, more important than *believing* in God, is *loving* God. This idea is expressly stated in the opening of the *Shema* prayer. We are commanded: *V'ahavta eit Hashem Elokecha* – "You are to love God"[1] – there is no corresponding biblical mitzvah to believe in God. Love, as an emotion and a deed, can be more powerful than a faith statement or logical proof. It moves us toward experience. Consider this poem from Leonard Cohen, titled "Fun":

> It is so much fun
> to believe in God
> You must try it sometime
> Try it now
> and find out whether
> or not
> God wants you
> to believe in Him[2]

---

1. Deuteronomy 6:5.
2. Leonard Cohen, *Book of Longing* (Toronto, Ontario: McClelland &

Perhaps all of the language trying to explain God is merely a crutch that we find ourselves using even as we ultimately need to get beyond that point. We can use the idea of a personal God, a relatable God, an anthropocentric vision all expressed through human language, to realize that Divinity is beyond it all (this concept is referred to in *kabbalah* as *ein sof*, literally meaning "there is no end"). Our intellectual and spiritual lives cannot be reduced to purely physical terms. The physicalist-materialistic world view (that all reality is concrete) has major flaws, and thus any secular logical attempts to prove or disprove God through language is flawed. While Nietzsche famously proclaimed that "God is dead" he also wrote: "I am afraid we are not rid of God because we still have faith in grammar." We are very wedded to language as a means to communicate, to learn, and to pray.

Language is about ways to share a common experience of living in the world, of articulating a shared reflection of reality as it has been presented to us. Edmund Husserl (German philosopher and founder of phenomenology), in his 1931 book, *Ideas: A General Introduction to Pure Phenomenology*, argued that we must liberate ourselves from the captivity of the accepted world. We have come to see everything through an accepted filter of facts and truths and bracketed off most of reality and the depths of consciousness. But we can see more and experience more. Indeed, moving beyond convention and into the depths of subjective experience is the essence of spiritual seeking. We find ourselves so limited because we consider the options that have been presented to us. But, at every moment, there are multiple ways of being, multiple ways of engaging, multiple ways of leading. Before we can go deeper and even beyond the depths, we need to find our inner calm and turn off the noise. We must be aware of our inner turmoil and discover strategies to keep inner peace within these tense moments.

Before we can calm our broader emotional experience, we

Stewart, 2007), p.49.

will, perhaps, first need to overcome fear. Fear, like anger, is one
of the great barriers toward growth. What are the main steps to
overcoming fear?

1. Name the Resistance
2. Surrender
3. Welcome
4. Embrace/love

We can reopen choice for ourselves and disempower our small
inner voice of critic. We must stand tall and push out our inner
saboteur. Each of us is capable of moving beyond language,
conquering internal barriers, and going deeper.

Let's look to the East:

Buddhism is based on the Four Noble Truths (the truth of
suffering, the truth of the cause of suffering, the truth of the
end of suffering, and the truth of the path that frees one from
suffering). Buddhism suggests that in order to end suffering, one
must follow the Noble Eightfold Path.

In Jainism,[3] one of the most basic ideas is *anekantavada*, the
idea that different points of view perceive reality differently, and
therefore, there are no points of view that are fully true. Great
emphasis is placed on equality of life, spiritual independence,
nonviolence, and the fact that an individual's behavior has immediate consequences. In Jainism, self-control is crucial for one
to understand the soul's true nature.

Turning back to the West, let's consider Avicenna,[4] one of
the most influential philosophers of the Islamic Golden Age.
Avicenna presented an idea called "floating man," according to
which he described the immateriality of the soul. He encouraged
his students to imagine themselves suspended in the air. When
one hangs in the air, one will experience an isolation from one's

---

3. An ancient Indian religion, also known as Jain Dharma.
4. 980–1037 CE.

senses and not have sensory contact with one's own body. With the isolation from the senses, Avicenna argued that a person would still have consciousness. He believed that one couldn't logically prove a soul, but rather one needs to experiment to find it and experience it. Rambam read Avicenna and was influenced by him.[5]

Prof. Daniel Matt (a noted contemporary scholar of *kabbalah*) writes:

> The creative pool of nothingness is the "preconscious" [*kad-mut haseichel*], which precedes, surpasses, and inspires both language and thought. Of this, [Rabbi] Dov Ber [of Mezritch] said, "Thought requires the preconscious, which rouses thought to think. The preconscious cannot be grasped. Thought is con-tained in letters, which are vessels, while the preconscious is beyond the letters, beyond the capacity of the vessels. This is the meaning of the verse (Job 28:12): "Wisdom emerges out of nothingness (*Or ha-Emet*, 15a)."[6]

The preconscious here can be imagined as the fetal pre-birth experience. Or for God, as the primordial creation of Divine solitude before there is an "other." God's self-consciousness, so to speak, might emerge out of creation of an "other."

One other way to understand this is through the idea that communication is about far more than just the words we speak. Albert Mehrabian (contemporary psychologist and pioneer in the field of nonverbal communication) offered the 7%–38%–55% Rule. His research showed that only 7 percent of our feelings and attitudes are conveyed through our words.[7] The tone of our voice

---

5. In his "Letter to Shmuel ibn Tibbon," Rambam refers to Avicenna as Ali ibn Sina. (Shalit ed. 2.553). Often when Rambam wrote in Arabic, he wrote it in Hebrew letters.

6. Daniel C. Matt, *God & The Big Bang* (Vermont: Jewish Lights Publish-ing, 2015), p. 61.

7. Albert Mehrabian, *Silent Messages: Implicit Communication of Emotions*

constitutes 38 percent of the communication, while 55 percent is conveyed by body language. In fact, communication happens in subtle and meaningful ways, beyond words. So, too, the soul and human consciousness at large perceive far more than the limited messages that words can convey.

Then we look at some stories in religious texts that appear fantastical, perhaps even absurd, and we wonder what they're doing there. Rabbi Dr. Arthur Green (contemporary scholar of Jewish mysticism) writes:

> I know that religious language is not just a collection of stories, but an attempt to put into narrative form a truth so profound that it cannot be told except when dressed in the garb of narration.[8]

The Chassidic teachers share that we live in an *olam sheker* (world of lies) that masks a deeper reality. Our spiritual work is to see beyond the garments on the surface. This is why it is an honor to receive *gelila* and wrap the Torah after it is read. We are reminded that to receive Torah, we must see past the wrappings. And yet, we also witness the power of dressing the Torah again to reverently preserve the sanctity. Consider the mitzvah of the *chevra kaddishah* to give the final dressing to a deceased person to honor their body and life while also acknowledging that the soul, beyond the body, is the true seat of consciousness.

Rabbi Binyamin Lau (noted contemporary Israeli thinker and activist) writes about the Sages' engagement with language:

> Better in his eyes was a single measure of reflection on what is written and given than massive speculation above and beyond to the very limits of apprehension. One who sees Rabbi Yishmael in

---

and Attitudes. (California: Wadsworth Pub. Co., 1981), p. 76.

8. Arthur Green, *Seek My Face: A Jewish Mystical Theology* (Woodstock, Vermont: Jewish Lights, 2003), p. xxii.

a dream should "anticipate wisdom:" Rabbi Yishmael's teachings contained straightforward logic, and with it, lucidity, simplicity of language, and an aversion to intellectual games. Attributions to him have no superfluity of language or florid expressions. He sought to strip Scripture of anthropomorphisms and to excise unnecessary metaphor and imagery. But Rabbi Akiva's teachings sought to penetrate to inner depths with profundity and potency of language. He did not shrink from anthropomorphism, but rather he preserved the concrete in Scripture, cherished imaginative meanings, added metaphorical embellishments, and created images of the supernal world.[9]

On Shabbat, we are encouraged to use verbal language (conversations, reading, praying, learning) but we are invited to consider a new relationship to writing. Through the process of writing, we create a lasting form of communication. Written language is positively transformative, but can also be deeply hurtful and damaging to others. This is all the more true in our age of interconnectedness where, on social media and beyond, words are not only saved and stored but can go viral. May we always choose our words so carefully, understanding that they can never adequately describe the full truth but also, nonetheless, how much they can affect others.

In doing so, we'll learn not only to be more cautious with our words but also how to listen (and read) more carefully. Martin Luther King Jr. said: "A riot is the language of the unheard." When we don't listen to others who need to be heard, moral complaints will grow. In learning to listen to the language that comes from our depths, we can learn to listen to others. Doing so is not only spiritually rewarding but also morally necessary.

There is a *chassidishe vort* (teaching) that one of *the shivim panim laTorah* (70 "faces" of the Torah) is not *panim mamash* (actual face or expression) but rather *shetika* (silence). It's worth

---

9. Binyamin Lau, *The Sages* (Jerusalem: Koren Publishers, 2010), 218.

thinking about what it means to be in a covenantal revelatory moral relationship through silence. How is it responsible not to be heard through the word? How is it healthy not to be understood through the limited human channel of language?

With all of that said, I think that communication by silence is mainly for God. I think we should exercise "silence as resistance" with great caution since silence has the potential to be political and politically dangerous. While committing to *shemirat ha'lashon* (the ethics of speech), I think speaking out in resistance (even slightly too much and even slightly with imperfection), when the moral stakes are high, is often more in line with Jewish values than waiting for perfect speech to bubble forth, often time in the privilege of our silence. There is, of course, a time for silence. But each of us must learn the art of emerging and retreating. The *avodah* (spiritual growth curriculum) is different for each of us.

The *melacha* of *koteiv*, then, reminds us to be mindful of not only our oral speech but also our written word. Reflecting on writing on Shabbat allows us to take a step back and contemplate the writing we have engaged in during the past week and will again do so in the coming week. *Koteiv* is the reminder we all need to choose carefully when to be silent and when, and how, to speak up.

33.

Mocheik (Erasing)

T HE PREVIOUS *MELACHA* looked at the ethical dimensions
of writing two or more letters. The *melacha* we want to
focus on now, *mocheik*, is about erasing in order to write
more. To be biblically culpable, one must erase two or more letters. The Talmud, interestingly, indicates that this *melacha* applies
to erasing even one letter if there was space for two letters to be
drawn in its place.[1]

Let's step back for a moment: What does it mean to erase?
Does it mean the complete denial of something that previously
existed? Sometimes our memories can be erased for better or
worse. Consider Rav Kook's suggestion in connection with the
Exodus from Egypt:

> God wanted the Israelites to leave with a sense that some of
> the debt had been settled, so that part of the stigma of slavery
> would be erased and they could leave without a deep sense of
> hatred and rage.[2]

To transcend toxic emotions, we sometimes need to erase the
full emotional impact of past hurt. We acknowledge that evil, or

---

1. BT, Shabbat 75b.
2. Rabbi Avraham Yitzchak Hakohen Kook in his *Haggadah Commentary*,
page 85.

simple misdirection, is real in the world, and we wish and work to erase it from the earth. We read in Psalms: "The eyes of God are on the righteous, God's ears attentive to their cry. The face of God is set against evildoers, to erase their names from the earth."[3] Some evil is simply so unbearable that it must be erased. We say *yemak shemo* about the chief Nazi – "May his name be erased" with this language of *mocheik*.

But erasing is not only something that we do to ourselves and to our memories. One can erase others, sometimes even violently. Consider this rabbinic teaching:

> Rabbi Akiva says: One who sheds blood erases the likeness [of God], as it says: "One who sheds human blood, by humans their blood shall be shed, for in the image of God, God made humankind" (Genesis 9:6).

The Maharal (16th century, Poland and Prague)[4] writes about how this type of erasing applies to the process of shaming as well:

> But what (the Talmud) said, whoever shames their fellow it is as if they shed blood, this is something inner, because one who shames one's friend it is that they are extinguishing the light of the face, which is the human being, as if they were extinguishing a candle, and this is called shedding the blood of a person, for this *tzelem* (image) has a most wonderful thing, ... that it is the form of the human being, and therefore one who shames (whitens) and nullifies the *tzelem* of the face (of his friend) until they whiten it and extinguishes its light ... For shedding of blood is nothing but the nullification of the person, and one who whitens (shames) the face of the other, they erase that through which the

---

3. Psalms 34:16–17.

4. Maharal (Rabbi Yehuda ben Bezalel Loew) served as the rabbi of Mikulov, Moravia and Prague, Czechoslovakia. He is perhaps best known for the legend of his creation of the Golem of Prague, an animated creature formed of clay.

person is recognized, their *tzelem*, and this is the erasure of the person as well, because the *tzelem* is the person....[5]

Through shame, one can feel marginalized, which is a social form of erasure. And so, indeed, the *image* of God ethically takes precedence over the *name* of God. One of the 613 *mitzvot* is the prohibition not to erase holy writings or written names of God.[6] The gemara lists several Divine names that we are forbidden to erase. It then lists several other names, such as *chanun* (compassionate) and *rachum* (merciful), which although they are often used in reference to God, do not contain any particular holiness and may be erased.[7] Even given the importance of the unerasable names of God, Rambam writes:

> If such a poor person has to choose between oil for both a house lamp [on the Sabbath] and a Chanukah lamp, or oil for a house lamp [on the Sabbath] and wine for *kiddush*, the house lamp should have priority, for the sake of peace in the household, seeing that even a Divine name might be erased to make peace between husband and wife.[8]
>
> Great indeed is peace, inasmuch as the purpose for which the whole of the Torah was given is to bring peace upon the world, as it is said, "Its ways are ways of pleasantness, and all its paths are peace" (Prov. 3:17).[9]

---

5. Ben Bezalel, Judah Loew. "Path of Love of your Friends." *The Pathways of the World*. https://www.sefaria.org/Netivot_Olam.

6. *Sefer Hachinuch*, mitzvah 437.

7. BT Shevuot 35a. This is so perhaps because the terms *chanun* and *rachum* aren't necessarily names per se, but are rather descriptives of God.

8. Indeed, the very reason for lighting Shabbat candles is for *shalom bayit* (piece in the home). Consider, of course, that pre-electricity, people would have often sat in the dark if not for the use of Shabbat candles.

9. Mishneh Torah, *Hilchot Megillat Esther v'Chanukah*, 4:14. Also see *Derech Eretz Zuta*, chapter Perek Ha'Shalom 11:9: "Said R. Yishmael: Great is peace, for we find that the Holy One blessed be He conceded that His name,

We feel guilt when we go through a spiritual evolution, as if we are erasing a part of our past projection of God. We can feel like we have betrayed God in some way. But this can be a mistake because our sense of guilt might form a barrier to religious and spiritual growth. In some sense, we may need to "erase" God from our hearts to give birth to a new consciousness of divinity.

What would it mean for Torah to be erased? In the Jewish tradition, we don't erase ideas we disagree with. Rather, we debate them, record them, learn them, even limit their application, and sometimes even denounce them.[10] Torah can only be erased in death. This is best expressed by the Talmudic view that one is no longer obligated in *mitzvot* upon death.

> The Sages taught in a *baraita*: With regard to a garment in which diverse kinds, a prohibited mixture of wool and linen, was lost, i.e., it is a wool garment into which a linen thread was sewn or vice versa and it is not known where on the garment the thread is located, one may not sell it to a gentile and one may not even fashion it into a saddlecloth for a donkey. This is prohibited lest one remove a piece of the garment and sew it onto his own clothing. But one may fashion it into a shroud for a corpse, as there is no concern that one might remove it from the dead. Rav Yosef said: That is to say that the *mitzvot* will be nullified in the future. If this were not the case, then when the dead are resurrected, they will be deriving benefit from the garment of diverse kinds in which they were buried.... Once a person dies, he becomes *chofshi min hamitzvot* (free from the [performance of] *mitzvot*).[11]

It is as if the *mitzvot* have been erased for someone as they are elevated to the heavens. But this position goes even further,

---

that is written in holiness, be erased in the water, in order to bring peace between a man and his wife."

10. Of course, the denouncing of ideas is not applicable to mitzvot of the Torah itself.

11. BT, Niddah 61b.

suggesting that the *mitzvot* are not eternal. Maimonides later rejects this view, suggesting that in the messianic era, not only will *mitzvot* not be erased but even more *mitzvot* will be restored (which could not heretofore be observed in exile).[12] Moreover, he suggests that belief in the eternity of the Torah and *mitzvot* is one of his 13 essential tenets of faith. For the Rambam, *mitzvot* cannot be erased.

But, indeed, erasing can be a sign of maturity. In Pirkei Avot, we learn:

> Elisha ben Avuya said: "One who studies Torah as a child, to what can they be likened? To ink written on fresh paper. And one who studies Torah as an old person, to what can they be likened? To ink written on smudged paper."[13]

Smudged paper could be understood as paper that has been corrected through erasing. One may write with a high degree of intellectual confidence, represented in the sharp clear mark of a fine pen. But one with more uncertainty, and perhaps humility, writes with a pencil so they can correct, change, and erase. A "smudged paper" is not merely the ragged page of the aged but rather the sign of a humble introspective life.

For another example, let's look at the work *Erased de Kooning Drawing*, "created" by the artist Robert Rauschenberg in 1953. Rauschenberg was part of a collective of artists who formed the New York Avant-Garde scene in the mid-twentieth century. Along with his contemporaries, such as Jasper Johns, Rauschenberg tried to expand what art meant via deconstruction. The starkest example of that is the work, *Erased de Kooning Drawing*. The title is literal. Rauschenberg, an admirer of Willem De Kooning, an abstract expressionist, took a painting that De Kooning had worked on and, using an eraser, stripped the art

---

12. Hilchot Melachim 11:1.
13. Pirkei Avot 4:25.

back to its bare canvas. In the final piece, "Rauschenberg set out to discover whether an artwork could be produced entirely through erasure – an act focused on the removal of marks rather than their accumulation."[14] Rauschenberg literally went to the home of de Kooning and erased his art to make a profound, albeit transgressive, statement about the nature of art.

Indeed, when we engage in *teshuvah* (repentance), we are attempting to erase our mistakes of the past. But we also realize that we are an ever-evolving spiritual canvas. While our past mistakes can never be erased from history – the smudges will always remain – repair is possible, and the beauty of what is underneath becomes real. This is why Benei Yisrael carry the broken *luchot* (tablets) along with the new fresh tablets. We bring all of ourselves into our spiritual service in the world. We don't erase parts of our history or memory that we simply disapprove of. To be sure, sometimes, to help we need to work to forget. Other times, like in psychoanalysis, we seek to un-erase the hurt of one's unconscious youth to re-explore it. Or for some with PTSD, they need to (through virtual reality or another way) re-emerge into the trauma in order to find themselves safe again. Here, in therapy, we are not seeking erasure but transformation.

So why on Shabbat Zachor are we commanded to remember the mitzvah to erase the name of Amalek? If we want to forget the name, then we shouldn't be commanded to remember the mitzvah to blot out the name, right? Here, we learn that erasing doesn't mean something about passive memory. Rather, it is about actively uprooting an evil in the world. To erase or blot out the name of Amalek means to remember that it's always here and always needs to be contended with. We say "Never again" to remember what we must blot out in our day.

On Shabbat, we reflect on how we erase and correct in the world. In some ways, might we be erasing others? Canceling others? In what way might we work to erase ideas or memories

---

14. https://www.sfmoma.org/artwork/98.298/.

from our consciousness in order to evolve from them? But we must remember, erasing is not enough. The *melacha* of *mocheik* is not about mere erasing, but erasing in order to write. When we erase, we must also prepare for new creativity to emerge onto our own life page.

34.
Boneh (Building)

WHILE THE LAST two *melachot* were about the creation and destruction of lines on paper, the thirty-fourth *melacha* is *boneh* (building), which involves the creation or assembling of a structure. Building perhaps seems like the most obvious *melacha* of Shabbat, given that the *melachot*, by definition, are the very same activities that were used in the building and construction of the *Mishkan*, and given how inherent physical labor is to the enterprise. On a practical level, playing with interlocking building blocks would be forbidden. Non-locking blocks, such as plain wooden building blocks and games involving stacking blocks, are not problematic, as long as one intends the building to be merely temporary.[1]

God built the world, which resulted in what we see, feel, and hear all around us. But, as we also know, God rested. While the world was complete, the human being – the apotheosis of Creation itself – was left incomplete. That final decision to rest gives us a profound insight into the Divine mind: God passed on the task of completing this fragile world to each and every person. Consider this fascinating passage in the *Zohar*:

> R. Yohanan said: Why were people created in the image of God? As it says, "God created humans in [God's] image" – it

---

1. Similarly, word-building games such as Scrabble are not *boneh* if one intends to dismantle the game shortly after its conclusion.

is like a king who ruled his kingdom and built small fortresses and repaired works in the city, and all the members of the city were subjugated to him. One day, the king called to all the city dwellers and appointed his minister over them. He said: "Until now, I would see to all the needs of the city and build towers and fortresses; from now on, [the city resident] will be as I am."[1]

As humans created in the image of God, we have been endowed magisterially with the holy responsibility to be in "palaces," a responsibility to use the structures we build for holy purposes. We are not to overuse the glorious world we have been given by being gluttons or spendthrifts, or otherwise wasting what we have. Instead, we are tasked to look after the world and to care for creation. Consider why Abraham built mansions:

> Abraham ... would go forth and make his rounds, and wherever he found travelers, he would bring them to his house. To the one who was accustomed to eating wheat bread, he gave wheat bread to eat. To the one who was accustomed to eating meat, he gave meat to eat. To the one who was accustomed to drinking wine, he gave wine to drink. Moreover, he built stately mansions on the highways and left food and drink there so that every traveler stopped there and thanked God. That is why delight of the spirit was vouchsafed to him. And whatever one might ask for was to be found in Abraham's home.[2]

Sadly, materialism rules the world, and many people seem to care more about the palaces than about peering out from their turrets upon meaningful responsibility. Consider the Midrash that says that when a worker from the Tower of Babel would fall no one cared, but when a brick fell the builders wept. We can build cold towers of isolation or we can build bridges of

1. *Zohar Haddash I* [Torah], Parashat Bereishit 2a.
2. *Avot d'Rabbi Natan* 7.

empathy and compassionate understanding. We need, of course, to strive for elevated motives for all that we build. The Rabbis famously record:

> "And behold it was very good" (Genesis 1:31). This [refers to the] evil inclination. But is the evil inclination very good? How strange! However, were it not for the evil inclination, a man wouldn't build a house, wouldn't marry, wouldn't procreate, and wouldn't engage in business.[3]

Indeed, self-interest accompanies higher motives when we are building a home and building the world.

What kinds of structures do we wish to build in the world? Rav Kook writes:

> For the building is constructed from various parts, and the truth of the light of the world will be built from various dimensions, from various approaches, for these and those are the words of the living God.... It is precisely the multiplicity of opinions which derive from variegated souls and backgrounds which enriches wisdom and brings about its enlargement. In the end, all matters will be properly understood, and it will be recognized that it was impossible for the structure of peace to be built without those trends which appeared to be in conflict.[4]

Rav Kook teaches that to have a structure of peace, it must be built upon the foundations of conflict. This is to say that only by embracing the messiness of real-life can we achieve a sustainable peace. Healthy relationships of course entail disagreements, but disagreements where all parties are treated with dignity; we work to build a safe and more peaceful world. To do so, we must often

---

3. Bereshit Rabbah 9:7.
4. Rabbi Abraham Isaac Kook, *Olat Raya*, vol. I, p. 330.

embrace conflicts to advance societal progress. This is not only work for us but for our children.

The Talmud teaches that "sages increase peace in the world,"[5] but Rav Kook explains that they only increase peace through argumentation. Commenting on the verse *V'chol banayich limudei Hashem, v'rav shelom banayich* ("All your children are learned of God, and great is the peace of your children"), this Talmudic passage instructs us to read the word *banayich* ("your children") as *bonayich* ("your builders").[6] Our children will have peace as the builders of a new world where earlier conflicts have been surpassed. These children are the dreamers and the idealists we need to shatter our skepticism, or, God forbid, our cynicism.

What children so often don't understand, however, is how to transition from being mere receivers to becoming builders. Learning how to transition takes years of experience. When I entered adulthood, I knew a lot about change (entering into new situations, new contexts), but I knew little about transitions (the psychological process of adapting to change). The most important step I didn't know about was how we need to mourn and to let go of the past before we can adequately start to adapt to the future. I wish I knew that when I switched from an earlier childhood interfaith mindset to an immersed Jewish context. And I wish I knew that when my family hit major immediate financial hardship and when my parents got divorced. I needed to learn to mourn a certain type of family model I once took for granted. I needed to learn how to let go of a past type of stability.

I wish I knew that when I celebrated the birth of my first child. I thought it was pure joy, but I hadn't yet let go of an identity, an early marriage lifestyle that I knew so well.

We often think that growth means we need to change. But it is more; we need not only to change (behaviorally and intellectually) but to transition (psychologically).

---

5. BT Berachot 64a.
6. "Builders" is a euphemism for sages.

In a book called *Managing Transitions*, the authors write: "Chaos is not a mess, but rather it is the primal state of pure energy to which the person returns for every true new beginning."[7]

Indeed, we don't achieve a state of peace and then remain there. Rather, in each major transition, we return to chaos, a chaos of "pure energy." The authors write that there are three phases of transition:

1. Letting go of the old ways and the old identity people had. This first phase of transition is an ending and the time when you need to help people to deal with their losses.
2. Going through an in-between time when the old is gone but the new isn't fully operational. We call this time the "neutral zone": it's when the critical psychological realignment and repatterning take place.
3. Coming out of the transition and making a new beginning. This is when people develop the new identity, experience the new energy, and discover the new sense of purpose that makes the change begin to work.[8]

When we discover this new energy, we reignite our sense of purpose. Antoine de Saint-Exupery said, "If you want to build a ship, don't drum up people together to collect wood and don't assign them tasks and work, but rather *teach them to long for the endless immensity of the sea.*"

We will build a future by transcending our resentments and anger of the past. Rabbi Jonathan Sacks wrote:

> I cannot build the future on the hatreds of the past, nor can I teach them [the children] to love God more by loving people less.... The duty I owe my ancestors who died because of their

7. William Bridges, PhD with Susan Bridges, *Managing Transitions: Making the Most of Change* (New York: Hatchette Books, 2017), page 14.
8. Ibid., page 5.

faith is to build a world in which people no longer die because of their faith. I honor the past not by repeating it but by learning from it – by refusing to add pain to pain, grief to grief. That is why we must answer hatred with love, violence with peace, resentment with generosity of spirit and conflict with reconciliation.[9]

This is not just a sweet idea about how we build the future but actually a codified Jewish law about building. The Talmud records a fascinating disagreement:

> The Rabbis taught: If a person wrongfully takes a beam and builds it into a palace, Beit Shammai says that they must demolish the whole palace and restore the beam to its owner. Beit Hillel, however, says that the latter can claim only the monetary value of the beam, so as not to place obstacles in the way of penitents.[10]

The practical Jewish law followed Hillel, as usual:

> According to the letter of the law, whoever steals is required to return the stolen object itself, for it is said, "they would restore the robbed item which they robbed"[11] ... even if they stole a beam and built it into a large mansion ... biblical law would require that they destroy the entire building and return the beam to its owner; but the Sages instituted, as an ordinance for the

---

9. Rabbi Jonathan Sacks, *The Dignity of Difference: How to Avoid the Clash of Civilizations* (London/New York: Continuum, revised edition 2003), 190.

10. Babylonian Talmud, Gittin 55a. The notion here is that the Talmudic sages were concerned that if this individual were indeed required to demolish the entire structure, he would not bother to do so, and would thus not repent and replace the misappropriated item.

11. Leviticus 5:23.

penitents, that they should repay the value of the beam and not forfeit the entire building.[12]

To build a more just society, we cannot destroy those who make mistakes. We need to make it possible for everyone to engage in *teshuvah*, moral growth.

Traditionally, we refer to God three times a day in the *Amidah* prayer[13] as the *Boneh Yerushalayim* ("Builder of Jerusalem"). Indeed, we are partners in that holy work. Today, on the one hand, we need to be builders and guardians of Jerusalem, and at the same time guardians of the idea of Jerusalem. We have to physically build the earthly Jerusalem, and keep alive the power, energy, and uniqueness of the heavenly Jerusalem.

Building is not only about expanding but also about protecting. Consider the Torah commandment to build an enclosure around the roof of a house so that no one falls from it. Part of building is about securing as we build. This notion is also true as we build the future of Torah life. We do not merely confine and conserve. Rather, when we encounter new ideas, we often have the opportunity to expand upon the Torah. Rav Kook put it best:

> We should not immediately refute any idea which comes to contradict anything in the Torah, but rather we should build the palace of Torah above it.[14]

We don't enter the world with fear but rather with an eagerness to learn and to serve. It can be much harder to rebuild than to build. Often, when a structure doesn't work, we seek to dismantle it and then try to build anew. It can be exciting to escape and to build anew but this can also be an easy way out. To rebuild is not

---

12. Shulchan Aruch, *Choshen Mishpat* 360:1.

13. The *Amidah* prayer is the formal name for the silent meditation known as *Shemoneh Esrei*. The word *amidah* literally means standing, as one typically stands when reciting this prayer.

14. *Iggerot*, 134.

to abandon a project we are committed to but to work through adjustments, repairs, and evolutions as is needed.

As it says in Psalms 89:3, *Olam chesed yibaneh* ("The world shall be built of love"). Rabbi Yehuda HaChasid wrote: "I will build an altar from the broken fragments of my heart." Indeed, building involves pain and tears. But it is precisely from this toil and purpose of life that we will bring our ultimate offering, our truest contribution: cultivating lives of service to peace and love so that this world will no longer experience hate, fear, and needless conflict. The *melacha* of *boneh* calls upon us to build accordingly.

35.

Soteir (Destroying)

THE THIRTY-FIFTH *MELACHA* is *soteir* (destroying), and specifically refers to the act of destroying built structures in order to build new ones. It is directly related to our previous *melacha* of *boneh* (building) in that anything that was put together in a way that constituted *boneh* could potentially be destroyed in a way that would be called *soteir*. If one destroys something *shelo al menat livnot* (not in order to rebuild), then it would not be the biblical *melacha* of *soteir*, but would rather fall within the category of rabbinic destruction referred to as *mekalkeil* (ruining). In fact, *mekalkeil* is at times not a halakhic problem. For example, some *poskim* (halachic decisors) feel that opening a food or drink container on Shabbat is problematic, yet permit it if one opens the container in such a way that it is now destroyed and no longer usable.[1]

There is another biblical prohibition of destruction not limited to Shabbat called *bal tashchit* ("do not destroy").[2] The Sefer HaChinuch explains:

---

1. For example, opening the container from both ends. In this case, rabbinic *soteir* (*mekalkeil*) allows one to engage in an otherwise forbidden activity.

2. The term *bal* is Aramaic for the Hebrew *lo* or *al*, meaning "don't." This name for the prohibition to destroy is derived from the verse (Deuteronomy 20:19) which forbids one to chop down a fruit tree during war. This prohibition is not limited, however, to fruit trees, and applies to destroying all food, and even other items, unless necessary. In the context, non-fruit-bearing trees are

It is likewise included under this negative precept not to cause any damage or loss: for instance, to set fire, tear clothing, or break a vessel for no purpose....

The root reason for the precept is known: for it is in order to train our spirits to love what is good and beneficial and cling to it; and as a result, good fortune will cling to us, and we will move well away from every evil thing and from every matter of destructiveness. This is the way of the kindly people of piety and the conscientiously observant; they love peace and they are happy at the good fortune of people, and bring them near the Torah. They will not destroy even a mustard seed in the world, and they are distressed at every ruination and spoilage that they see; and if they are able to do any rescuing, they will save anything from destruction, with all their power.[3]

It is hard, in our time of mass consumerism and constant transactions, to remove ourselves from destruction. And yet, we are called upon to re-sensitize ourselves to this. Rabbi Moshe Cordovero, known as the Ramak, teaches that:

One's compassion should extend to all creatures, and one should neither despise nor destroy them, for the wisdom above extends to all of creation – inanimate objects, plants, animals, and humans.

Even further, we should consider the need to avoid unnecessary destruction not only as a matter of personal responsibility. Indeed, we should also exercise empathy, taking account of how others feel when their objects have been destroyed. Rabbi Yisrael Salanter, the founder of the *mussar* movement, teaches that when

indeed permissible to chop down in order to create a fortress, as it serves a necessary function.

3. Mitzvah 529. Translation taken from Rabbi Charles Wengrov, *Sefer haHinnuch* (New York: Feldheim, 1984).

a child's toy breaks, we should assume the child feels as bad as an adult would feel if his or her factory were destroyed.

There has been so much destruction in the past – and that occurs in the present – that it is difficult to know how or where to rebuild.

The late Adrienne Rich (1929–2012) offers us this meaningful poem:

> My heart is moved by all I cannot save:
> so much has been destroyed.
> I have to cast my lot with those
> who age after age, perversely,
> with no extraordinary power,
> reconstitute the world.[4]

While we can't stop all destruction, the most important choice for us is to be on the side of rebuilding. This is not easy.

Throughout history, many have tried to destroy the Jewish people. Consider that the Arch of Titus in Rome, which was built as a moment to celebrate the destruction of Jerusalem in the first century CE. According to leading archaeologists, the first record of the Jewish people in history (outside of the Torah's accounting) is in the Merneptah Stele which contains a text about an Egyptian Pharoah dating from the thirteenth century BCE. It states: "Israel is laid waste – his seed is no more." This first allusion to Jews in history boasts that they are destroyed. Indeed, one way to tell the Jewish story is through the various attempts of nations obsessed with *soteir*. Only by destroying the eternal "Chosen People" could a nation view itself as truly victorious.

Consider the national catastrophe for the Jewish people found in the destruction of the Second Temple. How do we rebuild from that?

---

4. Adrienne Rich, *The Dream of a Common Language: Poems 1974–1977* (New York: W.W. Norton, 2013).

At the beginning of his book *Community of Faith*, Rabbi Jonathan Sacks writes:

> A Jewish legend says that when the Temple was destroyed splinters from its stones entered the hearts of the Jewish people. When they gathered as Knesset Yisrael, the congregation of Israel united across space and time in the collective service of God, they became a kind of human Temple and in their lives the Divine presence found its earthly home.[5]

Sometimes we rebuild something exactly as it was before it was destroyed. Other times we build something new in place of what once stood (consider the Twin Towers). Concerning the Temple, while many yearn for a third, permanent one, let's consider how we can rebuild a less lofty holy space in the meantime until the final Redemption takes place.

Sometimes, we are so filled with righteous indignation that we end up bringing more heat than light to a situation. Consider how Rashbi[6] and his son left the loving mystical experiences of the cave only with fury at commoners and a desire to destroy them:

> [Rashbi and his son] went out and they saw men plowing and sowing. They said, "They forsake *hayei olam* (eternal life) and busy themselves with *hayei sha'ah* (temporal life)?!" Every place they turned their eyes [in disapproval] was immediately burned. A heavenly voice went out and said to them, "Did you go out to destroy My world?! Return to your cave!"[7]

---

5. The source is by Hakham Moses Gaster – Sephardic chief rabbi of London in "Great Britain, Palestine and the Jews: Jewry's Celebration of Its National Charter," Jan. 1918. It seems to be a celebration of the Balfour declaration.

Jonathan Sacks, *Community of Faith* (London, United Kingdom: Halban, 1995), cites Barbara Tuchman's 2011 *Bible and Sword: England and Palestine from the Bronze Age to Balfour* where she quotes Hakham Gaster.

6. Rashbi is an acronym for Rabbi Shimon bar Yochai.

7. BT *Shabbat* 33b–34a.

It is challenging to be loud enough, yet not too loud, in our advocacy to create change. The Talmudic rabbis imagine that God had this problem too:

> We read in the Midrash: Rabbi Yehuda bar Nechemia said that since Moses was a beginner when it came to hearing God's word, the Holy One reasoned: "If I reveal myself to him in My awesome voice, I run the risk of destroying him. On the other hand, if I speak with a soft voice, he will regard My word as trivial."[8]

Here, we strive to learn how to be both courageous yet humble, to be bold yet quiet, to be fierce yet gentle. This is also true in the halachic tradition. We wish to prohibit all that is bad but also to be honest and measured. Consider the Maharshal's[9] view on that which is morally disgusting but not technically halachically forbidden:

> If a behavior is halachically permissible, but regarded by distinguished rabbis as destructive either personally or communally, it must be presented as such, but not as halachically prohibited. To do so would be akin to heresy in terms of the Maharshal's view.[10]

Of course, there are limited cases where destruction may be necessary. Consider God's flooding of the world or God's destruction of Sodom for being purely wicked. But those are for God to decide; we are called to restraint.

On Shabbat, we have the spiritual opportunity to reflect not only on how we build but also on how we destroy. We can de-

---

8. Exodus Rabba 45:5.

9. Maharshal is an acronym for Rabbi Shlomo Luria, a 16th-century Polish halachist.

10. *Yam Shel Shlomo* to tractate Baba Kama, as recorded by Berel Wein and Warren Goldstein, *The Legacy: Teachings for Life from the Great Lithuanian Rabbis* (New York: Maggid, 2012), 112–113.

stroy dignity with cruel words. We can destroy self-esteem with neglect of others. We can destroy, as a society, another country through military hawkism. We can destroy the planet through overconsumption, waste, and greed. It is not easy to remove oneself from being complicit in this *melacha* of *soteir*, but the first step on Shabbat is coming to realize this reality and contemplating one's own means of engaging in the act of *boneh*, and at the same time fine-tuning one's, at-times, necessary *soteir*.

We can reflect on the spirituality of disassembling. The *melacha* of *soteir* was about disassembling the *Mishkan* in order to travel and then stop and reassemble. So, too, in our lives today, we frequently have to disassemble. Consider our tasks of cleaning up the dinner table after a meal is done, or folding laundry once again. These tasks can be tiring and monotonous. But, through the lens of *soteir*, we can recharge through these tasks by engaging mindfulness. On Shabbat, we can reflect on the meaning of our disassembly in order to reassemble in the coming week.

36.

Mechabeh (Extinguishing)

THE THIRTY-SIXTH MELACHA is *mechabeh*, extinguishing
a flame. In the *Mishkan*, extinguishing was done in order
to make charcoal. And so, flames were not to be doused
or even decreased on Shabbat. While the above example entails
extinguishing for a constructive purpose, *mechabeh* includes
extinguishing even for its own sake. Modern-day applications
are turning off an electric light[1] and the ignition of a car.

How are lights relevant to the Jewish experience today? Jewish
life is about sparks. With each encounter, we have the chance to
ignite or to extinguish, to create or to destroy. This idea is the
secret to Jewish resilience. We must never lose hope. On Shabbat,
we reflect on extinguishing light to be sure we are correcting our
path so that we never remove light from the world or add un-
wanted darkness. This starts with the realization and recognition
of our own inner light. As the distinguished poet Maya Angelou
writes: "Nothing can dim the light that shines from within."

Rabbi Shlomo Wolbe writes:

> If not for the night, we would not know the stars. During the
> day, the light of the sun conceals them from our view and limits

---

1. The issue of electric lights (and appliances run by electricity) falling
under the rubric of *mechabeh* (and its counterpart, *mav'ir*, kindling) is quite
complicated and beyond the scope of this work.

our focus to earthly life. But when darkness descends upon the earth, new vistas – virtually infinite in reach – are opened to us and the stars are revealed. It is the same with a person's inner world. While one is among others, one's focus is entirely on practical matters; one is aware of only the "earthly" aspect of one's personality. When one withdraws for a time from social interaction, dusk envelops one's earthiness and the "heavenly" aspect of one's soul is revealed to them. One discovers emotions and inner yearnings for holiness that they never knew existed within them. If one truly desires a glimpse of the heaven within one's soul, with its myriad shining stars, one needs to dim one's earthly activities for a while. Through introspection born of seclusion one will uncover new worlds of nobility and purity, sanctity and longing for the eternal, in the recesses of their soul.[2]

It is our obligation to see our dignity and keep our flames alight and burning. Rabbi Israel of Rizhyn taught:

When a person walks through a forest on a dark night and meets up with another person who has a lantern, they no longer grope and stumble in the dark. But, at the crossroads they part, and the one without a light must again find their way in the darkness. If a person carries their own light, they need not be afraid of any darkness.[3]

Yes, we live in society and in community. Yes, we take care of each other and sometimes need to do the difficult work of lighting up one another. But we also must learn how to avoid extinguishing our own flames and how to carry our own lamps as best as possible.

---

2. Rabbi Shlomo Wolbe, *Alei Shur*, Vol. I (Jerusalem, Israel: Bais Hamussar, 1967), p.179.

3. Martin Buber, *Tales of the Hasidim: The Later Masters* (NY: Shocken Books, 1975), page 62.

On this point, we ponder the experience of mentorship from great people. We want to receive their light, strength, and inspiration, but we also want to be sure not to lose our own unique light. Rabbi Michael Rosen wrote in his book on the life and teachings of Rav Simhah Bunim:

> He also taught that it was forbidden to extinguish the light of one's own inner world to conform to the charisma of a *tzaddik*. Just as intellectual acumen requires independent judgment and a sense of autonomy, so too – he argued – in matters of emotion and spirit one could only make contact if one were truly present, if one took responsibility for oneself, even at the moment of encounter with the *tzaddik*.[4]

Indeed, even while each of us has our own unique talents, gifts, stories, and light, there is something universal and even primordial about the light we share as well. Rabbi Lawrence Kushner writes:

> There is another Kabbalistic legend that tells of all humankind descending from another Adam: *Adam Kadmon*, the primordial archetype man, which the Kabbala is careful to distinguish from *Adam HaRishon*, the first mythic man of the garden, lest the distinction between man and God be confused. By allowing them both to share the name "Adam," the blasphemous-holy confusion is nevertheless intimated. The primordial *Adam* was some kind of giant who contained within him the souls of us all. After the Fall they were scattered about the universe like sparks. They are never extinguished. There are only so many of them. They are each an eternal life force that gives life to one creature after another in one generation after another. And each of them began in the same *Adam Kadmon*, the same archetypic man,

the same primordial giant. And at the end, they will return once again to their same ancient unity.[5]

While tapping into that energy and power, we also remember that each of us has our own unique calling. The Baal Shem Tov taught: "It is incumbent upon every person to pursue that particular aspect of healing of the world that is meant for their soul alone."[6]

In addition to our human light that is universal and our individual light that is personal, there is a third dimension: our shared Jewish light. Rav Yosef Stern writes:

> These two categories – the repentant Jew and the constantly righteous one – are not necessarily mutually exclusive. Rather, aspects of both exist in each of us. On the one hand, all of us are guilty of sin, to some extent, as King Solomon says:[7] *For no man is so righteous in the earth that he does only good and does not sin.* Yet, no matter how far one strays, there exists in every Jew a sincere love for the Creator, and a spark of Jewishness that is never extinguished, as the prophet Yeshayahu writes:[8] *Your people are all righteous.* Thus, every Jew is, in one respect, totally righteous, and his *pintele Yid* never ceases to flicker. On the other hand, we all err, and are in dire need of *teshuva* (repentance). Consequently, both the *succah's* canopy of peace for the returnee to Judaism, and Shabbos' shelter for the righteous are equally necessary.[9]

What it means to be a Jew is to continue to play music even when the lights go out. Rabbi Harold Kushner illustrates this point beautifully:

5. Lawrence Kushner, *Honey from the Rock: An Introduction to Jewish Mysticism* (Vermont: Jewish Lights Books, 2015), page 109.

6. Baal Shem Tov's commentary on Parshat Nitzavim, comment 8.

7. Kohelet 7:20.

8. Isaiah 60:21.

9. *The Three Festivals: Ideas and Insights of the Sfas Emes on Pesach, Shavuos, and Succos*, Anthologized and Adapted by Rabbi Yosef Stern (Brooklyn, NY: Mesorah Publications, 1993), p. 299.

In 2003, with memories of 9/11 fresh in many people's minds, [Dr. Gordon Livingston's] patient was attending a concert of the Baltimore Symphony Orchestra. At one point, the lights in the hall went out. Many people wondered if Baltimore had been attacked. But "*the orchestra kept playing.* Sitting in the dark, unable to see the conductor or their scores, the musicians played on flawlessly . . . The ovation at the end of the piece [was] especially heartfelt." We too, in a time when darkness threatens to envelop us, can do nothing more helpful or more courageous than to ignore the darkness and go on playing.[10]

When we recite *Kiddush Levanah* (the prayer sanctifying the new moon), we reflect on the Torah thought of the Sfat Emet that as brutal empires of the oppressive sun have faded, the small people spiritually interconnected with the humble lunar calendar continues to shine a modest but indissoluble light amidst even the darkest layers of darkness. When we welcome the new moon, we seek the potential of a month of undimmed luminosity, spiritual renewal, reawakened potential, and freedom for all!

We don't just focus on the light. We know we must also enter the darkness. Rabbi Menachem Mendel of Kotzk, known as the Kotzker Rebbe, teaches on the verse in Parshat Yitro: "And all the people trembled, and stood far away; but Moshe entered the dark cloud where God was." It is easy to be attracted to loud sounds and bright lights. Consider how celebrities and the entertainment they provide are so powerful at drawing us in. But Moshe understood that the deepest treasures are found in the quiet, dark, humble, spaces of uncertainty. Elijah also saw that God is not found in the raging fire, but rather is in the still, small voice.[11] When we see something that looks perfect that attracts

---

10. Rabbi Harold Kushner, *Conquering Fear: Living Boldly in an Uncertain World* (New York: Anchor Publishing, 2009) pg. 32–33.
11. 1 Kings 19:12.

us with its bright lights, we can be wary. The deeper truths are hidden in the darkness.

Light and darkness require one another. Dr. Erica Brown writes:

> The pre-Socratic philosopher Heraclitus (535–485 BCE) created a theory called The Unity of Opposites. A thing can only be properly understood through contrast with its oppositional object. Objects are formed and changed through a confrontation with their opposites. Heat exposed to cold makes an object colder. Something dry exposed to moisture becomes wetter. This is true not only for objects but for ideas and emotions. Later philosophers, Hegel in particular, believed that ideas are shaped and sharpened by their dialectical opposites. Light requires darkness in order for one to understand either state. An identity can best be understood through both its similarity and its contrast to an opposing idea. This tension is dynamic.[12]

Children can be scared of turning off the lights. Darkness leaves one feeling alone and confused.[13] Sigmund Freud wrote about this feeling with a powerful anecdote.

> For [the] explanation of the origin of infantile anxiety, I have to think of a three-year-old boy whom I once heard calling out of a dark room: "Auntie, speak to me! I'm frightened because it's so dark." His aunt answered him: "What good will that do? You can't see me." "That doesn't matter," replied the child, "if anyone speaks, it gets light."[14]

---

12. Erica Brown, *Jonah: The Reluctant Prophet* (Jerusalem: Maggid Books, 2017), pg. 38.

13. In fact, the reason for lighting Shabbat candles is so that (this concern was of great significance prior to modern-day electric light) one wouldn't sit in the dark at the Shabbat meal. The Shabbat candles provide a sense of *shalom bayit* (peace within the home).

14. See Sigmund Freud (ed. Elisabeth Young-Bruehl), *Freud on Women: A*

It's not just children. Many adults are scared or suffering from the darkness of depression where they cannot see a light at the end of the tunnel. Of course, they may need therapy and medication. But we also have a role as friends and family members. The best way to show someone in a dark place that there is a light at the end of the tunnel is not to describe that light or dismiss the darkness.[15] The best way is to sit with them so they're not alone and to listen to them so they feel heard. Loving companionship can inspire hope and help enable another in narrow straits to rekindle a lamp that appears extinguished.

To be sure, when someone's light is extinguished, we can sometimes light up the room for them with something as simple as comforting, soothing words. On Shabbat, we reflect on the energy we put into the world. Perhaps the greatest legacy we can strive for is to have added more fuel to our own lamps and to the lamps of others. Only with death is our lamp extinguished, and even then, if we have shared light with others, our sparks of light continue to shine brightly on this earth for generations to come. *Mechabeh* serves as a reminder to us of the power we have to constructively extinguish when necessary, and at the same time to bring light to ourselves, to others, and to the entire world.

Reader (New York: W.W. Norton & Co., 1990), pg. 140 fn. 31.

15. In fact, one who is suffering generally needs to have their feelings validated. Validation alone, together with simply having someone to listen, can indeed be very therapeutic.

37.
Mav'ir (Igniting, Kindling)

THE THIRTY-SEVENTH MELACHA, *mav'ir* (igniting or kindling), is perhaps the quintessential *melacha*. When one thinks of *melacha*, one often thinks of the act of lighting a flame. It is the only *melacha* that the Torah addresses explicitly: "You shall not light a fire in any of your dwelling places on the day of Shabbat."[1] In fact, when Shabbat ends, it is the first *melacha* we do as we light the *havdalah* candle, symbolizing the difference between Shabbat which has just ended and the rest of the week. As *mav'ir* is the counterpart to the previous *melacha* of *mechabeh* (extinguishing), modern-day applications include turning on a light and appliances.[2]

And yet, *mav'ir* is about so much more than striking a match or igniting a lighter. *Mav'ir* is, perhaps, the most important act we do in our lives: lighting up souls around us. Unfortunately, we sometimes bring negative energy to others and drag them down. But we also have the option of *mav'ir*, to lift others up with energy, encouragement, and light.[3] We can be like solar panels that receive light from a major source and then channel that light illuminating spaces all around us. In the creation story, God

---

1. Exodus 35:3.
2. See the previous chapter, footnote 1.
3. *Mav'ir* is, by definition, the only *melacha* which is inherently both constructive and destructive. The same fire that provides light has the power to destroy.

creates light before the sun, teaching that we are not referring to solar light but to spiritual light. God created an *ohr haganuz* (hidden light) that can emerge from within dark spaces. We learn that "The flame of The Compassionate One is the human soul"[4] and so God, as it were, is present on earth through our inner sparks that we ignite, protect, and share. Just as in classical religious art forms, a saintly figure has a halo and is radiating light and a satanic figure is in darkness, we can seek a type of religiosity that is not about self-glorification but about dwelling in, and sharing light.

We don't just light up others from a place of charity. Rather, when we use our energy to elevate our spiritual consciousness toward the unity of all life, we realize how interdependent we all are. In this sense, by lighting up others we also light up ourselves. Dr. Martin Luther King, Jr. wrote:

> As long as there is poverty in the world, [he writes,] I can never be rich, even if I have a billion dollars. As long as diseases are rampant and millions of people in this world cannot expect to live more than twenty-eight or thirty years, I can never be totally healthy even if I just got a good checkup at Mayo Clinic. I can never be what I ought to be until you are what you ought to be. This is the way our world is made. No individual or nation can stand out boasting of being independent. We are interdependent.

Similarly, Rabbi Jonathan Sacks wrote in his final book:

> A free society is a moral achievement. Over the past fifty years in the West this truth has been forgotten, ignored, or denied. That is why liberal democracy is at risk. Social freedom cannot be sustained by market economics and liberal democratic politics alone. It needs a third element: morality, a concern for the welfare of others, an active commitment to justice and compassion,

---

4. Proverbs 20:27.

a willingness to ask not just what is good for me but what is good for "all of us together." It is about "Us," not "Me"; about "We," not "I." The market will be merciless. Politics will be deceiving, divisive, confrontational, and extreme. People will feel anxious, uncertain, fearful, aggressive, unstable, unrooted, and unloved, they will focus on promoting themselves instead of the one thing that will give them lasting happiness: making life better for others. People will be, by historic standards, financially rich but emotionally poor. Freedom itself will be at risk from the far right and the far left, the far right dreaming of a golden age that never was, the far left dreaming of a utopia that will never be.[5]

Oftentimes, we may feel a sense of community when we're feeling great and celebratory. But when we're suffering, we may choose isolation. Suffering, however, can be a bridge to human connection like no other. James Baldwin wrote:

I can only tell you about yourself as much as I can face about myself. And this has happened to everybody who's tried to live. You go through life for a long time thinking, no one has ever suffered the way I've suffered, my God, my God. And then you realize- you read something or hear something, and you realize that your suffering does not isolate you; your suffering is your bridge. Many people have suffered before you, many people are suffering around you, and always will, and all you can do is bring, hopefully, a little light into that suffering. Enough light so that the person who is suffering can begin to comprehend his suffering and begin to live with it and begin to change it, change the situation. We don't [actually] change anything; all we can do is invest people with the morale to change it for themselves.

5. Jonathan Sacks, *Morality: Restoring the Common Good in Divided Times*, "Introduction: Cultural Climate Change," (New York: Basic Books, 2020), pg. 1.

How much richer we can be when we feel connected to all beings that suffer. And we can also experience a radical elevation when we feel love, responsibility, and respect for all beings. Rabbi Moshe Cordovero writes:

> [One should] respect all creatures, recognizing in them the greatness of the Creator Who formed humans with wisdom, and Whose wisdom is contained in all creatures. One should realize that they greatly deserve to be honored, since the Former of All Things, the Wise One who is exalted above all, cared to create them. If one despises them, God forbid, it reflects upon the honor of their Creator.
>
> This may be likened to an expert goldsmith who fashions a vessel with great skill, but when they display their work, one of the people begins to mock and scorn it. How angry that goldsmith will be; for by disparaging their handiwork, one disparages their wisdom. Similarly, it is evil in the sight of the Holy One, be blessed, if any [one] of the Divinely created creatures is despised.
>
> This is [the meaning of] the verse, "How many are your works, O Lord."[6] [The Psalmist] did not say "how vast" but "how many." ... Since You imbued them all with Your wisdom, Your workers are important and great, and it benefits one to contemplate the wisdom in them and not disparage them.[7]

We light others up when they need it and ask for it. We also seek to lift others up when they don't know they need it and aren't asking for it. Consider the Israelites in slavery in Egypt. They never cry out for freedom. Their cry is only a verbal expression of their immediate experience at the moment of that cry: an experience of pain born of the difficulty of their lives in an en-

---

6. Psalms 104:24.

7. Erica Brown, *Jonah: The Reluctant Prophet* (Jerusalem: Maggid Books, 2017), p. 38.

slaved status. They don't demand liberation. They just cry from
the burden. God hears not their request but their pain. So too,
we can rise to meet the moment when we hear the cries.

This requires that we wake up from a slumber of isolation
and self-focus. It requires that we view ourselves in the light
that will illuminate our reality as responsive moral agents. Recently, during a boring, routine moment while I was in my car,
my head-space returned to that of a carefree teenager. I tried to
remember why I felt so free – like everything was possible – in
that head-space; it's been so long since I was a teenager that I'd
forgotten what it felt like. My windows were rolled down, the
music was turned up, and I was singing at the top of my lungs
without a care in the world.

Why did I feel that way? Why had I not felt that way in so
long? And then I realized … mortality!

When I was a teenager, I really didn't know people who had
passed away. I witnessed a few deaths of loved ones and friends; I
could count them on one hand. On some level – as only a teenager
could – I believed I was immortal. Yes, there were strange cases
of young deaths I heard about, but they were mostly distant. Yes,
there were elderly people who died, but for me that was a whole
lifetime away. Yes, I must not have believed I could ever actually
be an older person.

Today, understanding the depth and fragility of compassionate
relationships and empathetic to the national and global human
condition (not to mention my own aging and the aging of those
I love!) means that mortality is so much more tangible to me.
It's so much more real and ever-present. It has finally entered my
mind as a concrete possibility more than an abstraction meant
for others.

It is a gift to reach consciousness of the finite time that we all
are allowed to enjoy. This consciousness is not only something
we can appreciate in that it gives us personal perspective, but
also because we are in the world of compassionate relationships,
care, grief, and interconnectivity.

It was nice to be naïve to, and oblivious about, the effects of mortality years ago, but given the choice, I'd rather live with an open heart with all of us together recognizing our individual limitations in terms of the quality, and also the quantity, of our lives, but at the same time recognizing our collective strength. We know that at every celebration of a milestone in someone's life there is someone also dying. And at every death, there is someone somewhere celebrating. When we think of mortality, we shouldn't think only of its inevitable conclusion. That's a distraction from the bigger picture. Instead, let us ride this journey together in the messy, productive turmoil that constitutes the ups and downs of life.

The Kotzker Rebbe asks: "If the heavenly gates of tears are never closed, why are there gates at all?" I'd suggest they're a mere projection of the gates around our hearts. If we can learn to ignite – that is, to light up – our hearts and break through the boundaries of our emotional limitations, we can then break through the gates of heaven, igniting the cosmos.

Let's keep reading, writing, leading, and building. But please, let's add prayer, meditation, reflection, therapy, and healing practices to our individual and collective agenda. We should lead by focusing on the light (without naivete of crises of course) rather than leading by primarily focusing on fear.

The Bnei Yisasscher teaches: "What is Shabbat? It is the name of HaKadosh Baruch Hu,[8] a name that is complete in every aspect."[9] He then connects this point to mercy: "There are thirteen different ways of fully spelling the Name HaVaYa"H, and they correlate with the thirteen attributes of mercy."[10]

Indeed, embracing Shabbat means becoming more God-like, more merciful, more kind, and more gentle. On Shabbat, we can

8. *Hakadosh Baruch Hu* is the Hebrew term for "the Holy One blessed be He."
9. Zohar II 88a.
10. Bnei Yisasscher, Ma'amar 1.

reflect on the unseen energy found in spiritual light. We can reflect on how much more powerful than our words and deeds is the emanation of our being. The energy we put out can ignite others around us. Healing and recuperating on Shabbat can enable us to be sure we're putting out the type of energy, the type of warmth and light, the type of *mav'ir* that we do want to be generating.

38.
Makeh b'Patish (Striking with a Hammer)

THE THIRTY-EIGHTH *MELACHA* is *makeh b'patish* – literally, striking with a hammer – which refers not only to this specific action, but also to finishing the job. In the construction of the *Mishkan*, the final hammer blow was administered to the gold sheets to connect them to the boards. This *melacha* doesn't only relate to the completion of something newly created; it also applies to a repair to a broken item that makes it workable again. A practical example would be screwing back in the temple piece of a pair of glasses.[1]

Finishing a task can be rewarding. In human psychology, it can be so uplifting to feel a sense of completion. We like to commemorate such events. Think of graduations, of a *siyum* (celebrating the completion of learning a section of Torah, Talmud, or the like), the last day on a job before starting a new one, or retirement, divorce, closing the door of an old home for the last time, and even death. Some endings are simply bitter. Others are just sweet. Most commonly, they are bitter-sweet.

It's interesting to note that, in Jewish spirituality, we traditionally don't just recite a blessing before eating food but also afterwards, referred to as the *berachah acharonah* ("the final

---

1. It would not be *melacha* to reattach a temple to a pair of glasses in a temporary manner, such as inserting the screw but not tightening it or by means of a paper clip.

blessing"). We say thanks before eating, and then when we finish, we express gratitude once again to mark the completion of our eating. This practice is connected to the first Jew and his love of welcoming strangers as a way to repair the world:

> Said Rabbi Isaac: Abraham used to welcome wayfarers. When they had finished eating, he would invite them to give thanks. They would turn to him and ask him what they should say. Abraham would answer: Bless the everlasting God of Whose bounty we have partaken. Whereupon God said to him: My name was unknown to My creatures and you introduced Me to them. I, therefore, regard you as being a partner with Me in the creation of the world.[2]

Some tasks in life have no end, and so we break them up into segments to feel a sense of completion within a never-ending long-term journey. Consider the journey of marriage, or the journey of parenthood, or the journey of spiritual growth. These experiences never truly finish, but we celebrate their milestones by marking *b'nei mitzvah* and *b'not mitzvah*, birthdays, graduations,[3] and weddings – even, often, after the death of a person whose life events we mark (*yahrtzeits*).

In community organizing, we know that we never completely win and find ourselves in a utopia. Rather, the path toward a more just and holy world is never-ending. So, we celebrate little wins to keep up the momentum, but never take our eyes off the grander prize.

Rabbi Harold Kushner offers a fascinating distinction between the "life" of an angel and the life of a human:

> In the Bible, we often read of angels appearing to people at crucial moments of their lives to bring them a word from God.

---

2. Bereishit Rabbah 43:9.

3. Notice that the formal term for a graduation is commencement, literally meaning beginning!

We don't have to picture them as ethereal creatures with wings and halos; they usually seem to take on human form. But one interesting thing about angels sent by God is that when they have completed their mission, they disappear, which happens to the angel who tells Samson's mother that she will have a special child in Judges 13, and to the angels who come to Abraham and to Lot in Genesis 19. One by one, their message delivered, they vanish.

That is the difference between angels and human beings, and between human beings and less advanced forms of life. We [humans] find ample reason to go on living even when our biological mission has been completed. Nature may have designed us to bear and raise our young and then fade away ... Nature makes the rules for things like sex and childbirth, health, and illness. But nature cannot comprehend such qualities as love, wisdom, or creativity. We cannot expect Nature to understand our drive to see grandchildren grow up, to read (or write) another book, to hear [a] symphony, follow a pennant race, or take pleasure in the emergence of a talented young actor or actress. That is why we, in the last third of our lives, fight back against the natural process of decay. It is not out of greed or vanity. It is because there are things we still want to do and enjoy, proudly and defiantly, proclaiming that we are not yet finished living.[4]

As humans, we continue to affirm life even after the completion of activities that make up our lives. We don't complete our tasks and then call it a day, call it a life. Rather, we set new directions, new goals, and new aspirations. An angel has one calling and disappears after its mission.[5] But as humans, we continue to evolve and grow and realign with the calling of our time. But this

4. Rabbi Harold Kushner, *Conquering Fear: Living Boldly in an Uncertain World* (New York: Anchor Books, 2010), page 132.
5. Bereishit Rabbah 50:2.

never-ending journey can be quite exhausting. Rabbi Kushner continues:

> In my nearly fifty years as a clergyman, I have been at the bed-side of many, many dying people, young and old, religious and freethinkers, successful in life and less successful. They taught me the profound truth that terminally ill people are not afraid of death. When you are very sick, when little by little your body stops being able to do the things it has always been able to do, death may be the only cure that ails you. There are three things that terrify the very ill person more than the prospect of dying.
>
> They are afraid of pain, they are afraid that people will aban-don them while they are still alive, and they are afraid that they will die having wasted their lives, having never accomplished anything that will cause people to remember them when they are gone. For most people, the prospect of nullification, of having left no mark on the world, is more frightening than the prospect of not living forever. The real fear of dying, I am convinced, is the fear that we will leave this world with our tasks unfinished, and the best way, indeed the only way, to defeat death is to live fearlessly and purposefully.[6]

Indeed, we may seek completion, we might want to ride out into the sunset to a standing ovation. But life is far messier – along with being more beautiful – than something that can be tied up perfectly with a bow. To live in an open-minded, open-souled, manner, we need to control the fears that hold us back so frequently.

And yet, there are moments so great and transitions so radical that we can taste completion. Consider the Israelites on the far side of the sea watching their oppressors drown in the water through which they had just passed. Think of the moment at Mount Sinai hearing the pronouncing of the Ten Commandments

---

6. Ibid., pg. 151–152.

when these same Israelites knew that the world's moral compass would be altered forever. Consider the words of President Abraham Lincoln from his second inaugural address:

> With malice toward none, with charity for all, with firmness in the right as God gives us to see the right, let us strive on to finish the work we are in, to bind up the nation's wounds, to care for him who shall have borne the battle and for his widow and his orphan, to do all which may achieve and cherish a just and lasting peace among ourselves and with all nations.

Indeed, there are some tasks that are never-ending and others that we seek to complete, to close an era of division. Consider how Rav Pinchas Hurwitz wrote about our work of completing creation:

> It is said after deep inspection [that] the way of giving through [using one's] body is more glorious and praiseworthy than giving through the pocketbook.... However, just because this type [of giving] is more glorious, a person should not abandon the second type [of giving], for truly the second type is more needed for repairing the community of humanity (*l'takanat kehilat min ha'enoshi*). And it's better in the eyes of God and humanity to furnish the poor from the blessings of one's house, to supply the poor from one's own money and to free the captives and give ransom for their lives and not feel [the loss of] the ransom money, to give one's bread to the hungry and to cover the naked with clothing, to loan money to the poor, and things like this. And the essence of fulfilling the obligation of loving one's neighbor is of this second type, even though "both of them as one are good"[7] for the fixing of the world (*l'takanat ha-olam*), and for the value of joining together the human species....

---

7. Ecclesiastes 11:6.

And now let us explore how many levels there are in these three kinds of doing good [through ideas, through one's body, and through property], and they are: 1) that one should help a single person ... 2) that one should do this for many, for example, if there were a town without a source of water ... and one dug with one's strength a well for them ... 3) that one does good for all the people in the world, for example, one use[s] one's body and one's strength to make a bridge for a road that many pass through ... or that one would hire workers to make the bridge and pay them from one's pocket, or through the power of one's intellect invent some new tool that is good for the whole world, like Noah invented plowing tools in the world, and similarly any tools that complete the establishment of the world (*hamashlimim tikkun ha'olam*) and its well-being....

And one who does good for the people of the world, such as one who invents a new tool that is good for the world, or a good book, it is appropriate for someone who is enlightened on the subject of loving neighbors that at the least he would buy it in order that [the inventor or author] would expand and strengthen his heart by means of this to invent more good tools for the world, and so for the rest of all those who are wise of heart, that they should strengthen themselves and strive also to invent good things and necessary tools for the improvement of the world and its completion (*l'takanat ha'olam ul'hashlamato*).[8]

We learn famously in Pirkei Avot: *Lo alecha hamelacha ligmor,* that "the work is not for us to complete" yet we still cannot desist from participating.[9] This incredibly powerful directive reminds us that none of us can complete our missions and yet our work is still meaningful. Consider how the Creator of the world allowed each day to pass in the days of creation without having finished

8. R' Pinchas Hurwitz, *Sefer Habrit*, "On Loving Neighbors" (Yerid Hasefarim, 1990), ch. 19.

9. Avot (Ethics of the Fathers) 2:16.

creation. And even after a week's worth of creativity, the apparent completion of creation was followed by a Divine command to humankind to participate in the continued completion of the task, as it were, by populating the earth and mastering it.[10] So too, when we go to sleep at night, we can find solidarity with the Divine in knowing that the work is not done but that we did what we could that day.

What's so inviting about theologies of a messianic era, is the sense that we can and will live in a redeemed world. Rabbi Avraham Yitzchak HaKohen Kook writes:

> The holiness that is in Nature is the holiness of the Land of Israel, [while] the *Shekhinah* [God's presence] that descended into exile with [the people] Israel [has] the capability of preserving holiness [even] in opposition to what is natural. But holiness battling against Nature is not holiness [that is] whole – it needs to be absorbed into its highest essence, in supernal holiness, which is the very holiness of Nature herself, which is the foundation of repairing the world in its entirety (*tikkun olam kulo*) and its complete rapture, and [then] the Holy in the exile will be joined to the Holy of the Land.... Then war will stop completely, the attribute of judgment will be enraptured, and all will incline toward lovingkindness.[11]

On Shabbat, we can dream of that redeemed world where our work is complete. In the meantime, we will need to engage in our own *makeh b'patish,* to continue to work each day tirelessly to build a redeemed world. To do so, we will need to pause, rest, recharge, and reflect on what work we're doing. Shabbat can give us a temporary sense of completion, an inkling of what it

---

10. Genesis 1:28.

11. R' Avraham Yitzhak Hakohen Kook, *Orot Hatechiyah (Lights of Resurrection),* chap. 28, 77.

could feel like to see the work as finished. After Shabbat, we are reminded of just how broken the world is and how incomplete the dream of completion is. Shabbat gives us a respite, allowing us to dream of that final hammer blow.

39.

Hotza'ah (Carrying)

THE 39TH, AND final, *melacha* is *hotza'ah* (carrying, or more literally bringing out). When the *Mishkan* was utilized in the desert, it would be disassembled for transportation as the Israelites traveled from place to place. They would place the parts of the *Mishkan* in large wagons, each of which was its own *reshut hayachid* (private domain) in the midst of the larger *midbar* (desert) which was a *reshut harabim* (public domain). And thus, *hotza'ah* is about carrying objects from a *reshut hayachid* to a *reshut harabim* and vice versa.[1]

In the midrash,[2] a heretic once asked how God could bring rain down on Shabbat since it should be the *melacha* of *hotza'ah*, transferring water from one domain to another. The Rabbis responded that since the whole world belongs to God, the transfer of water is not from one domain to another but all within God's domain. "The world is filled with Your possessions."[3] Indeed, from a theological perspective, one might suggest there is only

---

1. There are four halachic domains: *reshut harabim* (public domain), *reshut hayachid* (private domain), *carmelit* (neither a fully private nor fully public domain; a domain that fits neither category), and *mekom petur* (a domain of "exemption"; one that fits none of the above categories). It is permissible to carry from a *mekom petur* to one of the three other domains and vice versa. *Reshut harabim* and *reshut hayachid* are biblical in origin, and *carmelit* is rabbinic in origin.

2. Bereishit Rabbah 11:5.

3. Tehillim 104:24.

one domain. But from our societal constructs of public and private property, we make practical legal distinctions.

Interestingly enough, *hotza'ah* is the only *melacha* to have its own *talmudic* tractate (Eiruvin), which more technically is about a rabbinic workaround[4] to avoid the strictures of this *melacha*. The fact that the Talmud devotes an entire tractate to this topic is probably due both to the complexity of the matter and to the collective relationship to the *melacha*. *Hotza'ah* is the reason we don't blow the *shofar* on Rosh Hashanah when the New Year falls on Shabbat, lest someone come to carry it in a public domain. This is really radical – we refrain from the biblical commandment of blowing *shofar* merely out of fear that one might engage in *hotza'ah*.[5]

The transition from a private to a public space is so significant that it's marked by another biblical commandment that, on its face, seems disconnected from the laws of Shabbat: placing a *mezuzah*[6] on our doorposts and our gates. We must remember that we need to be our full selves in both domains, even while we

---

4. An *eiruv* is an imaginary boundary, usually constructed of vertical poles and horizontal ropes or wires, thereby creating the "frame" of a wall or fence. A property surrounded by an *eiruv* is considered a *reshut hayachid*, even if it is otherwise a large, public domain. Today, many cities and communities are surrounded by an *eiruv*. An *eiruv* enables carrying within its borders, which would otherwise be forbidden in the public outdoors.

5. The same is true for using the *lulav* and *etrog* when Sukkot falls on Shabbat and reading the *megillah* when Purim falls on Shabbat. (While nowadays Purim does not coincide with Shabbat, it did in pre-fixed calendar times. Even today, Purim in walled cities such as Jerusalem, known as Shushan Purim, does indeed fall on Shabbat).

In the *Beit Hamikdash*, the *shofar* and *lulav* were indeed used on Shabbat, based on the concept of *mora mikdash* (being in awe of one's presence in God's home), which, if actualized, would by its very nature serve as a safeguard against carrying on Shabbat. (In such a case, the *lulav* and *shofar* were brought to the *Beit Hamikdash* prior to Shabbat).

6. It is interesting to note that while the term *mezuzah* is used to refer to the item placed on the doorpost, namely the parchment (often encased in an adorned cover) on which is written the biblical passages referring to this mitzvah, the word *mezuzah* in its origin actually refers to the doorpost itself.

alter our respective styles in each domain. The *mezuzah* reminds us of our values. We check to see what parts of ourselves we are carrying from society into our homes and from home back out into the broader world.

Tragically, many do not have the privilege of crossing the threshold from a public domain back into the refuge of a private domain. Homelessness is indeed a modern plague.[7] Having served as a rabbi in homeless camps on many occasions, I have seen firsthand what deep despair can look like: indeed, a modern plague. The despair that comes in the form of homelessness is a plague that crushes the spirits of anywhere between a half-million to one and a half-million people in America each year.[8]

Jews are morally mandated to feed and tend to the most vulnerable in our midst. In the *Shulchan Aruch*, Rabbi Yosef Karo writes: "If someone comes and says, 'feed me,' you don't check them to see if they are an imposter, but you feed them right away."[9]

In the Torah, a society that punishes those who feed the homeless is analogous to Sodom, a city that was riddled with moral perversion. Not only are we encouraged to engage in hospitality and acts of kindness, we are also warned that there will be collective consequences for those who mistreat the downtrodden.[10] The citizens of Sodom not only avoided welcoming guests and abused

---

In fact, the verse states, "And you shall write them [the words of the Torah] on the doorposts (*mezuzot*) of your home."

7. A plague is defined as a force so robust that one cannot hide from or escape it, an unfortunately apt description of the brutally harsh reality of housing insecurity and homelessness in America today.

8. On a Single Night in January 2020[,] 580,466 people – about 18 of every 10,000 people in the United States – experienced homelessness across the United States. The 2020 Annual Homeless Assessment Report (AHAR) to Congress." *U.S. Department of Housing and Urban Development's Office of Policy Development and Research*, www.huduser.gov/portal/sites/default/files/pdf/2020-AHAR-Part-1.pdf. Over the course of a year (October 2009–September 2010), the 2010 AHAR found that 1,593,150 individuals experienced homelessness.

9. Shulchan Aruch, "Laws of Tzedakah," Yoreh Dei'ah 251:10.

10. BT Sanhedrin 109b.

them, but also punished those who helped others. "They issued a proclamation in Sodom saying: 'Everyone who strengthens the hand of the poor and the needy with a loaf of bread shall be burnt by fire!'"[11] How can we ensure that America does not resemble Sodom? As we ask that practical question, we should ask the parallel moral question: how can we not ensure that we will do all we can to avoid having America resemble Sodom?

This is a life-and-death issue. To ignore it is to absolve ourselves of our sacred responsibility; to wait around for action is to betray the very essence of justice itself. From Henry David Thoreau to Martin Luther King, America has a strong tradition of objecting to and even defying laws that violate core spiritual values. It is not enough to provide meager soup kitchens to which the poor must travel. Many people without shelter need more, and find themselves so desperate that they are begging in the streets. We must respond compassionately. The Jewish people need to be at the forefront of this call to action. We must engage in *hotza'ah* during the week to bring forth supplies to those in desperate need.

When we go forth into the world, we don't only carry objects. We carry our past, our stories, our identity, and our future aspirations. I was recently carrying my oldest son to his bed after he fell asleep and I noticed that he was … his own person. In the past, I saw a little bit of this grandparent's nose and that grandparent's eyes. In some ways, he looks like his mom and in some ways like me. But this time was different; he looked just like HIM! Beautiful HIM just as he was created to be! Yes, in God's image but also in his own image, as a unique beautiful creation.

And I realized that this is our human story. We have inherited "our people's" narratives (the traumas and glories). We carry the richness of our past with us but every one of us is also profoundly unique and a radical new beginning in the human story.

We are so gracefully "carried" asleep from the past (by our families, our ancestors, our own DNA) to this present moment.

---

11. Pirkei DeRebbe Eliezer 25.

And yet in this present moment, we can wake up and realize the two key components of who we are: both that we were carried so gently and lovingly to this moment by others who molded us so deeply, but also to the deeper existential reality of our unique purpose (never untied from where we have come from but never blocked from liberation to start a new path). The world needs the richness of our past to be understood and honored. But the world also needs each of us to actualize our unique potential. It's about particularism and universalism, traditionalism and progressivism, a focus on others and the self, determinism, and freedom – it's about the old and the new.

What we also "carry" in the world is our usefulness, something that is deeply needed and meaningful in human experience. Consider part of the poem "To be of use" by Marge Piercy:

> The people I love the best
> jump into work head first
> without dallying in the shallows
> and swim off with sure strokes almost out of sight ...
>
> I want to be with people who submerge
> in the task, who go into the fields to harvest
> and work in a row and pass the bags along,
> who are not parlor generals and field deserters
> but move in a common rhythm
> when the food must come in or the fire be put out.
>
> The work of the world is common as mud.
> Botched, it smears the hands, crumbles to dust.
> But the thing worth doing well done
> has a shape that satisfies, clean and evident.
> Greek amphoras for wine or oil,
> Hopi vases that held corn, are put in museums
> but you know they were made to be used.
> The pitcher cries for water to carry
> and a person for work that is real.

"A pitcher cries for water to carry and a person for work that is real." Indeed, work is not only hard and demanding; it can also be deeply fulfilling when it is of use. To carry what we feel we are meant to carry. One of the most meaningful forms of being of use through carrying is carrying the casket of a loved one, thereby performing the mitzvah of *kevod ha'meit* (honoring the deceased), a true *chesed shel emet* (truest act of kindness), since it can never be repaid by the deceased and is thus not an act of reciprocity.

In addition to "carrying" what is positive and useful, we must learn how to put down and let go of that which is not serving us and others, such as toxic emotions. In dark, scary times, where all moral foundations of truth and decency are being chipped away, how do we not fall into despair?

The *mussar* teachers instruct us to regain our balance between *emunah/bitachon* (faith/trust, i.e., having faith in the path we must walk, and letting go of control) and *hishtadlut* (striving forward with all our energy).

There is so much we cannot control today. Let's breathe it out. Let it go. Seriously, those of us who really "care" about the plight of the vulnerable are often carrying way too much stress and anxiety and fear and pain in our hearts. It makes us less effective. It makes us less healthy. And to be fully compassionate toward others, we need to act compassionately toward ourselves.

And yet there is so much we can and must control today. Let's roll up our sleeves, push ourselves beyond our normal comfort zones, and each of us actualizes our unique potential to bring light to our own corners! This is a crucial moment in world history that our descendants will read about in history books (and will feel the lasting impact from) for centuries to come. "Where were you?" our great-grandchildren will ask.

Each day, letting go of control where we must. Each day, taking control together of the fate and destiny of our society, of humanity, of our planet.

Breathing. Marching.
Breathing. Marching.
Breathing. Marching.

Moses brings down the first tablets. When he sees the golden calf, he breaks them. He goes back up the mountain for forty days, prays for the people's forgiveness, and comes down with new tablets. But the amazing thing is that the *aron hakodesh* (holy ark) must contain the first broken tablets and the second whole tablets. We carry our brokenness and our wholeness together.

We carry the word of God (the first tablets written by God) and the human word (the second tablets written by Moses). We carry perfection and imperfection, and that is how it must be.

Another really meaningful form of carrying is carrying a baby in the womb. This is indeed considered an enhanced status of holiness in the Torah.

> Leviticus 12:1–4 presents the rule that when a woman gives birth she descends in purity. Moreover, when a woman gives birth to a daughter, she descends twice the level of purity that she descends when [she] gives birth to a boy. The Ohr HaChaim explains that this perplexing formulation teaches us that during pregnancy [she has] a higher level of holiness, since she is carrying another life.[12] The conception of a daughter who will maintain within herself a greater creative potential, raises her to a higher level of holiness. After the potential leaves her womb, her level of purity descends. Inasmuch as a female fetus represents a higher level of potentiality, upon the birth of a girl the mother's level of purity descends doubly. For potential creation is indeed holy. And the level of creation potential is directly related to the level of holiness.[13]

---

12. Or HaChaim, Leviticus 12:2.

13. David Birnbaum, *God and Evil: A Unified Theodicy/Theology/Philosophy* (Hoboken, NJ: Ktav Publishing House, Inc., 1989), p. 69.

One of the startling phenomena of becoming a parent is realizing that one is taking on all the burdens of their child. There is a Hebrew expression *nosei b'ol*, meaning "carrying the burden of another," acting in empathy and solidarity. Just as an expectant mother views a fetus as a part of herself, almost inseparable, a parent views their child as one that they "carry."

We carry those we love in our hearts.

We also must be careful of what we carry, lest we come to use it inappropriately. A story is told about Rabbi Yisrael Meir HaKohen, known as the Hafetz Hayim (1838–1933):

> In 1913, Israel Medintz was a young boy attending the Yeshiva of Raden, which had been established by the Hafetz Hayim. One day young Israel and Hayom, two friends, went for a walk in the woods near the Yeshiva. They carried sticks in their hands. They had found the sticks during their walk. Then the Hafetz Hayim himself passed the boys. He greeted them in a friendly manner and stopped to talk to them. "*Kinder*," he said, "never walk with a stick in your hand. You might be provoked by someone and, before thinking, use the stick to hit or beat someone. A Jew should never carry a stick. Without a stick in the hand, physical violence will not be so easy."[14]

The Lubavitcher Rebbe wrote a powerful message to Rabbi Jonathan Sacks about how we carry faith in the world:

> The Rebbe wrote me ... in the form of a parable. Imagine, he said, two people, both of whom have spent their lives carrying stones. One carries rocks, the other diamonds. Now imagine that they are both asked to carry a consignment of emeralds. To the man who has spent his life transporting rocks, emeralds too are

---

14. Lawrence J. Epstein, *A Treasury of Jewish Anecdotes* (Maryland: Jason Aronson, Inc., 1977), page 104. This anecdote was supplied by Bernard Medintz.

rocks – a burden, a weight. After a lifetime, that is how he sees what he is asked to carry. But to the man who has spent his life carrying diamonds, emeralds too are precious stones – different, to be sure, but still things of value and beauty. So it is, he said, [with] different civilizations and faiths. To the person for whom faith is just a burden, so too are other faiths. He does not value his own. How then can he value someone else's? But to the person to whom his own faith is precious, so too are others. Because he cherishes his own, he values someone else's. His may be diamonds, the other emeralds, but he sees the beauty in each. So, the Rebbe ended, in most cases, if not all, you will find that your attachment to Judaism will heighten your appreciation of the gifts of other cultures. In other words, the more you will value the achievements of others.[15]

In learning how to carry the *Mishkan*, the Israelites had something else crucial to carry forth from Egypt. The Torah tells us that the Egyptians gave them gold, silver, and fabrics, supplies that would be used to build the *Mishkan*, and then we read: "Moses took with him the bones of Joseph, who had extracted a promise from the Israelites on his deathbed, saying 'When God takes note of you, you shall carry my remains from here with you.'"[16] We carry the bones of our loved ones out of Egypt and we request that our descendants carry us forth from a place of narrowness as well. This is done to keep Judaism alive, progressing into new generations, honoring the past while adapting to the future.

And so, we are given the gift of Shabbat each week to pause and reflect upon *hotza'ah*, on what we carry forth from our homes, our pasts, and our hearts, into the world. We pause to be sensitive to what must be left behind and what must be carried on further and further.

---

15. Rabbi Jonathan Sacks, *A Letter in The Scroll: Understanding Our Jewish Identity and Exploring the Legacy of the World's Oldest Religion* (New York: The Free Press, 2000), pgs. 210–211.

16. Exodus 13:19.

Conclusion

W HEN GENTILES AND less familiar Jews think about Shabbat, the holiday is often framed as a submission to piety and cessation from the conveniences of the week. No operating of electricity, no driving, or even riding in an elevator all come to mind. Instead of engaging in "work," people who observe Shabbat are meant to only perform holy rituals: prayers, special meals, singing, and spending time divorced from worldly affairs.

But this conception of Shabbat, while partially true, wholly misunderstands the transformative power of the holiday. Shabbat is not an anachronistic nor Luddite rejection of the modern world. Shabbat is not meant to hinder one's engagement with the community. Shabbat is not meant to curb the ability of one to act.

Rather, at its most foundational level, Shabbat is a powerful vehicle for social justice progress. Don't believe me? Consider the macro-ethic of Shabbat: not working. What does that mean? In the Biblical context, one may not work one's worker; Shabbat is about worker justice. One may not work one's animal; Shabbat is about animal welfare. One may not work the land; Shabbat is about environmentalism. One may not work oneself; Shabbat is about self-care. So, in a contemporary context, Shabbat is a radical response to the scourges of rampant materialism and the new idolatry of consumerism. But even more so, Shabbat is about realignment and the notion that once per week, we break free of the view that every person and thing is an instrument for self-interested needs. Rather than buy and sell, make and destroy, work and be worked, we rest.

And we reflect.

It is precisely from the meta-values of Shabbat that authentic ethics emerge. The enterprise of Shabbat is about developing an existential consciousness and awareness that other human beings do not exist to serve *our* desires. This interruption of economic activity and labor is about the development of an egalitarian ethos that fundamentally pushes us toward the recognition that human beings are equal and essential. The Talmud makes clear that the Creation story reveals a deep truth about human equality:

> ...[The] first human being was created alone to teach that all who destroy a single life are as though they destroyed an entire universe, and those who save a single life are as if they had saved an entire universe. Furthermore [the first human was created alone] for the sake of peace among people, so that no one could say to another, "My ancestor was greater than yours."[1]

After humans were created, they rested; God rested. In the world of work, inequalities inevitably emerge. But, through the Shabbat experience, all are equal. One might think from the Biblical verse prohibiting worker oppression that we're only dealing with fellow Jews since the worker is called a *rei'a* (neighbor) which the rabbis usually understand as a Jew:

> You shall not defraud your neighbor, nor rob him; the wages of he who is hired shall not remain with you all night until the morning.[2]

But another Biblical verse makes clear that this sentiment is also true for gentiles:

1. JT Sanhedrin 4:22.
2. Leviticus 19:13.

> You shall not oppress a hired servant who is poor and needy, whether he is of your brothers, or of your strangers who are in your land inside your gates.[3]

The Talmudic rabbis explained that worker rights may not seem like they are issues of life and death but should be treated as though they are: "All who withhold an employee's wages, it is as if he has taken his life from him."[4] It is precisely through the Creation narrative that we learn that every human being was and is created equally in the image of God. Rabbeinu Yonah (thirteenth century, Spain) explains how high the burden is if one chooses to take on an employee:

> Be careful not to afflict any living creature, whether animal or bird, and all the more so, one should not afflict a person who is created in the image of the Divine. If you want to hire laborers and you find that they are poor, they should be [regarded as] poor members of your household; and do not degrade them, for you were commanded to have a respectful manner with them and to pay their wages.[5]

Our obligations during Shabbat are not just to obey secular and even Jewish law but to go beyond the letter of the law to ensure that workers are treated with full dignity.[6] Indeed, commentators of past centuries argued that the commandment of Shabbat requires not only rest on the seventh day but also work on the previous six days.[7] More recently, Rabbi Joseph Soloveitchik argued that human work was at the core of our dignity and sanctified purpose. "When God created the world, He provided an opportunity for the work of His hands – man – to participate

---

3. Deuteronomy 24:14–15.
4. BT Bava Metzia 112a.
5. *Sefer HaYirah* of Rabbeinu Yonah.
6. BT Bava Metzia 83a.
7. *Avot deRebbe Natan* version A chapter 11, Ketubot 5.5.

in His creation. The Creator, as it were, impaired reality in order
that mortal man could repair its flaws and perfect it."[8]

The deep truth that emerges from the Sabbath is that no person can be owned by another person. Rather, we all belong to
our Creator:

> ... As it is written, "For me, the children of Israel are servants,"[9]
> and not servants to servants.[10]

Rabbi Yerucham Levovitz (known as The *Mirrer Mashgiach*,
late nineteenth/early twentieth century, Poland) taught that the
name *Noah* comes from the word *menuchah* (rest), since he was
a person concerned with the righteous comfort of the people
of his generation. Therefore, embracing *menuchah* is an act of
emulating God (as described in Genesis 2:2): "And He rested on
the seventh day." God created the concept of rest and personally enacted it among His creations. But what is the nature of
this rest? The Shabbat *mincha* (afternoon) prayer describes the
Jewish notion of rest in the following way: "A rest of love and
magnanimity, a rest of truth and faith, a rest of peace and serenity
and tranquility and security, a perfect rest in which You find
favor." Rest is about achieving the deepest of virtues, when we are
relaxed and focused enough to internalize their truths, thereby
actualizing the function of the soul. And indeed, every person
deserves the opportunity for self-actualization. One dimension
of self-actualization is made manifest through our social progress
in the physical world, which includes our spiritual actualization
achieved in rest. Indeed, we have demonstrated above that our
spiritual and physical selves are intertwined and are two parts
of the whole.

---

8. Joseph Soloveitchik (trans. Lawrence Kaplan), *Halakhic Man* (Philadelphia: Jewish Publication Society, 1983), p. 101.

9. Leviticus 25:55.

10. BT Baba Kama 116b.

Rabbi Abraham Joshua Heschel (twentieth century, America, originally Poland) explains:

> He who wants to enter the holiness of the day must first lay down the profanity of clattering commerce, of being yoked to toil. He must go away from the screech of dissonant days, from the nervousness and fury of acquisitiveness and the betrayal in embezzling his own life ... To set apart one day a week for freedom, a day on which we would not use the instruments which have been so easily turned into weapons of destruction, a day for being with ourselves, a day of detachment from the vulgar, of independence [from] external obligations, a day on which we stop worshiping the idols of technical civilization, a day on which we use no money ... is there any institution that holds out a greater hope for man's progress than the Sabbath?[11]

The social psychologist Erich Fromm explains that this consciousness must lead to freedom:

> The Sabbath symbolizes a state of union between man and nature and between man and man. By not working – that is to say, by not participating in the process of natural and social change – man is free from the chains of time, although only for one day a week.[12]

Another vital dimension of Shabbat's inherent dignity is letting go of our mastery of the world. We cultivate a humility that we are not in control and we submit to the inevitabilities of our frailty and mortality. Rabbi Aryeh Kaplan (twentieth century, America) explains:

---

11. Abraham Joshua Heschel, *The Sabbath: Its Meaning for Modern Man* (New York: Farrar, Strauss and Giroux, 1977 ed.), 13 and 28.

12. Erich Fromm, *You Shall Be as Gods: A Radical Interpretation of the Old Testament and its Tradition* (New York: Henny Holt & Co., 1991).

God did not rest because He was tired or overworked. Even creating the universe is not hard work for God. Our Sages teach us that it involved less effort than to pronounce a single letter. God rested in another sense. He rested when he stopped creating – when He no longer interfered with His world. This gives us an insight into the Torah's definition of Sabbath rest. We rest in a Sabbath sense when we no longer interfere with the world.[13]

During the week, we immerse ourselves in the responsibilities and commitments to work, family, community, society, and the world. A primary purpose for human existence is to toil, to serve, and, yes, to work. Certainly, the value of work is expressed throughout Jewish sources. The Jewish tradition, overall, places a high priority on the value of work. In Pirkei Avot (Ethics of the Fathers), the sage Shemaya taught: *Ehav et hamelacha* ("love work").[14] And, Rabbi Shimon ben Elazar said:

> Great is work because even Adam did not taste food until he had performed work, as it is said, "The Lord God took the man and placed him in the Garden of Eden to till it and preserve it" (Genesis 2:15). Only then do we read, "The Lord God commanded the man: From every tree of the garden you may eat."[15]

But we might ask: is there a truly religious value to rest and leisure? Here, consider that leisure was once a high priority for Americans. Those who grew up in the post-Second World War period experienced a world of increasing leisure time, usually within the framework of a husband earning the income and a stay-at-home-mom taking care of home and children, and new

---

13. Aryeh Kaplan, *Sabbath Day of Eternity* (New York: National Conference of Synagogue Youth, 1974).

14. Pirkei Avot 1:10.

15. Genesis 2:16, Avot deRebbe Natan, chapter 11.

inventions designed to increase productivity and entertainment in the household.[16]

Yet, by the turn of the millennium, an ABC News report noted, "not only are Americans working longer hours than at any time since statistics have been kept, but now they are also working longer than anyone else in the industrialized world."[17] (In the ensuing years, some studies contend that there has been a reversal and that now Americans have more leisure time than ever, or work less than people in industrializing countries.)[18] These studies often use faulty methodology, however, including assuming that it takes less time to do housework, errands, and other tasks, so there is more time for leisure. This conclusion ignores the additional tasks that have been added to modern housework as a result of living in larger homes with more devices and furniture, longer commutes, and an obligation to check work-related text messages and emails at every moment. Indeed, many Americans do not even take their full amount of vacation days (already much fewer than for European workers) annually for fear that they might lose the "competitive edge."[19]

Yet, regardless of the causes of this trend, there is a consensus that working long overtime hours is deleterious to one's health. Studies based on data from the Centers for Disease Control and Prevention, the American Psychological Association, and peer-reviewed journals, reveal that workers with the most overtime had:

16. For more, see Seth Masket, "How Leisure Time Transformed Society and Politics," *Pacific Standard*. October 02, 2017. Accessed April 17, 2018. https://psmag.com/economics/how-leisure-time-transformed-society-and-politics.

17. Dean Schabner, "Americans: Overworked, Overstressed," *ABC News*. May 2000. Accessed April 17, 2018. http://abcnews.go.com/US/story?id=93604&page=1#.T-JVJhxdWEt.

18. "The Land of Leisure; Work and Play," *The Economist*, February 2, 2006. Accessed April 17, 2018. https://www.economist.com/node/5476124.

19. Steve Yoder, "Is America Overworked?" *The Fiscal Times*. February 16, 2016. Accessed April 17, 2018. http://www.thefiscaltimes.com/Articles/2012/02/16/Is-America-Overworked#page1.

- An increased risk for injury, illness, and mortality, along with poorer perceived general health
- Higher levels of anxiety, depression, and stress
- Greater interference with their responsibility to family and home

Conversely, companies that try to balance work and home life reap rewards; their employees demonstrate greater innovation, creativity, and productivity, and make fewer mistakes. In short, physical and psychological health is enhanced by leisure time. Thus, one might suggest that rest is not only a Shabbat ethic but a quotidian necessity. Rabbi Baruch Epstein (nineteenth/twentieth century, Lithuania) elucidates:

> Consider ... that for a young man working on Talmudic analysis for five or six hours straight can certainly affect his health ... and I therefore came upon you at daybreak and told you to go have some tea, and my focus was not the tea but rather the fact that you would have a break ... And this, too, I believe, that when one rests in order to reach a certain goal, then that rest is as valuable as the goal itself ... for the goal of the rest is to add strength and power to the actual pursuing of the goal, whether it be learning or good deeds.[20]

From a Jewish perspective, there is greater value to *mindful* rest than *mindless* rest. The opportunity to take a break does not mean the primary value is to turn off one's own core faculties. Rather, it's the opposite. Mindful rest, where we engage our mind, heart, and soul in different and meaningful ways, is not only more effective to recharge, but it also ensures that our rest helps promote true self-actualization. Maimonides teaches the importance of engaging in pleasures that do not just feel good but also strengthen us and assist us in moving toward our core goals:

---

20. *Makor Baruch*, part 4.

One should try to achieve through his eating, drinking, intercourse, sleeping, waking, movements, and rests – the goal of his body's health, and the goal of having a healthy body should be that one's soul finds its tools whole and ready to engage in wisdom.... And in the same vein one should not be considering only how pleasurable those actions are – which might cause him to choose only that food and drink which tastes good, and so too with the other physical aspects – but rather one should choose that which will be most helpful and effective, whether pleasurable or not.[21]

There is something spiritually great and morally necessary about "seeing the fruits of our labor." We are created to work, to change the world for good. But we must not dismiss the religious and ethical value of rest and leisure, for through its responsible actualization, we can truly learn to live fully. Concomitantly, there is a humble dimension to humans (powerless beings that return to the earth), but there is also a majestic dimension (powerful to create change in the world). We must embrace the limits of our work (humility) but also embrace our work to be as effective as possible (majestic). It is not accidental but intentional that our lives should be consumed with labor. Rabbeinu Bachya (thirteenth century, Spain) writes:

Mankind's livelihood requires his active participation. Apart from the period of (the Israelites') wandering in the wilderness, and other times of miraculous intervention, there is no manna from heaven. This active participation of man in the creation of his own wealth is a sign of spiritual greatness. In this respect we are, as it were, imitators of God.[22]

In addition, Rabbi Joseph Soloveitchik teaches that there is a fundamental duality to humans:

---

21. Introduction to Pirkei Avot, Ch. 5.
22. *Kad Kemach*, Tamari, 31.

The dual religious experience of *majesta* and *humilitas Dei* has had its impact upon Judaic morality. There are … two moralities: a morality of majesty and a morality of humility. The moral gesture of cosmic man aims at majesty or kingship. The highest moral achievement for cosmic man is sovereignty; man wants to be king. God is king of the world; man, imitating God, quests for kingship, not only over a limited domain, but over the far and distant regions of the cosmos, as well. Man is summoned by God to be the ruler, to be king, to be victorious. Victory, as the most important aspect of kingship, is an ethical goal, and the human effort to achieve victory is a moral one, provided the means man employs are of a moral nature.[23]

Sadly, many today work only to survive. The ideal is for individuals to work pursuing their passions and actualizing their unique talents. I truly dream that this is not an impractical ideal, a reality only for the privileged, but that labor can help us all to ascend to perfecting our souls and the world. It is important that we encourage everyone to experiment with various types of work. We must inspire the up-and-coming generation to seek out new professional experiences so as to find what they are truly passionate about. It is imperative that we work to create a more just world where people can have the ability to seek out the work that best suits them and not merely be forced into a lifetime of unchosen monotonous labor.

Ahad Ha'Am (19th–20th-century Zionist thinker and essayist) was correct when he wrote that, "More than the Jews have kept the Sabbath, the Sabbath has kept the Jews." Shabbat is about keeping Jewish continuity in a survivalist sense, and keeping Jews on our singular moral mission: the mandate to honor the inner dignity of all people.

So, what does it mean to "keep" Shabbat today? The Soches-

---

23. Joseph B. Soloveitchik, *Majesty and Humility*, Tradition 17, no. 2 (Spring 1978), 33–34.

hever Rebbe, the son-in-law of the Kotzker Rebbe, once remarked: "You can keep every [Shabbat] to the letter of the law, but unless Shabbat reaches the deepest and highest place in your heart, you haven't kept [Shabbat]." Indeed, one dimension of keeping Shabbat today, in addition to mindful rest, is internalizing the dignity of all laborers in our workplaces and our homes.

The Torah's promise of Shabbat is one of a subversive revolution that reminds us that as important as work is in our lives, rest is a great aim. Rest does not merely mean fun, but *elevated leisure*. Our character is best assessed by how we choose to use our free time. Does it elevate ourselves and those around us? Does it give us more energy, ideas, and positivity? Does it bring repair to brokenness?

Shabbat is a day for rest, for learning, for prayer, for self-care, for Divine worship, and for spiritual reflection. It is one of the greatest gifts that God has bestowed upon the Jewish people and upon the world. No one can be purely instrumental. Everyone and everything is given their chance, and responsibility, to rest and heal. Shabbat can also be, and must be, about moral and spiritual transformation.

In this book, I have offered a model for how the thirty-nine *melachot* are the necessary spiritual tools we need to embrace the perfect fullness of Shabbat. Through these *melachot* and concomitant ethical practices, we refrain from mundane work so that we are able to reflect on the power of the *melachot* on the other six days of the week. We see how our days are interwoven, how people are interconnected, how all is one within God's glorious kingdom.

I hope that this journey presents for you the opportunity to dive into what the thirty-nine *melachot* mean to you and how they can be personally transformational. This is my attempt to make meaning of the *melachot*, but there are so many other ways, each Shabbat, to make meaning of our Shabbat experience through humble restraint from the *melachot* and our weekday courageous engagement with them.

The world suffers horrible burns from pollution, hate, war, and corruption. To sustain a peaceful, loving, just world, we can return to rebuilding the world. God created the world through the *melachot*. We, the Jewish people, were in turn empowered to use the *melachot* to build the *Mishkan*. And now, once again, as God takes a step back, we are empowered to employ the *melachot* to sustain and build this world. This project, both my book and its charge for each of us, has never been more urgent. If we choose to get the most out of it, Shabbat is truly a gift for renewal, reflection, and transformation.

About the Author

Rabbi Dr. SHMULY YANKLOWITZ has twice been named one of "America's Top Rabbis" by *Newsweek* and has been named by *The Forward* as one of the "Most Inspiring Rabbis" in America as well as one of "America's 50 Most Influential Jews." Rabbi Yanklowitz is the author of 22 books on Jewish ethics and his writings have appeared in outlets as diverse as *The New York Times*, *The Wall Street Journal*, *The Washington Post*, *The Guardian*, and *The Atlantic* among many other secular and religious publications. He has served as a speaker at the World Economic Forum in Davos, Switzerland, and a Rothschild Fellow in Cambridge, UK.

Rabbi Shmuly received a Master's degree from Harvard University and a Doctorate from Columbia University. He serves as the Founder & President of *Uri L'Tzedek* (the Orthodox Social Justice movement), the President & Dean of Valley Beit Midrash (Torah learning center), the Founder and CEO of *Shamayim* (Jewish animal advocacy), and the Founder and President of YATOM (Jewish foster and adoption network). Rabbi Shmuly, his wife Shoshana, and their four children live in Scottsdale, Arizona. Rabbi Shmuly and Shoshana have also served as foster parents to several children.